Also by Phil Strongman

Cocaine: A Novel
John Lennon & the FBI Files (with Alan Parker)

PRETTY VACANT

A History of

UK Punk

Phil Strongman

CHICAGO
REVIEW
PRESS

An A Cappella Book

Library of Congress Cataloging-in-Publication Data
Strongman, Phil.
  Pretty vacant : a history of UK punk / Phil Strongman.
      p. cm.
  Includes bibliographical references and index.
  ISBN-13: 978-1-55652-752-4
  ISBN-10: 1-55652-752-7
  1. Punk rock music—Great Britain—History and criticism. 2. Punk culture—
Great Britain—History. I. Title.

  ML3534.6.G7S77 2008
  781.66—dc22

                                        2007038680

Cover design: Trudi Gershenov
Front cover photos: © Jupiterimages/Creatas/Alamy (Queen Elizabeth II on
Canadian twenty dollar bill); © Hulton-Deutsch Collection/Corbis (Johnny
Rotten on Stage with the Sex Pistols); Steven Puetzer/Photodisc/Getty Images
(Tiara on black background)
Interior design: Orion Books

First published by The Orion Publishing Group, London,
as *Pretty Vacant: A History of Punk*

This edition published in 2008 by
Chicago Review Press, Incorporated
814 North Franklin Street
Chicago, Illinois 60610
ISBN 978-1-55652-752-4
Printed in the United States of America
5 4 3 2 1

Dedicated to the memory of

DAVE GOODMAN
NILS STEVENSON and
JOE STRUMMER

without whom . . .

Acknowledgements

Phil would like to thank Jay, Steph R, Don, Jeannette, Dave, Ray, Olga, Gary L, Ian Marshall and Ian Preece @ Orion, Robert Kirby and Catherine Cameron @ PFD, Sophie Richmond (for reading between the lines) and, last but not least, Alan Parker, for the research.

Contents

PRETTY VACANT

Preface

I first heard about the Sex Pistols while sitting in the Acme Attractions' basement in the Antiquarius Market, King's Road. It was a few days before Christmas 1975 and Steph Raynor – Acme's co-owner – happened to casually ask, 'You know Malcolm, up the road?' He spoke knowingly, so I nodded in reply. 'Well, he's got a group, a rock group. They've started to do some gigs apparently.'

I didn't know who Malcolm (McLaren)[1] was then and, though I'd heard of 'a trendy sex shop' at the far end of the King's Road, I hadn't actually gone there. Well, it was just a sex shop, wasn't it? I'd naively assumed. A sex shop with a couple more t-shirts. Why would anyone bother, unless they were after porno . . . ?

I should have asked Steph more serious questions at this point but all my 17-year-old self could come up with was the banal query, 'What's this group called then?' 'The Sex Pistols,' Steph answered, and my immediate thought was, 'What a dumb name! They sound like a bunch of male strippers . . . '

And so it was to be almost five more months before I finally caught up with the Pistols. It was to be years – in some cases decades – before I really got to know most of the prime movers present that steamy night: Malcolm 'the manager'; Glen Matlock, the songwriting Pistol; Dave Goodman, 'the sound wizard'; Ray Stevenson, the most important rock photographer of his generation; Ray's brother Nils, the band's charming road manager; Joe Strummer, the future Clash legend; Bernard Rhodes, The Clash's

---

1 MacLaren's name was so regularly misspelt as McLaren that according to at least one former colleague, he eventually just accepted it.

bittersweet'n'sour boss; Jah Wobble, the Stepney tough guy who's turned into a supremely talented musical survivor; Vivienne Westwood, the finest designer to emerge from the seventies; Steve Severin, future Banshee and soundtrack expert . . . Others I spoke to only briefly: John 'Rotten' Lydon, Sid Vicious, Siouxsie Sioux, Steve Jones and Paul Cook – the former three are now icons, Sid's death making him the most well known, from Korea to Canada, from LA to Moscow.

These people were, *are*, all amazing: prime movers that no novelist could make up, characters any playwright would kill for. But Malcolm McLaren was perhaps unique in that he was the one man there with strong links to the parallel scene in New York. And he remains the most highly rated – and, in some quarters, the most highly hated – of all of them. For many reasons, both good and trivial.

But what this unique bunch inspired, 'punk', soon leapt way beyond the Pistols–Clash–Ramones, beyond two shops, beyond Manhattan and the King's Road, way beyond any one person or group. It became a genuine movement – musically as intense, exciting and diverse as any before or since. (Bands such as Stiff Little Fingers, 999, X-Ray Spex and The Buzzcocks were, are, as different from each other as from the originals.)

Personally, it probably warped my view of how things work. My brother Jay and I went to our first Pistols' gig with little expectation of them or the forthcoming summer. Within a few months the band were on magazine covers and I was working as a designer at Acme. By the end of the year, the Pistols were, quite literally, world famous, while I was seeing new, innovative bands four or five nights a week and Jay had started on the long dusty road that led to him being, for a long time 'the world's greatest club DJ'. All of which probably gave us the false impression that it was easy to launch something, or someone, with little money or back-up. Whereas the truth is somewhat different. Especially now.

'It was the least boring thing since the sixties,' as Charles Shaar Murray put it, 'and everything since, at least in terms of white rock, has seemed a bit of a comedown.' That comedown has involved, for

2

far too many people, an orgy of depression, drugs, debt and self-destruction.

And because it all went too far, too fast, for a time it really seemed as if it was about to vanish, leaving almost no trace. Another victim of the Cold War. But the truth is, punk kicked up a helluva lot of dust and much of it still sparkles. It was, is, both PRETTY and VACANT, and it will now, quite simply, never be forgotten. What follows hopefully gives some of the reasons why . . .

Phil Strongman

Prologue

London, 1975. It is one in the morning on a warm Friday in August. In the East End, two teenage boys have broken out onto the darkened roof of a council tower block. It is almost an hour since the last faint strains of the national anthem could be heard, coming from the flats beneath their feet – a sound indicating that BBC television was closing down for the night.

Both young men – John Lydon and John Wardle – are buzzing, mainly because of a heady combination of grass, speed, alcohol and, in the case of the older one – Lydon – lysergic acid. But they stand in silence on the very edge of the block, defying the danger, surfing on the warm smog breeze as they watch the lights below go out, one by one. From the faraway street it looks like a double suicide that's about to happen . . .

In the suburban west of the city, in an enlarged garden shed in Hounslow, musician and would-be producer Dave Goodman endlessly plays back and forth his four-track recordings of his band Polecat. The latter's blue-eyed jazz funk pumps out of the headphones as Goodman painstakingly teaches himself the skills of bouncing down, delaying, double-tracking, compressing and expanding – the art of blending noise into music and music into noise. He doesn't know at this point if the Polecat album he's working on – their first and last – will ever be released. Or if he – a professional bassist who's played Hamburg, Manchester and even Wembley with the likes of Ben E. King, The Drifters and The Jackson Five – will ever be near the big time again . . .

In the north of the city, in a Stoke Newington squat, another bass player – beginner Glen Matlock – struggles to turn a new riff into a song. Struggles to turn nothing into something. The song is for his band who, after a year, still have no full set and no singer to sing it – just a string of head-bangers, refuseniks and no-hopers. A band that Matlock, an art student, increasingly fears will never play a gig.

In south London, within a stone's throw of Clapham Common, Malcolm 'Edwards' McLaren flicks, with tired resignation, through the thick pad of fabric swatches his girlfriend, Vivienne Westwood, has placed upon the 'table' (the latter consists of a huge slab of oak placed on four dusty piles of books – volumes by Marx, Lenin, Trocchi and various, anonymous, porno authors). McLaren dutifully nods an interest in the cloth put before him but the 29-year-old's mind is still on his vision of something that will combine his own interests – clothes, politics, sexuality and rock'n'roll. Billy Fury meets Youth In Revolt – Paris '68. At the start of the year, with the revamped New York Dolls briefly under his management, that vision had seemed so close to fruition. Now it seems as distant as ever, as dead as the UK music scene. On his way to the kitchen McLaren almost trips over his tenant for the night, the homeless would-be guitarist and street thief Steve Jones, who sleeps fitfully in the corridor.

In a north-western suburb of the city, one-time rock photographer Ray Stevenson prepares for bed, bored already by the prospect of yet another day churning out snaps by numbers for the BBC.

Back in the East End, on the tower block roof, Wardle's silence ends as he relights a joint before enthusing about some new reggae he's heard, imports he's borrowed from a girlfriend. Lydon murmurs in reply, sucks on the proffered joint and continues to stare down. Another hit off the joint and he smiles as if he has some secret. Which, of course, he has. For Lydon knows, though his friend does not, that he's decided to join the rock'n'roll band he auditioned for just a few days before. An audition meant for his friend John Beverley. Lydon had to be bribed into attending and it took physical threats before he actually treated the audition seriously. But he has now made the decision, the decision that will eventually help transform the lives of all of the above, and they, in return, will ensure that it also transforms the lives of millions of others. Headlines will be made, deals sealed, movies filmed, millions of pounds earned and millions more blown, the reputation of cities and even entire nations will be affected, lives will be changed, lives will be lost – on several continents.

And at that moment, nobody knows it, nobody sees it, nobody even suspects it is possible – nobody except for the daydreaming McLaren, 'only 29 with such a lot to learn' . . . and, perhaps, the skinny youth, shoulders hunched, windsurfing on top of an East End council block . . .

Side A

PUNK: GOING UNDERGROUND

.

THE 100 CLUB – Whatcha Gonna Do About It?

All art worth its salt starts out wanting to change the world.
(Lindsay Anderson, film-maker, 1979)

The true story of punk isn't easily divided into bite-sized chunks. It blurs into too many fields: the cultural and social, the musical and sartorial. It comes with equal amounts of baggage and prejudice, both from its detractors and from the often dark days of the eighties when much of it – or, at least, much of its superficial trappings – fell among hustlers.

This is the messy background against which all this is written, although, it must be said, clarity and culture are not words that easily mix anyway. For just as the 'word' rock'n'roll can evoke both the fifties *and* the latest indie rock group, so punk is, at one and the same time, a flash of a past decade *and* a never-ending chord, a feedback whine that stretches out across the years, touching – and often encompassing – not just yesterday's and today's biggest groups but most of tomorrow's. U2, Nirvana, Green Day, the Arctic Monkeys . . .

And even a serious, straightforward chronology of punk presents problems. For during the years 1976 to 1979 an incredible amount happened, both in terms of rock music and in a much wider, cultural, sense. Britain itself – where the first flames of 'pure punk' burned fiercest for longest, providing a launching pad for what little success the original American acts enjoyed – changed enormously in terms of politics and economics.

In the areas that really counted for its first prime movers – music, fashion, design and street politics – punk succeeded beyond its creators' wildest dreams. 'Every design team wishes it had invented the use of kidnap writing in packaging,' says Malcolm McLaren now. 'Everyone wants to appear anti-corporate these days,' insists the man who was one of punk's key people, 'even the corporations want to at least *appear* anti-corporate in their ads, in their styling . . . '

And the short hair and narrow jeans that led to dirty looks and police harassment in 1976 and 1977 had, by the end of 1979, been adopted by almost everyone under 30 – from disco dollies to university graduates and even young NCOs in the British Army. This new look completely ended the ten-year domination of the long mullet haircut and denim flares – a combination that has, ever since, been seen only as comedy fare. The cutting-edge music of the flared jeans generation, Prog rock – or progressive music as it was always known then – was reduced to a state of parody from which it will never fully recover. And, while some of the big pre-punk 'stadium dinosaurs' still linger on, it is purely as expensively priced nostalgic 'rock theatre' (either literally, as in the case of Queen and their coach-party musicals, or metaphorically, as with the Stones and the tours designed to please those wanting a last glimpse of Mick'n'Keef while they're still alive and kicking).

Even the Teds – the young, and middle-aged Teddy boys who spent 1977 trying to fight the incoming tide – saw their next generation seduced. For the future will not be denied and a new wave of rockabilly groups, spearheaded by The Stray Cats, The Polecats and The Meteors, swept away most of the old bands in bri-nylon drapes. And among the rockabilly fans of these new 'rockin' groups' were kids with punky dyed hair, often decked in the chains and ripped Levis that would have had them labelled punks just a couple of years before.

The vast majority of these changes – a few of them quite stunning in the cold, retrospective light of day – had their roots in a period not much longer than 18 months. During this time punk went from being almost unknown to the most infamous music on the planet. Even within this short space of time, this growth in public awareness did not happen gradually. The change came, literally, in a matter of hours.

This book is therefore roughly divided into two sections – underground and overground. Or, to put it in crude terms, before and after Grundy. For it was the live TV 'swear-in' on Bill Grundy's *Today* programme in December 1976 that first sent punk shockwaves, and headlines, around the UK and then, albeit more faintly, around the entire world. For many, perhaps most, of those then involved, it irrevocably damaged the small, original 'scenes' in both London and Manchester, but it also made sure that those scenes would become legendary – that their influence would also be felt across continents, cultures and then-unimagined genres. Because one of the most important things about punk – hiding beneath its tendency to divide – was its ability to bring people together. In the bloody streets of seventies' Northern Ireland, young people from both sides of the Catholic–Protestant barricades were involved and 'none of them argued about religion because in Northern Ireland, punk *was* a religion'.

Similarly, the original London prime movers included those from borstals, comprehensives, grammar schools and even, in a few cases, public schools. Teens and twenty-somethings with working-class and lower middle-class backgrounds, did, admittedly, make up a clear majority – as well as a clear majority of those considered most influential. But then those classes did represent a majority of Britons (as they do now). This diverse mix was projected onwards into the years that followed.

In that sense, punk was a successful forward-facing return to the genuine roots of a nation's youth culture: fifties skiffle, sounds that anyone could make – the genre that led John Lennon into music-making – had come from the streets, as had the beat boom that Lennon's Beatles led almost a decade later; as revered in the halls of privilege as it was in the most run-down of council estates.

Yet, by the mid-seventies, those musical genres not concerned with the past, as pub rock and its return-to-R'n'B was, were all heavily tainted with commercial artifice. Something was needed that would blow away the glittery cobwebs and the increasingly fake tinsel (as well as the sheer po-faced pretension of most Prog rock).

McLaren had initially wanted the fuse for this explosion – the now near-mythical Sex Pistols – to be a mere backing band for either a New York Doll or a teenage Midge Ure. The Pistols were to be, in Anthony Wilson's words, 'a new Bay City Rollers, but this time a Bay City Rollers of outrage'.

But, although McLaren's personal magic brought the Pistols together and, crucially, kept them there long enough to spark an entire genre, he was never wholly in charge. And he never got his new Bay City Rollers. For he hadn't bargained on the likes of John Lydon or Glen Matlock – or Paul Weller, Pete Shelley, Steve Diggle, Mick Jones, Bernard Rhodes, Joe Strummer . . . For some, like the latter duo, punk was a last chance to apply talent that had seemed destined to be wasted. For others, only distantly connected, such as Ian Dury, Hugh Cornwall, Jean-Jacques Burnel, Sting and Elvis Costello, it opened doors that looked like they'd always be closed.

The same applies in a different way to female performers – from Siouxsie Sioux and Poly Styrene to Pauline Black and Lene Lovich – and to those of a different sexual orientation. All who wanted to be were empowered by this bizarre new music.

The boot-boy aggression of Oi-punk, the fascistic notions of many of its eighties followers, make it easy to forget that the lesbian club Louise's was an essential punk hang-out in 1976 and that the first openly gay chart artist – Bowie and his 'bisexuality' notwithstanding – was one Tom Robinson, a man whose TRB group lurked, in 1977 at least, on the blurred borderline between what was considered punk and what was called 'New Wave'.

Because, despite being launched – and sometimes spearheaded – by those whose stock-in-trade was hype or double-think, punk's essential claim to worth, to durability, to cultural importance, was – *is* – honesty. It was this that led to moral outrage, shocked head-lines across the globe, questions in Parliament and even – at one point – MI5 wiretaps.

Today, half a decade into an increasingly corporate 21st century, in a world that is itself physically threatened by commercial greed, the core of punk – its questioning, challenging spirit – is as relevant as ever. Its history is a tale that – in cultural terms at least – *has* to be fully told.

And, like all stories, it begins with a time and a place. . .

The seventies. Everyone complained, comparing them unfavourably with previous decades. Even the forties were now looked back upon with a certain nostalgia. Yet the time would inevitably come when the seventies would themselves be remem-bered as a time of peace and plenty. So they were, for all their alarms. (Brian Aldiss, *Life in the West*, 1980)

Spring 1976. A Tuesday night 'Rock Special' at the 100 Club jazz joint on London's Oxford Street. If Ronnie Scott's club is a kind of jazz flagship – glossy, expensive, air-conditioned and with three-course meals – then the 100 Club is a much-loved tramp steamer: cheap, cheerful, hot. The only food is a small Chinese take-away that nestles in one corner. The dimpled sheen on the 100 Club's sticky floor is perfectly mirrored by the condensation that gathers on its ceiling.

The band appearing this evening got this gig – and an ongoing residency – by the most curious of methods: they gate-crashed the Valentine Dance of High Wycombe College of Art, an event held at the Nag's Head pub where Screaming Lord Sutch, ageing rock'n'roller and leader of the Monster Raving Loony Party, was topping the bill. Uninvited, the future heroes of the 100 Club jumped on stage and played a brief but shockingly chaotic set. Some people applauded, most booed and several walked out before a mini-riot erupted. Most promoters would have run a mile but Ron Watts, the 100 Club's 'rock night' manager, was sufficiently impressed to book this new group for a one-off gig on 30 March.

The shambolic set that emerged that evening – cut short after less than 15 minutes, when the sneering, boozed-up singer tried to pick a fight with his own bassist – was incredible theatre, if nothing else. The singer left the venue and was waiting outside for a 73 bus home to Finsbury Park when the manager caught up with him. 'Get back on stage now or you're finished!' the manager had shouted.

The singer reluctantly agreed but only actually climbed onto the club's battered wooden platform after he'd seen his distraught guitarist rip the strings from his stolen Gibson. Ron Watts responded by booking them again, in April, and three times in May.

Outside, on Oxford Street, people stroll by in what has become the West's unofficial, post-sixties uniform – tight patterned shirts with collars as flared as the denim baggy trousers that complete the look. The few women who wear skirts wear them mid-calf length, in the same muted pastels the men wear. With minor variations people have looked like this since late 1967. The fashion look of teens and twentysomethings – once so cutting-edge – is now, like most of the music played on the radio, a matter of routine. Safe, tired, everywhere.

The current, overworked, variation is rounded off with the shoulder-length hair that everyone has, from school kids to football hooligans to factory workers to advertising executives to pop stars to TV newscasters . . .

The look that was 'youth being a little extreme' in the last half of the sixties is all-encompassing now. Smart-casual – though on most people it looks neither smart nor casual. It is, curiously enough, the uniform of an age of individuals. For the youth movements of the past – zoot suiters, Teddy boys, beatniks, rockers, mods, hippies, skinheads, suede-heads – have all but disappeared. Young people everywhere look like young people everywhere. Individual singers, and individual bands, sing individual songs. They sing about love, sex, romance, romantic disappointment, etc. . . .

And they wear The Uniform.

The warm night has tempted both sexes to undo a button or two more than normal . . . Cortina, Mini and Rover cars rumble past, faintly leaking music, mostly the current number one, a work of banal, childlike simplicity by the Brotherhood of Man: 'Save All Your Kisses For Me'. They too already enjoy a faint connection with tonight's group . . .

The heat in the 100 Club's gloomy basement is phenomenal, it is almost steamy down there. The warmth is almost as striking as the appearance of the audience – almost two-thirds of them have short, almost cropped, hair. One of the girls, a fashion student, has tiny ripped denim shorts and a sphinx haircut, another wears a daringly brief mini-skirt and another is clad only in underwear; a peep-hole bra, French knickers and suspenders. Her dark ponytail almost reaches the black and red Nazi armband on her elegant, stork-like arm.

The men, again mostly in the 17 to 22 age bracket, are similarly outlandish. See-thru t-shirts, baggy zoot suit trousers that narrow at the hem, drainpipe jeans, shirts with small collars, the occasional studded wristband, drastically pointed shoes. Black, leather, threatening.

Some have dyed discreet flashes of colour in their hair. They wear a smorgasbord of all that the 'outside world' has forgotten – forgotten or consigned to the brothel or bedroom – to look like bisexual vandals from some future-shock urban nightmare. Most shockingly of all, they are *not* wearing The Uniform. The implications of this are all and nothing – mere fancy dress with attitude and yet also something disturbing, tribal, quasi-military, polysexual, political. Brutal yet camp yet also, possibly, communistic (despite the swastikas). This new 'look' – with its myriad variations – is 'subversive' is every sense of the word.

Several weeks before the May 100 Club gigs, a concert given by the same band had ended in bloody fisticuffs (although fists were not the only weapons used) and many of tonight's onlookers have a tingle in the pit of the stomach – as you might have going to a high-profile football match or a particularly seedy area, expecting trouble and excitement in equal measure.

As these characters drift past, like actors on a split-level stage, eyes adjust to the semi-darkness and inadvertently fall on a male couple, arms draped around each other. Blatantly gay – or blatantly pretending to be. Another guy, with the dark wedge haircut of the soulboy, has a homemade t-shirt bearing the words 'The Pistols Shot A Hole In My Soul!'.

Arcane garage sounds of sixties Americana play through the PA – '96 Tears', 'Pushin' Too Hard' – as the mood of expectancy grows. At the bar there are a dozen 'normals', jazz students sweating in their long hair and army surplus greatcoats.

A band come on . . . but not *the* band. This lot look pretty much like 'normals' too. They announce their name – 'We're Krakatoa!' – then play a mix of pub rock and 'progressive keyboard blues'. They are met with a smattering of polite applause.

After an unexplosive half-hour, Krakatoa give up the struggle and, with the help of a stressed roadie, quietly take their stuff off stage. The promoter glances at his scuffed Timex. It is 10.15 already and the new band has still not turned up. He chews his lip, recalls talk of the group already being banned from the Marquee and Nashville Rooms. There have been several cancellations too. Perhaps the future of rock'n'roll won't show at all.

It is at this point that the band finally walks in, kind of separately but kind of together. First in is the bassist, hair two inches longer than the others (but still shorter than the straight Uniform). His clothes are magnificently different – a tab-coloured sixties' shirt and black jeans artfully dribbled with white paint, in the style of paintings by 'Jack the Dripper', the late Jackson Pollock.

The guitarist and drummer follow, moddy hair and 'boot cut' parallel jeans.

Last in is the singer. He is thin, just under average height, with orange spiky hair over piercing eyes. He is clad in a neat blue fifties overcoat with pegged trousers – black with grey and silver needle stripes – and a t-shirt that bears a huge screen print of what looks like a dark movie Oscar (actually a naked basketball player, an image ripped from a gay porn magazine).

The singer looks very precise and controlled, and speaks quietly in streetwise tones that are part uptight Cockney, part something softer. He looks like a star. Already. There is an unearthly quality about him, something not quite real. He seems in his self-contained self-confidence to be in his mid-twenties but is actually only four months out of his teens (though his manager's latest press hand-out claims that the entire band are still teenagers).

Two curious characters appear as if from nowhere and speak to the singer. The shorter one – though even he is taller than the singer – has hair that is a mass of dark orange curls, almost the same orange as the singer's hair. But 'curly' is obviously older, in his mid- to late-twenties. He talks in an unselfconsciously arcane fashion, with theatrical mannerisms as he steers the group towards the stage, a discreet herding action that shows he's smoothly desperate they should play before the club closes.

The other curious character is more unsettling. He is almost as skinny as the singer though he is several inches taller. He has tight jeans worn into rips at the knee and an oversized studded wrist-band such as might be seen in some S&M gay bar. His eyes are dark and the rings around them tell the well informed that he is some kind of speed freak – addicted to amphetamine sulphate. He seems to be half fashion victim, half psycho.

All of this is a little unsettling but the unpleasant cherry on the cake is his dirty white t-shirt. Upon its white cotton front is screen-printed a truly hideous image – a pile of dead bodies from some Nazi slave labour camp. When the speed freak turns round, it's possible to see that there are some related words that he's carefully written on his t-shirt's back panel. 'This is how we treated the victims at Auschwitz, first selections were made as they came off the trains, heads were shaved and . . .'

As far as many of those present are concerned, the speed freak is a nutcase. The girl in the French knickers and swastika armband is perhaps just some liberated fashion innovator who's seen the movie *Cabaret* too often (maybe on a double bill with *The Rocky Horror Show*, a stage version of which is still running near the King's Road).

She's wearing one thing. A sick joke – albeit of an extreme nature. But the speed freak in the Auschwitz t-shirt is quite another matter. Ten minutes later the speed freak enters the toilet, giving out a death's head grin to the punters he runs into.

The speed freak carefully puts a bloodstained bike chain to one side of the sink before washing his hands several times. The blood is his own – for the moment . . .

It is now almost 10.30. A 19-year-old soulboy with a brown wedge haircut and striped sixties shirt nudges the guy next to him – an unreformed thirty-something mod from the first time round.

'Are these boys actually gonna play or what?'

'Sssh!'

The mod points to the stage where the singer and the other three are plugging in mics and guitars. The front man is now wearing a ripped Pink Floyd t-shirt. Above the logo of the progressive band are stencilled the words 'I Hate'. It makes up a slogan the singer presumably agrees with – 'I Hate Pink Floyd'. But the last two words are almost superfluous, for the real message is far simpler – 'I Hate'. The singer 'who hates' suddenly gives a nod and plunges the venue into absolute audio chaos.

The band is earth-shatteringly loud. And the 'music'? A complete mess. The singer gives the occasional sneering yelp while the guitarist slams out random doomy chords as his Gibson – far too close to his amp – fills the room with howlingly painful feedback. The bassist makes run after run down his deepest strings, making the crowd's tooth fillings throb, while the drummer punches out the kind of haphazard fills and crashes that you might expect to hear on an experimental jazz rock album for the deaf . . .

Just when the crowd thinks it can't get any louder – or crazier – the singer puts his thin lips to the mic and 'plays' it, making it hum like an electric kazoo. The long-haired Richard O'Sullivan looka-like at the mixing desk adds reverb and echo to the havoc and the audience's fingers begin to inch towards their ears.

After 30 or 40 seconds, and with a final clatter from the drums, the racket stops – as abruptly as it had started. The band suddenly snaps into a 'proper' song – verse, chorus, verse, chorus, brief solo, chorus, end. To the surprise of some of the newcomers, the band *can* actually play. Among the crowd is a soft-faced man in a mohair jumper; he stands a few feet from a tough-looking type in a straight-zipped leather jacket. Behind him is a black man still in his late teens. Behind him is a woman with straggly blonde hair and a black wet-look ciré t-shirt. All have one thing in common – their eyes are locked onto the band on stage.

By the time the group power-chord their way through The Who's 'Substitute' almost everyone is hooked – heads bobbing, feet tapping – although some like the verbal ad libs as much as the sound.

Most bands – then and now – beg to be liked. But this lot don't care whether you like them or not, don't care whether you get 'it' or not – if you do, fine, if you don't, so what? You know where the bleedin' door is . . .

'Just heard the new Deep Purple album today, maaan . . .', sneers the singer, 'just sooo far out.'

'What's wrong with Purple?' bellows a baffled long-hair.

'Oh Jesus,' says the singer dismissively, 'thank God I'm not accountable for human taste . . . '

The singer's psychotic stare is abetted by the one thing that can

make his arrogance bearable – barbed criticisms of his own performance. 'That one was quite mediocre, wasn't it?' he shrugs after
another song 'That was *really* unimpressive, wasn't it, maaan?'
after another.

The stretched-out 'maaan', first heard on Bowie's 'Suffragette
City', a track from his 1972 *Ziggy Stardust* album, seems to mock
not just the actual word – a piece of beatnik-hippy punctuation –
but the casual solidarity it is supposed to stand for. The entire
Woodstock philosophy mercilessly parodied in a single, elongated
syllable.

But, for all the sneers and bitterness, the singer's raw voice fits in
perfectly with the musical barrage the band throws up. In fact,
the ringing, surging guitar underpins a truly tight rhythm section –
the drumbeat just loose enough to be compellingly human while the
bassist skilfully walks the line between power and melody (even
when he delivers backing vocals as he jumps up and down with the
singer).

It is the jumping up and down – the tight, twisted little pogo, like
a repressed footballer heading a ball – that nearly does for the
thirty-something mod. The speed freak is standing right in front of
him when, halfway through the set, he suddenly leaps into a pogoing dance of his own. His fourth or fifth jump brings him down
hard on the mod's plimsoled left foot. The ageing mod immediately kicks back. The speed freak stops his hiccuping dance and fixes
the older man with an evil stare.

'Well, you kicked me, mate, you jumped on me foot,' the ageing
mod blusters as he shouts above the music, into the speed freak's
ear.

A few of the others who know the speed freak turn to look – the
promoter recalls that a dozen people were involved in the fight at
the Nashville. Including the speed freak. The victim that night had
to be carted off in an ambulance. The mod's friend, standing right
next to him and already identified as a potential target, begins to
get ready to punch his way out of the club, his racing heart locked
into fight-or-flight mode.

The stairs are only seven feet behind the mod but he is well within reach of the speed freak's bike chain, a chain that seems more than capable of shredding his face.

But the paranoia, while understandable, is unjustified this particular night. The speed freak merely stares a moment longer then nods, smiles a death's head grin and pats the mod veteran on the shoulder. The others turn back to the band and the speed freak moves away, nodding his head to the beat as he says something to a guy with ice-blue eyes. The mod and his friend breathe a silent sigh of relief.

Remembering the speed freak's attitude – and his DIY Auschwitz t-shirt – the soulboy suddenly recalls Bowie's 'Diamond Dogs' song. It had been recorded just two years before and its introductory words told listeners that this wasn't rock'n'roll, it was 'genocide' . . .

'Get me a drink, Malcolm,' the singer unwittingly interrupts from the stage. It is barked in a half-joking way, but there is a hint of menace there too, 'Get me a drink or I can't do any more for the boys and girls . . .'

'Curly' stares defiantly for a moment or two then strolls off towards the bar.

There was to be no violence at all that night although, several months later – with a foreign TV crew and dozens of photographers present – a crescendo of scuffles and fist-fights will end in broken glass, deportation orders, at least one case of grievous bodily harm and a girl blinded in one eye. By then, though, the band will be the talk of the town, 'London's Outrage!'

The band was, of course, the Sex Pistols, as led by singer Johnny 'Rotten' Lydon.

Within seven months of that hot May night they would make

every front page in Britain, feature in news stories worldwide and be banned from every major venue in the UK. They would also grab the first of half a dozen record deals that would earn them, in today's terms, over £10 million (of course, where there's a hit there's a writ – and not one of the group would see more than 10 per cent of that figure). Later, a feature film of these events would get a theatrical release and be seen by millions.

The man with the orange curls at the 100 Club was Malcolm McLaren who, over the next three decades, would be linked with the Sex Pistols, Adam Ant, Bow Wow Wow, fascism, communism, anarchy, satanism, under-age exploitation, cassette piracy, porno movies, square dancing, world music, funk opera, bankruptcy, Hollywood and the electoral race to become London's first mayor . . . He created none of it entirely on his own – and yet none of it would have happened without him . . .

The soft-faced stranger was feature film director Julien Temple, then a National Film School student, who would go on to 'make' the Pistols' movie *The Great Rock'n'Roll Swindle* – with a vast amount of uncredited help from McLaren – as well as *Absolute Beginners*, Hollywood's *Earth Girls Are Easy* and *Pandemonium*. Like fellow directors Derek Jarman and Don Letts, Temple had already seen the Pistols once before that night in May.

The soulboy was Jay Strongman, now a top DJ at Chinawhite, London's most exclusive nightclub, and the black man in his teens was Norman Jay, now Norman Jay OBE, a BBC broadcaster.

The straggly blonde was another future OBE, the leading designer of her generation, Vivienne Westwood, the woman who'd sparked the fearsome bloodbath of a fight during an earlier Sex Pistols gig at the Nashville Rooms – the same woman who was to later shock even her friends by calling the queen 'a moron' during the latter's Silver Jubilee year. The same queen who was later to give Westwood an OBE.

The Richard O'Sullivan lookalike was fledgling 'sound wizard' Dave Goodman, who'd already toured Europe with Michael Jackson and The Jackson Five and who would go on to produce some of the finer tracks by acts as diverse as the Sex Pistols, Eater, and The Mobiles. His Polecat album will be issued because of the invention of the Brotherhood of Man's producer, Johnny Goodison. Goodman would also pioneer the solar-powered Green Field stage at Glastonbury. Twenty-nine years later he would die, still allegedly owed money by the Sex Pistols, his legal case – the music industry's longest-running ever – still unresolved.

The girl in the ponytail, French knickers and swastika was Siouxsie Sioux, whose Banshees group would have a string of successful albums as she, almost single-handedly, inspired the entire Gothic cult and all its various messy metal children.

The tough-looking character in the leather jacket was Tony, then a *New Musical Express* cub reporter who, a few months later, would bring his girlfriend Julie Burchill to punk gigs. Tony is now, of course, million-selling novelist Tony Parsons.

The youth with the ice-blue eyes was tough guy John 'Jah Wobble' Wardle, a close friend of John Lydon and Vicious, who would be present at virtually all the key events of the year to come (and whose solo music career would later blossom just as those of almost everyone else present began to flounder).

There were too, among the other 'boys and girls' at the 100 Club, future members of groups such as Public Image Limited, The Damned, Adam and The Ants, The Buzzcocks, Chelsea, Generation X, The Billy Idol Band, 999 and The Clash. There was also a drug novelist, milliner Stephen Jones and designers Sebastian Conran and Lloyd Johnson.

Not bad for a crowd of fewer than 65 people gathered in one dark little basement . . .

In fact, the Sex Pistols' residency at 100 Oxford Street would turn out to be the most spectacularly successful club residency since The Beatles conquered the Cavern and The Doors blew away the London Fog in LA. The Pistols started it as virtual unknowns with an audience of dozens and ended it having been filmed by British,

French and New Zealand film crews – as queues waited outside, queues that would form the core of the biggest mass art movement since Dada.

Within two months of their final gig there, at the tumultuous two-day Punk Festival, the Sex Pistols would sign to EMI, then the world's biggest recording organisation, in the label's fastest ever deal . . .

May 1976. The 100 Club. One in the morning. On the way out, the crowd are buzzing like an electric bee on heat – it has been a tense exhilarating night, a stoned stroll on the wild side, a glimpse of a new British underground – raw yet arty, sexual yet somehow asexual – and most there already know they'll be talking about that gig for months, maybe years to come. Even if the band go nowhere.

But they know that the band can't go nowhere – they are just too damn intense not to be propelled somewhere. Even if it takes two or three years. As the emotionally exhausted crowd passes the ticket office, one of them instinctively takes down a 100 Club calendar poster that has that night's event (mis)printed on it – 'Tuesday: Rock Special with Sex Pistols plus Roogalator!'

A trendy in black Smiths' jeans is watching from the top of the stairs. He smiles then shouts down at the poster thief: 'Necrophiliac! They're not even dead yet!'

Beside him the skinny speed freak slowly turns and gives another death's head grin . . .

The speed freak is McLaren's one-time protégé John 'Sid Vicious' Beverley. Vicious would achieve the rock stardom he craves by joining – and helping to destroy – the band he loves, the Sex Pistols. Within a year of their implosion he would have solo hits of his own and become a household name in Britain, then Europe, America and the rest of the world.

The only other love of his life, a New York groupie called Nancy Spungen, will die in Sid's presence. He will be arrested and charged with her murder. The publicity will turn him into an even bigger icon, one who, right up to the present day, continues to sell millions of badges, t-shirts, books, DVDs and CDs. As he leaves the 100 Club that May night, he has barely three years to live.

The fashion student with the sphinx hair – Tracey O'Keefe, later to be the lover of both Steve Jones and Vivienne Westwood – also has less than three years to live, as do four others who are to appear with her in the Pistols' *Swindle* movie.

The key members of the 100 Club crowd will, inadvertently, help to create a minor epidemic of the drug that virtually all of them then despised – heroin. They will also inspire a fourth generation of rockers and spark an anti-racist movement. Those who directly follow them will provide the audience – the foot soldiers – for both independent record labels and a CND revival. They will also, together, usher in the last great creative period of British culture.

MERCER ARTS CENTER – Too Much Too Young (Hey White Boy, What You Doing' Uptown?)

As with virtually all new 'modern music', the racket that energetically crashed out of London's 100 Club in spring 1976 had some of its tangled roots – and a little of its attitude – buried in the fertile cultural soil of pre-Carter America.

The most blatant manifestation of this first flowered in the unlikely setting of a Manhattan arts centre – but the road there was to begin with two equally left-field characters. The first was Lou 'Reed' Firbank, a cynical New Yorker who'd shocked many of his peers by openly flirting with bisexuality as early as the mid-sixties; the second was Welshman John Cale. Reed's poetry and journalism courses at Syracuse University, NYC, had left him with a lifelong love of the darkly Gothic – and an awareness of the power of a well-turned phrase. He was alienated from his parents – a wealthy accountant and a former beauty queen – so much so that they'd actually tried to have him incarcerated in an insane asylum on several occasions.[2]

---

2 Once, they succeeded, and their son was subjected to electric shock treatment at Rockland County Hospital – at the time, electro-therapy was an accepted treatment for both madness and homosexuality.

Reed was a 22-year-old singer-songwriter and novice guitarist when he started his first serious band, The Velvet Underground, in 1965. He took the evocative name from a soft-porn novel by Michael Leigh, a copy of which Reed carried around for months. Later he claimed he'd found it at random, abandoned in a New York gutter. His first recruit to the Velvets was fellow Syracuse graduate Sterling Morrison, a classically trained bassist, who was impressed by the fact that Reed was working as a professional in-house songwriter for music publishers Pickwick. This fairly well-paid job didn't actually last and Reed and other future Velvets were often reduced to pawning instruments, selling blood or posing as models for crime tabloids ('This Man Raped And Robbed His Way Across An Entire County!'). Drummer Angus McLise seemed to complete the band's minimal line-up but, in late 1965, John Cale met Reed at a party where the latter was strumming his own songs on an old guitar. Cale, a talented viola player, didn't really like Reed's acoustic music – he hated 'Dylan and Joan Baez and all that folk shit' – but he was impressed with Reed and his lyrics. Cale eventually agreed to leave the 'drug drone band' he was in, The Dream Syndicate – the group he'd co-founded with stoned New York trendy La Monte Young. And he soon completed the move by joining the Velvets.

Cale added a whole new dimension to the band with his electric viola – and with his determination to be part of something truly groundbreaking. At 26, he was the oldest of the bunch, a classically trained cellist who'd studied at Goldsmiths in London and then won a scholarship to study in the US, a choice dictated by his love of the American avant-garde. And the Velvets' sound was abundantly avant-garde; feedback-drenched performances were laced with the sardonic poetry of Cale's whirling mutilation epic 'The Gift' and Reed's odes to sado-masochism (most noticeably in the medieval-sounding 'Venus In Furs' – title again stolen from a soft-porn book – a disturbing piece from its slow, throbbing drum intro, through the meandering menace of its 'whiplash girl-child' verses to its ending in a blizzard of strings).

The increasing sophistication and popularity of songs by the likes of Bob Dylan and The Beatles had made a record deal seem inevitable for the Velvets, but it was not to be so easy. Even in an age starting to embrace sexual liberation, Reed's songs always seemed a step too far. He was writing about a late-night New York – a coffee-stained world of drugs, drunks, rip-offs, transvestites, hookers and 24-hour cafés – that even most hip young New Yorkers didn't want to know about. He was penning numbers like 'Heroin' at a time when Dylan was subject to press interrogations over whether he'd committed the heinous crime of ever puffing on a joint of grass.

Even a four-track demo got the Velvets nowhere, despite Cale blowing a small fortune by travelling all the way back to 'Swinging London' to tout it round.

But help *was* to come sooner rather than later – and it came in the unlikely form of would-be promoter Al Aronowitz, who wanted a support act for the new band he was managing, a combo called Myddle Class. The latter had a string of dates lined up in Manhattan's Greenwich Village and The Velvet Underground seemed different enough to hold audience attention and complete the bill, even though Aronowitz considered them to be a cynical bunch – 'crooks, hustlers, junkies . . .'

The new Aronowitz connection led to a residency at one of New York's most notorious tourist clip-joints, the Café Bizarre, and all seemed to be going well until McLise dropped out, apparently seeing multiple nights at the Bizarre as some kind of sell-out (a step towards the music biz normality that the group had previously avoided). Reed and company were *sans* drummer, about to cancel the gigs, when the sister of another Syracuse Uni connection led to the androgynous-looking Maureen 'Mo' Tucker. With the gigs just days away a desperate Reed auditioned Tucker in her parents' lounge and offered her the job there and then – partly for her undoubted percussion skill but partly, no doubt, because a female percussionist was still, in the mid-sixties, a major talking point in itself.

Aronowitz by now considered himself the Velvets' manager – a 'deal' he 'sealed' with a handshake with Reed – but present at the first Café Bizarre gig was Andy Warhol, along with Paul Morrissey, the in-house film-maker at the Factory, Warhol's artistic playpen. Warhol was by then a major player on New York's cutting-edge art scene – at least in terms of publicity. His early 'pop art' screen prints featured bold, cartoon-like images of everything from Campbell's Soup cans, Marilyn and Elvis, to police brutality, civil rights marches and Jackie Kennedy in mourning: this is America and the modern world, he seemed to be saying, in all its sheen, shallowness and horror. These screen prints weren't selling very well, however. Some – like the hammer and sickle series – generated virtually no cash at all. In 1965 it was possible that Warhol could go bankrupt – and perhaps even disappear back into obscurity. The Factory's short films cost very little, however, and had the bonus of enhancing the place's reputation.

So Morrissey, who later directed the full-length features *Flesh*, *Trash* and *Heat* for Warhol, knew his collaborator/boss could be talked into new ventures in that direction. And the Factory's film-maker felt that a pop band that could be filmed and could then become an 'on-going happening' would have massive potential. 'When you *direct* films you lose a lot of the qualities that Hollywood gave us,' Morrissey was quoted as saying at the time, 'so we look for stars and just let them do what they want.' In the Velvets, Morrissey had indeed found some potential stars and Warhol was soon in agreement – he already had a female singer for them, the glacially beautiful, German *chanteuse* Nico. Her arrival wasn't particularly welcome to Reed or Cale, but she agreed to sing only a few of her own songs, plus those numbers written especially for her by Reed – numbers that Warhol had quietly insisted he write. Nico even agreed to dutifully rattle a tambourine around during those songs she wasn't fronting.

Within months they were touring as part of Warhol's Exploding Plastic Inevitable, with tougher numbers much more to the fore. The driving, throbbing 'I'm Waiting For The Man' was deservedly given prominence; it was a future classic, with its simple but effective chord changes – effective because you had to wait for them. The lyrics – about *waiting* to meet a drug dealer 'with 26 dollars in my hand' – helped add to the threatening power of it all, as well as conveying the sense of young Americans crossing barriers that previous generations hadn't.

The Velvets live backdrop would usually be a light show and fetish dancers, plus colour footage, shot by Warhol, of the last gig or rehearsal.

Press write-ups, and the Warhol connection, finally led to an album, recorded in 1966 and released the next year. It was with left-field jazz label Verve via MGM, a set that was cut in 48 hours for $3,000. Warhol was the nominal producer though Tom Wilson and the band themselves did most of the actual tracking and mixing. The LP was given the imaginative title *The Velvet Underground And Nico* and it featured startling layers of scratchy guitars duelling with Cale's rasping viola as Reed's dry seen-it-all-before vocals leered over the top. The female contribution is equally strong: Tucker's mind-numbing pulse drums and Nico's dead-pan rendition of 'All Tomorrow's Parties', the latter sung with just the right amount of studied, decadent boredom. But despite all this, and Warhol's 'pop art' sleeve – featuring a banana and his own moniker – it took months for sales to crawl into the low thousands. Denied airplay or many seriously positive reviews, the Velvets' debut failed to climb higher than No. 171 in the US listings – it failed to chart at all in Britain, Europe or Japan – and was swiftly deemed a flop. And yet, amid the glad-handing and insincere air-kissing that made up much of the first Summer of Love, *The Velvet Underground And Nico* stood out, an alarm call that wouldn't be heard for years. It remains one of the most influential rock albums of all time.

The last northern tour before the album had seen the Exploding Plastic Inevitable reach the University of Michigan, close to the tough Detroit satellite known as Ann Arbor (the gig was timed to coincide with the Ann Arbor Film Festival). At an after-show party at her house, Anne Wehrer, a local trendsetter who'd been left with a wooden leg after an accident, had introduced Warhol and some of the others to a teenage drummer by the name of James Jewel Osterberg. Jim Osterberg was then busy moving from one band, The Iguanas, to another, The Prime Movers. 'I thought Jim was cute,' Warhol was later quoted as saying, 'and that's when he first met Nico and John Cale. That was the start of his affair with Nico, a record with John Cale and a movie with Francois de Menil . . .'

Jim Osterberg was equally impressed with the Exploding Plastic Inevitable show, particularly the Velvets. No one seems to remember Lou Reed saying much to Osterberg, which is a pity because Reed and 'Iggy Pop' Osterberg were both later hailed as the godfathers of punk – and there is a sense now that maybe their brief meeting was like some premature passing of the torch, from one demi-generation to another.

Iggy – the nickname came from his time with The Iguanas – was still a clean-cut percussionist and part-time vocalist at this point. 'Iggy Osterberg was a great drummer,' according to Wayne Kramer of the revolutionary MC5, 'he was unbeatable . . . pure power rock'n'roll beat.' Iggy was also fascinated by black blues and the women who hung around the R'n'B clubs of the day, clubs he'd often play ('They had such big asses, those women, I'd never seen bottoms so big!'). But a revelation in Chicago – halfway through his first joint, according to myth – told Iggy that real *blues* for a wiry white kid didn't mean just copying middle-aged black men, it really meant creating his own noise, his own genre. So, after recruiting bassist Dave Alexander and the Ashetons – the Nazi-obsessed Ron Asheton on guitar, his tough guy brother Scott on drums – Iggy launched his band The Psychedelic Stooges (whose name was swiftly shortened to The Stooges).

Danny Fields, Elektra Records' publicity director and in-house 'freak', caught up with them at the University of Michigan. It was 22 September 1968 and The Stooges were playing a benefit, supporting The Up and Detroit heroes the MC5.[3] Wayne Kramer's

---

3 MC5 is short for Motor City Five, appropriate for a band who started out playing hot-rod rallies before diving headlong into New Left's 'revolutionary rock'.

MC5 boys were strong but they were – in Fields's mind at least – blown away by The Stooges, with Iggy, in white make-up and white maternity dress, wriggling around like a well-oiled snake on speed (that's when he wasn't playing home-made 'instruments' such as blenders, vacuum cleaners and mic'd-up oil drums). 'You're a star!' Fields screamed at Iggy as he came off stage. 'I work for a record company, can I talk to you?' But Iggy had decided that the bedenimed Fields was just another weekend freak. 'Yeah, yeah,' he replied sarcastically, 'see my manager.' The lead Stooge then promptly walked away.

But Fields wasn't going to be deterred that easily and he phoned Jac Holzman, Elektra's boss, the very next morning. The label was riding high with The Doors at that point, so when Danny boy mentioned he'd seen two great bands, both of which should be signed, Holzman was genuinely receptive. 'Offer the main band twenty grand and the other one five,' he casually ordered before ringing off. Fields's informal, three-album offers – $20,000 for the MC5 and $5,000 for The Stooges (the latter sum later doubled) – were met with unrestrained glee by all concerned.

The MC5 were soaked in late sixties street credibility, partly because they were the only group who actually dared play the 1968 Democratic Convention in Chicago (where Mayor Daley's corrupt and brutal police force went berserk, attacking anti-Vietnam War demonstrators and tear-gassing young and middle-aged passers-by in an orgy of violence). The Five – singer Rob Tyner, drummer Dennis Thompson, bassist Michael Davis and guitarists Fred 'Sonic' Smith and Wayne Kramer – got away unscathed that day but they were to remain a target, mainly because of their manager John Sinclair and his stated manifesto of 'revolution, dope and screwing in the streets'. It was an attitude that meant a record deal – especially a major one – was unlikely. Elektra's walk on the wild side was just the break the Five were looking for. Not that it mellowed them – or their abrasive *Kick Out The Jams* album debut, which reached the edge of the album Top 20 – though the most noticeable thing about it, aside from the dynamically raw title track, was the use of the word 'motherf—er'. A well-known chain of record shops – Hudson's record stores – objected to the word and refused to stock the LP. The band immediately ran full-page adverts in the underground press proclaiming 'F— Hudsons!' To add insult to injury, the MC5 had the Elektra logo on the offending ads. (This was all small-time stuff compared with an incident a few months later, when one of the MC5's entourage bombed an empty CIA recruiting office before casually strolling back to the band's communal pad.)

But the MC boys themselves were eventually to become disillusioned with both Elektra's in-house 'company freak' Danny Fields and the alleged revolutionaries of the hairy New Left. The hardcore of one lefty organisation – the 'Motherf—ers', no less – had demanded 500 free tickets to the MC5's Fillmore East gig. The band had agreed but the freebies never got distributed and, to make matters worse, Fields had delivered the group to the East Village venue in a gleaming white limo. Murmurs of 'You've sold out!' became screams inside the hall when Tyner naively told the crowd, 'We didn't come to New York for politics, we came for rock'n'roll!' The Five were bundled off stage and, as the PA was trashed and the curtains set alight, the band were subjected to an impromptu show trial, the main charge being that they were 'pussies, not revolutionaries!'. Before the 'trial' was over, things got ugly – the band was pelted with glasses, and knives were pulled. Somehow, the Detroit musicians fought their way clear and ran to their now scratched and dented limo, which screamed away under a hail of bricks and bottles. The MC5 were pretty much through with direct politics after that – unfortunately, after such a riot, the music biz in the US was pretty much through with them (Fillmore East's promoter Bill Graham banned them from all his venues and plenty of other club owners followed suit). January 1969 saw Nixon's presidential inauguration and Elektra's sacking of Danny Fields – within months the label would make the first moves towards dropping the MC5.

35

One of the last gigs the MC5 performed with their 'little baby brother band', The Stooges, was at the NY State Pavilion in August '69 – a concert that was the start of a nationwide tour to promote The Stooges' eponymous debut LP. A wild-eyed Iggy stormed on stage wearing ripped dungarees and instead of ignoring the pair of beer cans that landed at his feet, hurled them angrily back into the crowd. 'F— you! F—you!' he shouted, until a few bottles crashed down before him.

After squirming on all fours moaning '*I wanna be your dog, baby*', Iggy launched himself into the crowd, dived back and then rolled in the broken glass centre stage over and over until his chest was a bloody red mess. Then he grabbed some drumsticks and a shard of broken guitar and cut his chest up some more. After less than 20 minutes, Iggy walked off stage as Bach's Brandenburg concerto thundered through the PA, silencing the handful of punters who'd been applauding him. Iggy's 'tactics' were new, if nothing else – no one had ever been quite that crazy live on stage before. Perhaps it was a response to the state-sponsored slaughter in Vietnam, some critics wondered; perhaps, said others, it was just Iggy's personal lunacy. It was OK for him to try and make rock as dangerous as it had first seemed in the mid-fifties . . . but not, surely, if the effort killed you. Or seemed to.

Pavilion promoter Howard Stein was actually in shock after The Stooges' 29 August show – and his pregnant wife responded to the night's events with a violent miscarriage (Stein promptly refused to work with The Stooges again). At their next major gig – supporting Ten Years After in Boston – The Stooges played to a completely silent audience; no one clapped until after the third number (not quite 'ten years after' they'd gone on stage but it must have felt like it).

But, despite a large amount of print coverage in publications from *Rolling Stone* magazine to the teenybopper rag *16*, The Stooges' tour was a comparative failure. They and their front man sank deeper and deeper into regular hard drug use and their album only just scraped into the Top 200, despite being a fine piece of blistering rock'n'roll. In fact, *The Stooges* had two serious stand-out tracks, bona fide classics of the near future, the searing frustration anthem '1969' and the power-chording 'No Fun'. The latter had a complicatedly simple drum pattern, that was followed by the distorted bar chords that usher in the birth of trash thrash – the guitar sound of the next generation. In many ways it was a future slammed out against an increasingly limp psychedelic present as represented by the stoned, and somewhat elitist, 'beautiful people'; the 'mainstream in-crowd' and their 'hippy drippy' mood, which was mercilessly parodied by Frank Zappa in the score of Haskell Wexler's doomy classic *Medium Cool*, perhaps the film that, more than *Easy Rider*, captured the 'real' 1969 (although Wexler's cameras covered much of the '68 Chicago Convention and the events that followed, they actually missed the MC5 performance).

Faint echoes of all this can be heard in 'No Fun', Asheton's swaggering guitar clearing the way for Pop's ironically dry yet maniacally powerful voice. The words he sings:

> No fun to be alone,
> alone and by myself,
> No fun to be alone,
> in love . . . with nobody else.

are straightforward enough to be almost bland and yet, despite Iggy's irony, the words do carry a charge; simply to be in one's teens is to give meaning to such words. Instrumentally 'No Fun' builds and builds into a racket that can only be described in superlative terms – it was, is, crudely magnificent. 'I wanted to write about how shit it is in the Midwest,' Iggy said later, 'there's nothing to do, nowhere to go . . .'

Yet, when combined with The Stooges' brutal guitar thrashings, his apparently directionless lyrics were to point the way forward for many.

This way forward was, itself, partly built on the racket kicked up by The Velvet Underground. The Velvets' own second album – *White Light/White Heat* – was even more challenging and uptight than the first. The shambolic beats and Cale's drones provided the perfect doomed background for dark gems like the powerful 'Sister Ray' (which managed to clock in at an epic seventeen minutes – less a horror moment, more a horror lifetime). Again, the album failed to sell in big numbers and by the summer of 1969 Lou Reed had ditched Warhol – just as he'd ditched Aronowitz, Nico and then John Cale. All such moves seemed designed to turn the Velvets into 'Lou's band' but, whenever anyone objected – and Tucker and Morrison were up in arms over the Cale expulsion – Reed would simply threaten to break up the band completely. As his sardonic 'charm' and bleak songs seemed to be the most noticeable feature of the Velvets – superficially, at least – Reed's bluff was not called.

Warhol never took music management seriously again, while Nico ended her affair with Reed with the bitter words, 'I cannot make love to Jews any more' – before she went off to give VD to a young Iggy Pop. John Cale responded to his 'sacking' by temporarily putting aside his keyboards and viola to concentrate on studio work (it was Cale who produced The Stooges debut album).

But the Velvets, and Reed, still continued to attract the young and talented – one such fan being Jonathan Richman, an 18-year-old Boston kid when he first 'arrived' in their inner circle during the last summer of the sixties. Steve Sesnick was the Velvets' manager at this point and he also co-owned the Boston Tea Party club, at which the band played on a regular basis – much to Richman's delight (he'd been 'really knocked out' by *The Velvet Underground And Nico* album). The awkward, alienated Richman had already written dozens of songs – including one about the long trips in his father's food delivery truck, driving 'past the Stop'n'Shops', a 'number with a Sister Ray' style riff which he called 'Roadrunner'. This and many others he'd play on a battered two-string guitar at the local Cambridge Common bar. It was commonly agreed that the songs were pretty good – certainly better, it was felt, than Richman's reedy voice. His quest for a spot on a Velvets' gig was finally rewarded when he became support for Reed's band and the Grateful Dead at a college gig in Massachusetts. Richman even followed the Velvets when they returned to New York – sleeping on Sesnick's sofa and working as, among other things, a bus boy at the once exclusive Manhattan venue Max's Kansas City, a steak and lobster restaurant-bar-club, situated at 213 Park Avenue South, off Union Square.

But Richman rapidly tired of the grimly urban and, when Reed finally left the Velvets, Richman returned to Boston. He did so partly to form his own band, 'because', in his own touchingly honest words, 'I was lonely and figured that that way, with a band, at least I'd make *some* friends . . .'

Believing that his songs were 'modern love songs', Richman decided his new band would be called The Modern Lovers. Getting the other band members together turned out to be surprisingly easy – the boy next door, literally, turned out to be budding guitarist John Felice. Bassist Rolfe Anderson then joined, as did Cambridge Common regular, drummer David Robinson. After a few months wandering around the kibbutz and desert wilderness of Israel, Richman returned to Boston ready for action. Two Harvard students – bassist Ernie Brooks and organist Jerry Harrison – replaced the equivocating Anderson and September 1970 saw the Modern Lovers make their live debut at Boston's Simmons College. It was, perhaps, the 'straightest' place they played – other gigs included art galleries, old people's homes and children's hospitals (and it was in such venues that the often besuited Richman would repeat numbers, recite lyrics or break down and cry while singing some of the more emotional pieces such as 'Hospital'). 'I'm Straight' was, ironically, one of the Modern Lovers' first songs – it was also their live opener for a long time – an ode to *not* being a long-haired, acid-popping 'head' ('Someone To Care About' was similarly direct – a song that was genuinely against both drugs and one-night stands).

39

Record labels began to gather as word of the Lovers' live power spread – Harrison's organ had just the right kind of edgy wail that the band could stretch out on, especially on masterpieces like the spiralling, staccato 'Roadrunner'. 'I'm in love with rock'n'roll and I'll be out all night!' – these and the later verses, about pine trees at night and the endless drives between Stop'n'Shop stores, are merely playful on the printed page, but when underlined by Harrison's jabbing, building keyboard, and the endless repeating 'Radio On!' backing vocal, they become magical – the defining electric core of a song that defines modern music's appeal to those who are young and/or isolated. Warner Brothers got the deal – partly because they promised to get in ex-Velvets' man John Cale to produce. Yet Cale was fated to work with LA music biz veteran Kim Fowley on this one (Fowley had produced novelties such as the 1959 Hollywood Argyles' smash 'Alley Oop' as well as working with singer-songwriter David Gates, drummer Sandy Nelson and legendary producer-arranger Phil Spector). The Modern Lovers' demo sessions went fairly well – usually with Richman and the Lovers working with either Cale or Fowley. But there was no doubting Richman's increasing disillusionment with his own material.

The Cale–Fowley produced Lovers' 'album' had been recorded on a haphazard basis between 1971 and early 1973, whereupon the increasingly single-minded Richman quietly informed Warners that he'd now changed his songwriting style completely and no longer wished to do live performances of the songs he'd just recorded. The furious label pulled the plug and refused to give – or even sell – the Modern Lovers the tapes.

Jonathan Richman wasn't too worried about his troubles with Warners – after all, he and the Lovers were still in demand live, no matter whether the songs he played were old or new. And one of his live dates in early '73 was in Manhattan's Mercer Arts Center, supporting an already infamous, but unsigned, band called The New York Dolls.

The Dolls came together in late 1971, a fusion-cum-evolution of various no-hoper New York groups – The Blonde Bombshells, The Dolly Daydreamers and Actress. All were proto-Glam bands, inspired not by Alice Cooper's music but by the fact the heavily made-up Vincent Furnier could give his group, and hence himself, a girl's name and yet still make a healthy living from music. Although Cooper's 'I'm Eighteen' and 'School's Out' had a certain raw appeal, the Dolls mostly preferred Spectoresque girl groups and Brit invasion bands, especially the pre-psychedelic Stones, Beatles, Kinks and Small Faces. After long hair and jeans had begun to lose their shock effect at the start of the seventies, what better way to get a second glance than with big hair, male make-up and hot-pants? But to look gay in an age when homosexuality was still heavily frowned upon – it was still illegal in many American states in 1971 – was brave to the point of foolishness. The Dolls didn't care though, partly, perhaps, because of some serious fashion links – and partly because worrying about what other people thought was not what rockers from the district of Queens did.

The original line-up consisted of guitarists Ronald 'Sylvain Sylvain' Mizrahi and Arthur Kane backed by the rhythm section of bassist Rick Rivets and drummer Billy Murcia. They had taken the group's final name from the New York Dolls' Hospital, which was situated on Jamaica Avenue directly opposite the Mizrahi family store where Sylvain and Billy both worked (Sylvain's own designer knitwear business, Truth and Soul, was only enjoying limited success). They were subsequently joined by one Johnny Volume – born John Genzale Junior – who had entered the band's orbit as a result of his having encountered a drunken Kane and Rivets one night in Greenwich Village while the pair were attempting to steal a motorcycle. Once in the group Johnny switched instruments with Kane, and changed his name to the more upbeat sounding 'Thunders'. His volatile personality swiftly led to rows with the rest of the group – especially Rivets, who was swiftly thrown out. Rivets's replacement was the flamboyant Jagger-esque David Johansen, a front man before he'd ever boarded a stage. He could also camp it up – when Danny Fields first met the Dolls he'd instantly assumed they were all gay (maybe because they all knew the influential Fields *was*). 'In fact, none of them were gay,' rock photographer Bob Gruen says now, 'they were all after girls, all the time. And those clothes they wore – they weren't women's dresses, they were *men's* dresses, stuff they found in thrift stores and so on. I mean, no woman ever looked like that!'

The year 1972 had started with Bowie announcing he was gay – well, bisexual – in the pages of *Melody Maker*, still a music-biz bible for New York's anglophiles. The fact that Bowie could get a record deal, and hits, with RCA – and sponsors for his make-up, dresses and mime troupes – confirmed to the Dolls that they were heading in the right direction. Yet many would-be fans were inevitably put off by the fact that the Mercer Arts Center – the venue for the Dolls' longest-running and most influential residency – was frequented by junkies, transsexuals, transvestites, gays and hookers. The socio-sexual avant-garde were the mandatory sacred cows at any non-mainstream post-Factory event in the Big Apple.[4]

Even Bob Gruen had been discouraged when he first went to check out the Dolls at Mercer's. 'First thing I see is a guy in make-up and so I'm outta there. It was not my scene at all, I thought. Second time someone talked me into going and there were quite a few girls in mini-skirts hanging around and that seemed more fun. The third time I *finally* go into the back room, the Oscar Wilde room, where all these amazing people were and the Dolls are play-ing and, of course, they're fantastic, just fantastic.'

By keeping the music raw and simple the band appeared to be reclaiming rock'n' roll from jaded superstars and their 20-minute solos played ponderously in over-priced stadium gigs. With the Dolls, the audience could genuinely feel as though they were a part of what they were witnessing on stage. The driving songs – 'Personality Crisis', 'Pills', 'Subway Train', 'Looking For A Kiss' – rarely strayed beyond the three-minute mark and were virtually all delivered at a frenetic pace, fuelled all the while by Thunders's droning guitar. In short, the Dolls' sound mirrored their hedonis-tic and mock-decadent lifestyles – they were not merely 'talking

---

4 Most of them could only afford to live in the Big Apple because, post-Kennedy, America's race riots, soaring crime rate and growing economic insecurity had led to 'white flight' to the suburbs, thus reducing city rents and staving off gentrification for a few more years.

the talk', they were also 'walking the walk', albeit in hookers' heels.

Although some of those who saw them felt they were merely talented Stones' imitators – Johansen and Thunders as Jagger and Richards – Johansen himself was more than ready to defend the band's stance. 'The Stones thing I don't think about any more, we owe more to those sixties girl groups,' he defiantly told reporters in early 1973.

What Johansen and Thunders also had – something that was far more important – was the right attitude, a harking back to the golden age hid their love of originality. And they had, perhaps inadvertently, hit on something else that was special in their own material – the growing distance between non-bubblegum rock and that music's target audience. Most 17-year-olds didn't have 'a woman', or 'a Cadillac' or troubles with their leases or mortgages. What they had, in many cases, were both raging hormones and raging emotions – neither of which were being particularly addressed by the new rock gods in their tax haven ivory towers.

It was the emotive power of the Dolls' songs that drew in people like record dealer Don Hughes, a top mod in sixties' Hounslow, whose music deals – and increasingly unhappy marriage – had him prowling the streets looking 'for a great new band four or five nights a week'. In the Dolls he thought he'd found them, 'I couldn't believe their "Jet Boy" track, that completely blew me away, it was so f—ing good with all those handclaps and that pushy guitar riff. And then seeing 'em live and then the album, them writing about Vietnam, you know in "Vietnamese Baby", when the war was still on and when no one else was daring to do it. They did fast, three-chord, three-minute songs and they did 'em with real feeling, it wasn't just some old millionaire rocker shrugging on stage, this was stuff from the heart. Passionate.'

'Trash' is perhaps, the most 'passionate' of all the Dolls' tracks – the perfect single that never was, actually, a single – from its straight-ahead pounding start, jumping in at the chorus, to its epic double-beat ending, enlivened by producer Todd Rundgren's use of high backing vocals that he'd skilfully lifted from The Herd's 'From The Underworld'. The lyrics are sung with enough desperation by

Johansen to be believable – they're also suitably dramatic, with the choruses begging the song's subject, 'my sweet baby', not to throw her life away. It is a desperate plea, seemingly delivered in the dirty alleyways and stopped sinks of *Midnight Cowboy* NYC and, in under four minutes, it tells a bittersweet'n'sour low-life love story – how does the girl call her lover-boy? 'Trash!' – in majestic trash-Glam style. These people might be hookers, rent boys, junkies, sneak thieves – or so the lyrics imply – but they're still human beings and their subject matter is still tragedy.

On another level the song's other constant refrain – about the need to pick up trash – made it one of the world's first ecology songs. 'To my mind,' claims Gruen, 'that's its main theme. "Trash, pick it up, don't throw my life away." On that level it's ecological. That's part of what David and Johnny intended and that's why I always thought the song wasn't just about girls or whatever. It always sounded too important for that . . . '

The song's soaring finale suggests that all these problems – chemical, emotional, environmental – might just be overcome by the sheer power of love'n'lust – young rock'n'roll romance, by the passion of young people.

But many saw this as a cheap kitsch fake. Bob Harris wrote the Dolls off as 'mock rock' when they appeared on his *Old Grey Whistle Test* TV show to promote their first album. The latter was a strong debut, though its own producer, Todd Rundgren, had described the Dolls, somewhat insultingly, as 'a novelty act' (words that showed the degree of hostility to the band within the rock mainstream). It was an album that only came about after Mercury's Paul Nelson had seen the band a staggering 80 times – a $100,000 signing that contradicted the wishes of Mercury's own vice-president. The Dolls' eponymous first album contained their finest songs and its power remains undiminished even now – but it failed to chart on either its US release, in late July 1973, or when it was issued in the UK some three months later. This failure was partly, perhaps, because the Dolls divided every crowd who ever heard them – even within the same magazine opinions could be blatantly, hugely, polarised by the Thunders– Johansen axis. *Melody Maker* in 1972–73 was a prime example: feature writer Mark Plummer seemed to take the Dolls' continuing existence as a personal affront, a band whose 'playing was the worst I've ever seen . . . musically dire', while Michael Watts, another *MM* reporter, instead saw them as 'a great kick in the ass to the corpse of rock'n'roll . . . maybe in a couple of years musicologists will be having their say but it doesn't even matter if the Dolls are around then. What counts is they're speaking for now. That's how it used to be. Remember?'

The hard-drug tag, which wasn't altogether true in the early days, also became difficult to shake. Or to market. The death of drummer Billy 'Dolls' Murcia during the band's first London trip in November 1972 only made things worse. He'd foolishly tried some speedballs for the first time, a mixture of amphetamine and heroin, and had overdosed almost instantly. The new 'friends' he was with ran off, leaving him to die. His replacement, Jerry Nolan, swiftly learned the ropes and summed it all up: 'Being a Doll wasn't a part-time gig. You couldn't arrive early and change into your costume – we had none of that. If you were a Doll you walked it like you talked it 24/7 and that was that.'

All this, though – like the make-up, dresses and urban anthems – could, conceivably, have added to the Dolls' appeal to 'alienated' youth across the US . . . but it didn't get through. The main reason is perhaps that they fell between two stools – the band were, after all, mostly in their mid-twenties, partly 'old school'. And their more superficial 'gimmicks' were too easily linked to the much more successful artists – Bowie and Alice Cooper – who'd immediately preceded them. The group *did* have a new attitude – they'd unwittingly combined Iggy Pop's iconoclasm with the Velvets' camp threatening sneer – but the heroin use, their birth certificates and their long hair really belonged to the generation before. Thus the Dolls could always cause enough outrage to ensure their records were effectively blacklisted (by all America's major radio networks)

but not enough to inspire teenage enthusiasm beyond their tiny Manhattan enclaves. Undiluted, their stance won them notoriety but little real American success (although, diluted, their look was to make millions for groups like Kiss). And this fatal pattern would be repeated with virtually all New York's original 'punk' bands . . .

The future Ramones had also checked out the Dolls in late 1972. 'They were great,' said Johnny Ramone years afterwards, 'even though they didn't play that well.' Another Dolls' 'regular' was Patti Smith, who was soon 'opening' for the band with a ten-minute poetry slot. Gaunt young feminist poet Patti – few dared call her a poetess – had been born in Chicago, although she was raised in a fairly poor, mixed-race area of New Jersey where she became pregnant at 16. She gave up the child to foster parents before finishing art school and moving to New York City in 1967. She was just 21 years old.

Smith had been publicly performing her stark, emotionally naked poems since February 1971, when her dynamic, rock-style reading at St Mark's Church, in the then still seedy Bowery district, had put her on the Manhattan art circuit map (the readings had been part of the edgily chic St Marks' Poetry Project – it was still cool to be a poet in late sixties/early seventies New York).

Smith was hanging out with art photographer Robert Mapplethorpe, then almost unknown. She and Mapplethorpe had briefly visited Paris – home of her hero Rimbaud, the 19th-century poet. Jean Nicolas Arthur Rimbaud was one of the creators of symbolism – in works such as *Les Illuminations* – as well as being someone whose *Les Deserts de l'amour* had predicted 'Freudian' notions before Freud was even a practising doctor. Arthur Rimbaud himself had given up poetry at just 20 and died young at 37. To Smith this made him a seeming pioneer of the 'live fast, die young' philosophy that The Who had encapsulated in their 'My Generation'. The fact that Rimbaud, like his friend and fellow poet Paul Verlaine, died in absolute poverty, only added to his romantic allure.

Smith had taken Mapplethorpe to France as her lover but, after an increasingly liberated Smith had gone out with several other guys, her photographer boyfriend made good on his threat to 'go off and go gay' – an event that, when it happened, seems to have shattered Smith, who allegedly saw it as some kind of betrayal of their months of intimacy. Back in Manhattan she was soon living a hand-to-mouth existence – that's when she wasn't contributing the odd article to *Creem*, *Circus* and *Rolling Stone*, or working part-time in Scribner's bookstore (often giving away volumes, and sometimes cash, to those bookworms who couldn't afford to actually buy anything). She acted in and co-wrote several plays, most noticeably *Cowboy Mouth*, put together with her then lover, the married actor-director Sam Shepard. He was then only in his mid-twenties, a man with six theatrical Obie awards to his name who was also a part-time rock'n'roll drummer. *Cowboy Mouth*'s title came from Dylan's 'Sad-Eyed Lady Of The Lowlands' song and the play itself, between a wide array of four-letter words, spoke of rock as being the new 'street religion' and of people wanting 'street angels'.

Nick Ray, director of James Dean's most dynamic film, *Rebel Without A Cause*, came to some *Cowboy Mouth* rehearsals and there was even talk of a film of the Shepard–Smith play – or at least, *à la* Frank Zappa's *200 Motels*, a videotape recording of a dress rehearsal. But Shepard couldn't take the domestic upheaval his blatant dalliance with Smith was causing and, after just one public performance of their play, he left both New York and Smith. She later described him as the 'most true American man' she'd ever met, someone who was 'hero-oriented', words that revealed her romantic streak (though she was also alleged to have said, not that long afterwards, that 'every man I've ever loved, or lived with, has shat on me . . .').

The Shepard affair only enhanced Smith's Manhattan reputation and in 1972 her first book of poetry was published. *Seventh Heaven* was a limited edition of a thousand copies issued by Victor Bockris's small Telegraph imprint.

A slimmer volume for Philadelphia's Middle Earth Books swiftly followed in autumn of the same year, but the girl who'd been disappointed by the 'straightness' of Glassboro art school was the same girl who didn't believe white men could be sexy . . . until she saw Mick Jagger and the Stones perform 'Satisfaction' live on TV. When she saw them live a few months later, at Madison Square Gardens, she suddenly saw that an exhausted Jagger – he'd already played two shows that day – was a dramatic enough performer to hold the audience's attention between songs, to hold it with mere words. It gave 'poetry such a future', in her own words. But some seven years later, that future had morphed back into rock. The ultimate modern poetry *was* now rock'n'roll – books, and poems without music, were never going to be enough. They lacked rhythm, at least on the surface, and Smith had recently told one interviewer that one of her three favourite poets was Muhammad Ali, principally because of his 'verbal rhythms, you know?'.

It seems inevitable now – but back then the rock–poetry schtick was a major revelation that took many months to be fully understood by Smith herself. After trips to Paris – to visit the graves of Rimbaud and Jim Morrison – and London – to read with Bockris, Andrew Wylie and ex-Warhol fave Gerard Malanga – Smith managed to blag herself onto the client list of Jane Friedman at Wartoke Concern (she got an interview within days by allegedly claiming that she was seriously ill with TB).

Wartoke was a major PR firm whose clients included serious music biz players such as Stevie Wonder and, by the spring of '73, Friedman had Smith doing readings at the trendiest place to be: the Mercer Arts Oscar Wilde Room with The New York Dolls. Within 12 months she would form a firm alliance – and then a band – with acquaintance and rock critic Lenny Kaye, the man who'd first encouraged her to write for the NYC rock press (the same man whose *Nuggets* compilation albums of raw sixties American garage bands – such as the Standells, Sonics, Trashmen, Shadows of Knight, etc. – were to prove so influential in their defiance of the soft, post-psychedelic tide).

Iggy Pop was one who'd irregularly attended the New York Dolls–Patti Smith concerts of that time. He was then flying back and forth between London and the US, promoting the *Raw Power* album he'd cut with David Bowie in 1972. Because of the Bowie–London link, in July of the same year, Iggy and his band – billed as The Ex-Stooges, for guitarist James Williamson now dominated the sound – performed their one and only gig outside of the USA. It was at the Scala, near King's Cross Station in north central London (a district already becoming a hang-out for young hookers and transvestites as well as the city's few hundred hardened junkies). The 'Stooges' were more a backing band by then, but they still kicked up a hell of a racket behind the glitter-jeaned, shirtless Iggy, who scuttled across the boards like some psychotic gay lizard – complete with silver body-paint and centre-spread poses.

In that stunned Scala crowd – which Iggy 'stared-out' and walked into several times – was one John Joseph Lydon, a 16-year-old from the 'English-Irish' ghetto of Finsbury Park, London, where 'punk' was to finally go beyond its arty American freak show roots and become a genuine mass movement . . .

CBGB's –
Blank Generation

At the end of January 1953, strong north-easterly gales, combined with surging high tides, had caused a devastating flood across the eastern coasts of Belgium, Holland and England. In the UK, one of the worst affected areas was around Canvey Island, in the south-east, where the 300-year-old sea wall broke. Since most of the isle was, is, below sea level, hundreds drowned and hundreds more saw their homes – and livelihoods – swept away. Britain then was still recovering from the Second World War and the Tories – victors in the 1951 general election, despite getting less votes than Labour – had still not fully fulfilled their manifesto pledge to remove the rationing and identity cards that the nation had endured since 1939. Canvey Island, subsequently, received comparatively little help as it struggled to return to normal – even though government neglect had undoubtedly made the size and impact of the disaster worse. An isolated, perhaps even alienated, mentality gripped much of the area. The fact that many of the isle's few summer tourists were 'fresh off the boat' black families from Brixton added to, rather than diminished, Canvey's subtle sense of separation.

Even when, in the sixties, some money arrived in the shape of the oil refining industry, there was a heavy price to pay in terms of water table contamination and air pollution. Despite being only half an hour from Southend, and less than two hours' drive from

London, Canvey did have something of a British 'Deep South' feel to it.

But British Beat did penetrate – the southern R'n'B variation as practised by the Stones and Pretty Things – and in 1964 16-year-old guitarist Wilko Johnson and his drumming pal John 'The Figure' Martin joined The Roamers. Within three years they'd mutated into rock band The Heap, but they'd done so without The Figure and Johnson himself left before the start of '68, bored with playing weddings and parties for £2 a night – and bored too with rock's increasingly indulgent direction. Having always seen his guitar as more a rhythm than a melody instrument, Wilko had little time for the endless curlicues of progressive rock. So, like Patti Smith and countless others before him, he set off for the big city, determined to become a poet. But Newcastle University didn't lead to a career in poetry so Johnson returned to Canvey – via Nepal and Goa – and in 1971 he pulled Lee Brilleaux and John 'Sparko' Sparks out of the jug band known as Pigboy Charlie and together they started a blisteringly tight combo with the name Doctor Feelgood (named after a Johnny Kidd and The Pirates' B-side – The Pirates' seminal guitar man Mick Green would remain a big Johnson influence). 'R'n'B is a much better word than rock, don't you reckon?' Brilleaux said later: 'Rhythm? Yeah, Blues? Definitely.' Muddy Waters, Bo Diddley and Little Walter were the key names – edgy, stripped-to the-bone chords and beats were the aim.

Just as Northern Soul – i.e. pre-Dolby Tamla, Stax, Spark and Gordy – had held on into the seventies in northern towns like Wigan and Sheffield, so in the less affluent parts of the south and east, rhythm'n'blues in the rawest sense continued to give a live platform for bands.

Infusing the older rhythms with a modern energy and sensibility seemed a good path to steer between the polar extremes of teeny-bop trivia and synth rock pretentiousness. Between them the latter two genres – and all the connected time-servers at the record labels, boutiques and radio stations – appeared to have it all sewn up. In many ways it seemed as if rock had returned to its pre-Beatles days, when insipid pop was the only music given a wide platform.

The Beat groups had shaken things up for a little while but the end of the sixties had seen the revolution quietly smothered. There were now shops selling flared jeans, loon pants and cheesecloth shirts in every other town and village in the UK (and most of the US). Long hair was allowed in most offices and colleges, and the generation gap seemed as narrow as it had ever been. Virtually all the major rock acts that broke through in the early seventies, from Pink Floyd to Led Zeppelin to ELP and Quo, had been gigging and recording in the previous decade. All of them swiftly graduated to playing vast stadia, and all of them were apolitical, in rock terms conservative with a small 'c'. The cultural and musical insurrection of 1964–68 seemed light years away, a feverish dream that was already half forgotten.

Crushed Butler were one of the few new bands attempting something genuinely different in the years 1969–70. A fast-talking trio – vocalist-guitarist Jesse Hector, bassist Alan Butler and mod pretty boy drummer Darryl Read – they'd toyed with using the name Clash and were, in many ways, Britain's first proto-punk band. Their gigs as a support band had the look, the energy and the on-stage aggression that shook headlining acts such as Slade, Mott The Hoople and Atomic Rooster . . . but, in the end, Butler were just too disorganised and brusque for the Woodstock era – '*Three ugly heavy musicians playing music to match,*' said one reviewer – and 'Combat mod' was then too recent to be successfully evoked by short hair and heavy sideburns . . .

But, by the end of 1973, Dai Davis of the Albion agency was getting the Feelgoods gigs in London, mainly at the Tally Ho pub in Camden and Holloway Road's Lord Nelson (another pub). The fact that Johnson and Brilleaux also looked the part, with shortish hair and well-worn suits – complete with manic stares for any hecklers or Ted purists who got too cheeky – only added to the group's live appeal.

In 1974 they played over 200 gigs on a circuit whose biggest acts – Kokomo, Ian Dury's Kilburn and The Highroads – were now being labelled as 'pub rock' artists. Dr Feelgood's choppy riff style soon had journos raving, especially at the *New Musical Express*.

The *NME* was then undergoing the painful transition from light-weight pop paper to something a lot broader and wilder. Writers like Mick Farren, Charles Shaar Murray, Nick Kent, Tony Tyler, Roy Carr and Neil Spencer were genuine music lovers and, though few, if any, had gone to journalist school – many came from either the underground press or failing bands – and they did manage to steer the weekly *NME* to sales of almost quarter of a million (a situation that added to the intense rivalry with the more 'progressive' *Sounds* and the more prestigious, if mainstream, *Melody Maker*). And all of the above writers liked Dr Feelgood – 'Tony Tyler raved about the Feelgoods, absolutely raved about them,' Roy Carr said decades later, 'he came into the *NME* office ranting about this great band he'd seen in this Holloway pub the night before.' This enthusiasm helped to set a new precedent when an unsigned band got front pages and two-page spreads in the *NME*.

'Feelgood were solid, a great band and they really did pave the way for the Pistols and The Clash and all those other guys,' said future Clash spokesman Kosmo Vinyl in 2005, 'and Bernard [Rhodes] and Malcolm [McLaren] did admit that to me, and a few other people, just after that time. They admitted it in private, of course. They wouldn't talk about it in public back then. But Feelgood were great, were different to other pub bands . . .'

What set Feelgood apart from the others was the intensity of their back-to-the-roots vision – that and Brillieaux's no-nonsense barking delivery as Johnson launched his staccato guitar runs across stage, 'machine-gunning' the audience with his battered instrument and madman stare. The word, of course, soon spread about a new band which was the hottest live thing around.

'John Gray put us onto Feelgood,' Wobble said some 30 years later. 'He'd seen 'em early on and thought they were pretty good – and they were. Me and John [Lydon] saw 'em at least once or twice and they did it, they could do the business live, no doubt about it.' A BBC radio session for John Peel – Radio One's late-night 'in-house freak' – led Wilko Johnson to take the giant leap forward of writing new material, since it seemed to Johnson 'pretty stupid to go on the air, to a couple of million people or more, and then only play other people's songs'. Previously they'd just been doing covers of numbers like 'Riot In Cell Block Number 9'.

Wilko's own songwriting efforts were impressive enough and United Artists signed the Feelgoods in 1974, seemingly intent on breaking the band properly – a nationwide poster campaign was launched and pop videos were shot for all the first four singles (a real rarity in those pre-'Bohemian Rhapsody', pre-MTV days). 'Roxette', the first 45, was too simplistic with its boom-boom-boom beat, but the follow-up – Johnson's 'She Does It Right' – was electrifying, capturing much of the band's raw live excitement with its jagged guitars and fast, pushing beat.

It was rhythm'n'blues, but faster and more savagely played than ever before, with bluesy lyrics about a fast woman and all that that entailed. The reviews were good; the Feelies had already captured the front pages of the music press. But the daytime jocks at Radio One and Capital, then Britain's most popular stations, refused to give it more than a few token plays and the Beeb's dominant *Top of the Pops* wouldn't air the accompanying pop videos. The unspoken feeling was, perhaps, that a band dedicated to rootsy integrity would somehow 'show up' the increasingly tatty round of Glam groups then ruling the *TOTP* roost.

The next two singles similarly failed to chart and UA began to lose interest a little, even though the stark image of the Feelgoods' frontmen and their Back To Mono stance – their first recordings were done this way – were always guaranteed to garner some media attention.

The Feelgoods' debut album, *Malpractice*, made the UK charts in October 1975, briefly getting into the Top 20, while several hundred copies eventually made their way into specialist shops in New York. Among those Americans listening were young, jobbing drummer Clem Burke and an ambitious young guitarist called Tom Miller, a songwriter/poet who'd exchanged his native Delaware for New York in 1968 when he was just 19. Someone he'd been to boarding school with – they'd run off together when they were 16 – was already in New York, one Richard Myers. He was another would-be poet, though one with a more streetwise sensibility than the more cautious Miller. They'd had their thoughts on music seriously redirected by the Mercer Arts Center's New Year's Eve bash of 1973 – 'The Endless Party', which had featured live performances by the Dolls, with Jonathan Richman's Modern Lovers, Wayne County's Queen Elizabeth plus 'special guests: Ruby and The Rednecks and The Magic Tramps'. Wave after wave of new sounds and chord-driven excitement kept the crowd there on their feet till dawn.

Inspired by the sheer nerve of it all, Myers and Miller quickly got together a band under the banner the Neon Boys, Miller swapping his acoustic guitar for an electric before teaching Myers the rudiments of bass-playing (the beat was provided by Delaware drummer Billy Ficca). By mid-1974 this group had been renamed Television. And by then the self-contained Miller had chosen another name, Tom Verlaine, an answer to Patti Smith's appropriation of Arthur Rimbaud.₅

Richard Myers joined in the name change fun, giving himself the suitably apocalyptic title Richard Hell. He now worked in the cine bookshop of gay fashion victim Terry Ork, a major Warhol associate, and used his wages to mimeograph pages of his poetry (this poetic output began to dry up after the revelation of seeing the Dolls). Any spare cash went on drugs after Ork had introduced Hell to the dubious 'joys' of heroin.

For many, Hell was – is – the founder of American 'punk'. Everything about him seemed right – from his spiky hair and rugged good looks to his narcotics, poems and ragged clothes.

Whereas Patti Smith's increasingly 'musical' readings with Lenny Kaye often sounded off the wall – Chris Stein later claimed they

5 Rimbaud's name would appear on Smith's live posters even when she wasn't performing the Frenchman's poems. Paul Verlaine was a symbolist poet who shot and wounded his friend Rimbaud – and served two years in a Belgian jail for his crime before dying in poverty.

were almost like a deliberate 'comedy routine' – Television swiftly became pretty damn serious (partly at the insistence of the determined Verlaine). Although the intelligent end of contemporary British Glam – Bowie, Roxy Music, Cockney Rebel, Mott The Hoople – was taken note of, Television were more influenced by the often stark, clipped chords of the Feelgoods, and by their own reading of two key strands from the mid-to late-sixties, British Invasion bands and US garage bands (including, of course, the latter's bastard child, The Velvet Undergound).

The Verlaine–Hell–Ficca trio was then augmented by new rhythm guitarist Richard Lloyd – a former mental patient that Ork had put them onto – after auditions that had also seen Chris Stein seriously considered and Dee Dee Ramone swiftly rejected (in true proto-punk style, Dee Dee only knew how to play bar chords). Television now had three strong frontmen in Verlaine–Hell–Lloyd, complete with 'duelling' guitars, and they were soon out looking for gigs in earnest. As luck would have it, they stumbled upon the one venue that would then have considered having them: Hilly Kristal's Bowery club CBGB's. This was originally a biker bar. Its full name CBGB-OMFUG stood for 'Country, Blue-Grass and Blues and Other Music For Uplifting Gourmandizers', genres that Kristal still, erratically, gave a platform to in early 1974. Former singer Kristal had been fixing the small club's outside awning one day when Verlaine and Lloyd had, almost literally, bumped into him. It was exactly the kind of venue they were looking for and they mentioned their 'new' band and its need for a live base (although they also claimed, somewhat disingenuously, that their music featured bit of country and 'a little bluegrass . . .'). Kristal had been running nightclubs, include the Village Vanguard, his own way since the dawn of the sixties and he agreed on the spot to give the former Neon Boys a Sunday night slot – three in a row.

One of Television's first gigs there, on 14 April 1974, saw Patti Smith and Lenny Kaye in the audience. Smith was blown away by the band's performance, a bizarre blend of the raw and the clinical, the earnest and the cryptic. American rock hadn't been that intense for years. As Hell had himself written a few weeks before, Bowie,

Patti Smith, Bruce Springsteen, and Bryan Ferry all created, or at least alluded to, other types of rock'n'roll. Their greatest talent was for 'attracting attention', which Hell thought was 'great'. The art of the future was going to be, he asserted, 'celebrityhood', which was why rock'n'roll 'is so appealing now', since 'it's an outlet for passion and ideals that are too radical' for any other form of expression.

Inspired by all they had seen and heard – Smith had became obsessed with Verlaine – she and Kaye decided to take their own music just a little more seriously. They auditioned dozens of piano-players before finding Richard Sohl, a keyboardist who'd been 'discovered' by Danny Fields. Despite, or maybe because of, this connection, Sohl was young and uptight enough to make Smith think 'he was auditioning us'. Sohl's other great advantage was a classical background that made it easy for him to jam with Smith and Kaye, following – or leading – them wherever they wanted to go musically.

In an attempt to expand her audience – and get closer to Verlaine – Smith agreed to gig with Television for six weekends in a row at CBGB's. The last gigs saw crowds so big they spilled out onto the street; New York's new music, still unnamed, had arrived and there were to be no more Saturday nights of bluegrass or country at the club.

The debut Patti Smith single, 'Hey Joe/Piss Factory', would be recorded and released later that year. It would be on her and Kaye's own tiny Mer label and this 45 is the first real punk single of the seventies – in some ways the first modern 'indie' single – the opening entry in a genre that was to be defined by those very formats, the single and the independent release. In performance, Patti's version of Hendrix's 'Hey Joe', the single's A-side, would often veer off into Smith's view of the breaking controversy surrounding another Patty, the heiress Patty Hearst.[6]

---

6 Hearst was a young heiress kidnapped by the far-left US terror group the SLA (Symbionese Liberation Army) in 1974 – their leader raped Hearst but they eventually became 'lovers', of a sort, and she took part in bank raids before most of the gang were killed in a police ambush. Hearst was later jailed, but was freed after just three years as many saw her as a 'brain-washing' victim.

The single version of 'Hey Joe' wasn't quite so exotic but it was backed by the brilliantly urgent sour'n'sour 'Piss Factory', the tale of a sparky girl stuck in an awful dead-end job – but the first-person protagonist is going to escape, Smith maintains, for she has 'something called desire'. As well as being an attack on industrial employment it also had a proto-punk sensibility and Sohl's spi-ralling staccato piano. The song was actually inspired by Smith's own teenage jobs, her summers spent in a children's bathroom fac-tory, surrounded by women so ignorant they regarded her Rimbaud books as 'being communist' merely because they were in French. The 'Hey Joe/Piss Factory' single got little airplay, even on the var-ious graveyard shifts, and was never in danger of being distributed enough to chart, but its very existence increased the tempo of the New York scene – and now it really was a scene. Its two leading groups in 1974 were Patti Smith, looking like an asexual Keith Richard, and her band – and Television, with their guitar trio in short hair and ripped clothes (and, on one occasion, a 'Please Kill Me' t-shirt . . . not a garment to be worn lightly in 20th-century New York). Hell also wore began to wear safety pins at this time; partly as decoration, partly to keep his artfully damaged clothes together (it was innovatory but not completely original, Warhol had worn clips of safety pins in his collar as early as 1968).

This tense, dense 'new scene' was based around several clubs; principally CBGB's and Max's Kansas City. Max's owner, Mickey Ruskin, had opened it in December 1965 with much fanfare. It had seemed very chic at the time; the staff were famed for their 'London-style' fashions and it was, initially, the favoured drinking hole of many fashionable and/or wealthy celebs. On any one of a hundred nights the Duke and Duchess of Windsor could be found eating a few tables away from actor Cary Grant while Senator Robert F. Kennedy and film-maker John Frankenheimer would be grabbing a quiet Irish coffee at the bar . . .

By the end of the decade, though, Max's was instead infamous for being a home for various hangers-on from Warhol's Factory crowd; plus it also had waitresses with the shortest skirts in town (and a backroom where grass and sex were occasionally enjoyed).

And Max's did still get irregular visits from the likes of Mick Jagger, Elton John and up-and-coming rocker Bruce Springsteen. By the mid-seventies it was firmly established on what some called 'the CBGB's poetry, art and rock circuit' – Patti Smith, with Kaye, had played the upstairs room at Max's, following in the footsteps of The New York Dolls who, in their turn, were following the band they were to eclipse, the near-legendary Magic Tramps. The latter had started out in 1968 as Messiah, an experimental LA 'theatre rock' trio with Youngblood Xavier on guitar backed by violinist Sesu Coleman and drummer Larry Chapman. Sunset Strip's Temple Of The Rainbow gave them a residency but, by late 1970, the band had started to spread its wings by going out and playing covers at various clubs and bars under the pseudonym 'The Magic Tramps'. In 1971 they had a new front man – singer Eric Emerson, another Warhol graduate, there in Hollywood just to help finish Andy's *Lonesome Cowboys* movie. And it was Emerson who suggested the move to NYC where, he felt, a stint at Max's could be arranged via Warhol's old pal Mickey Ruskin. The Tramps' residency at Max's swiftly became a high-fashion Mecca, mainly because of Youngblood's new flair for proto-Glam design (complete with thick white make-up for Coleman, something that a young Max's regular, Kiss founder Gene Simmons, seemed to take note of). Youngblood left the group to open an East Village fashion boutique with his girlfriend in St Mark's Place, within a stone's throw of where Patti Smith had launched her poetry readings some three years before. Xavier was replaced by guitarist Kevin Reece and bassist Wayne Harley-Harley, and with this new five-piece line-up The Magic Tramps were invited to a revamped off-Broadway theatre called the Mercer Arts Center. The Tramps became the Mercer Center's resident house band for a time; they turned down a couple of record company offers and didn't receive a third . . .

One Max's staffer who'd seen the Tramps there was Debbie Harry, who'd become a nightclub waitress after her career in folk had stalled,[7] despite her appealingly sweet voice and stunning looks

---

7 She'd recorded the wistful *Wind In The Willows* album in 1969.

(the latter helping to lead her, albeit briefly, into the life of a Playboy Bunny Girl and then a part-time beautician). The Miami-born girl's face and figure were youthful, although she was actually just a few months away from her thirtieth birthday in late 1974, a full year and a half older than Patti Smith. Harry looked younger, though, and could pass for 21; her age, in fact, had the adopted Harry mistakenly convinced that she was the pre-fame love child of Hollywood sex-goddess Marilyn Monroe.

In 1973 Harry had restarted her career as a vocalist by launching The Stilettoes 'singing dancing group' with two other singers, Elda Gentile and Rosie Ross. They rejected auditionee and groupie Nancy Spungen, despite her later claims to have been a member, and then recruited Chris Stein as the band's guitar player. Stein, at the tender age of 15, had been a part-time member of the Magic Tramps during the last few months of their existence.

The Stilettoes' own repertoire consisted of Supremes covers plus the songs Phil Spector-style girl groups had sung a decade before, 'Then He Kissed Me', 'Be My Baby', 'Walkin' In The Sand', 'He Hit Me (And It Felt Like A Kiss)', etc . . . The group split within the year, but not before Stein and Harry had become both musical partners and lovers. After a brief period as Angle and The Snakes, they mutated into Blondie and The Banzai Babes as 1975 approached. By the time of CBGB's Festival of Unsigned Bands on 16 July 1975, they were simply known as Blondie, with Debbie solo on vocals, new man Clem Burke on drums, and Gary Valentine playing bass after four-string regular Fred Smith had left to replace Richard Hell in Television. Harry's skimpy outfits and soaring vocals, and the band's inspired repackaging of the sixties sound, might well have had them topping the bill at CBGB's Unsigned Fest in other circumstances if The Ramones hadn't existed.

The Ramones were not brothers, of course, and merely used the name that Paul McCartney had once used as a pseudonym at hotels – an obvious declaration of the suburban New Yorker's love of pop.

The Beach Boys, The Kinks, late doo wop, Phil Spector's girlie groups – again – The Beatles, late-night pop radio shows – the boys from Queens loved it all. Unfortunately Dee Dee (Doug Colvin),

Joey (Jeffrey Hyman), Tommy (Erdelyi) and Johnny (John Cummings) couldn't play such a range (the latter two didn't have much of an excuse – they'd been in high school groups like the Tangerine Puppets as early as 1966).

In fact, the foursome couldn't play *that* much of anything *that* well at all, not with their voices and their limited, guitar-based instrumentation. So they simply turned their weakness to strength, by overloading the fuzz box guitar and making up for their lack of finesse with sheer speed and buzz-saw distortion – a *blitzkrieg* bop of a sound, as Johnny put it (the German word was appropriate for the genuinely right-wing Cummings, a man who'd been raised on US Army bases in West Germany). Lyrics were usually basic and, to the mainstream, as dumb-smart moronic as possible – cartoon lyrics for a 'so-called' cartoon band – all about sniffing glue and being afraid to go down to the midnight horror movie basement. They kept the standard longish hair of the time, though Dee Dee and Johnny's hairstyles were more mannered, but adopted a strong group uniform of sixties-style drainpipe Levis – jeans so old the knees were tattered and frayed open, worn with traditional leather bike jackets. They had an identity: wild ones so down on their luck they couldn't afford new clothes or haircuts.

The Ramones' first rehearsal was in January 1974, just a few weeks after Dee Dee and Johnny had seen The New York Dolls at the Mercer Arts. Barely two months later they were gigging their 20-minute sets, playing and/or socialising in all the Manhattan gig places – The 82, CBGB's and Max's Kansas City – that were soon to become legendary. By summer '74 the tall, gangly Joey had firmly established himself as lead vocalist. He'd been in a couple of other bedroom bands before and live performance was easy after months of cadging food and sleeping on the floor of his mother's paint shop. Dee Dee approved: 'The thing was, all the other singers [in New York] were copying David Johansen, who was copying Mick Jagger, and I just couldn't stand that any more. But Joey was unique, totally unique.' They had a small but dedicated following (many of them the fellow 'nerds' Joey couldn't help identifying with). Debbie Harry saw the band's first gig at CBGB's and thought it 'hilarious, Joey fell onto the stage and had to be helped up. It was ridiculous. But when they played it was exciting, all that energy.' It was energy that was partly anger: 'If I got angry with someone I'd go for the throat,' Dee Dee would later admit. 'That's what I thought was normal behaviour. Why'd you think I ended up in The Ramones?'

As with virtually all the New York groups, there was sporadic hard drug use in The Ramones, almost from the start, while others were disturbed by Dee Dee's alleged forays into male prostitution. But, for some, such things only added to the group's appeal – to jaded Manhattanites they were, by the summer of 1975, the biggest new band on the block. In terms of an entire package – cultural, sartorial, sexual, political – The New York Dolls before them and the Sex Pistols after, were to prove more influential than the brothers from Queens. But in purely *musical* terms, The Ramones, in attempting to re-create the excitement of pre-Dolby rock, were to cast a huge shadow – they had fused a blueprint for much of the indie future.

Two of those who'd checked out The Ramones in 1975 were Legs McNeil and John Holmstrom, the co-founders of New York's *Punk* magazine (originally to be called *Teenage News*, after the unreleased New York Dolls' track). *Punk* was a part-gushy, part-edgy guide to all that had happened, and was still happening, in New York; most noticeably all the up-and-coming gigs, all the gossip and the launch of David Byrne's Talking Heads (a launch aided by Byrne's borrowing of Jonathan Richman's persona – the deadpan yet hip nerd). But it was the thrill of seeing The Ramones that had really enthused the boys enough to see their magazine out onto the news-stands in time for Christmas '75: 'The Ramones were *so* great, it was like seeing The Beatles at the Cavern or something, it was unbelievable . . .'

Punk took its name partly from the sixties sub-genre of garage bands that had briefly flared up in the USA in the wake of both The Kingsmen's brilliantly moronic 'Louie Louie' song and the British Invasion (and that invasion's lesser-known heroes, the thuggishly but wonderful Troggs and Pretty Things). American garage bands that were still an influence in New York and, to a lesser extent, London. McNeil had also, though, opted for the four-letter 'P' word because he knew it would intrigue ex-Velvet Underground front man Lou Reed enough to grant the fledgling mag an interview, which he duly did. The bitterly entertaining Reed was now a solo star in his own right, with successful albums with Bowie in his recent past, and this interview coup convinced McNeil there was going to be some kind of market for what they'd written. He and Holmstrom consequently spent the fortnight prior to publication of the first issue plastering lamp-posts with the words 'Punk – coming soon!' Most people, including Debbie Harry, assumed it was 'just another new group with another really dumb name'.

Richard Hell, meanwhile, had been pushed out of Television by the control-freakery of Verlaine. To him, it was no big loss. For he had, up his sleeve, a new song that seemed to sum up the new world that was being slammed together in the small big city clubs he frequented. The song was 'Blank Generation', a number both anthem-like and anthemic, its taut beat and brisk guitar capturing the increasing tempo of NYC's brave new 'underground' scene of 1974–75. The word 'blank' was perfectly apt, Hell felt, not for the nihilistic reasons usually advanced but because, in his own words, 'blank was like a blank canvas, anything could be put on it, anything was possible'. The actual track, when finally released, was a minor classic; although apart from some major lyric changes, 'Blank Generation', as both a song and arrangement, was basically a steal from the B side of 'The Mummy', a 1959 novelty single. The flip of this 45 was called 'The Beat Generation', a casual, comic attack on 'welfare beatniks' by Bob McFadden and Dor – aka actor, poet and songwriter Rod McKuen (a 45 issued to little effect, or sales, by American Brunswick in 1959).

'Blank Generation' was the perfect 'slogan' for the time, though, and it – and Richard Hell – stuck in the mind of one visitor to New

York that year: 29-year-old Londoner Malcolm McLaren. The ex-art student had even taken a 'Richard Hell: Blank Generation' poster back to the other 'side of the pond', back to his King's Road shop, where it would soon 'add fuel to the fire' as well as inspiring one of rock'n'roll's finest songs.

WORLD'S END –
Revolt Into Style

Malcolm McLaren was born in January 1946, the son of Scots engineer Pete MacLaren and well-to-do Jewish girl Emily Isaacs. They'd split by 1948, a separation that came after pressure from the Isaacs family. Peter MacLaren was then effectively written out of the lives of young Malcolm and his older brother Stuart.

Emily changed her name to Eve and started a close on-off relationship with millionaire Sir Charles Clore – the owner of department store Selfridges in London's Oxford Street – after they'd met in Monte Carlo. Eve then remarried, tying the knot with Jewish businessman Martin Levi – later Martin Edwards – who owned a large dress-making factory in London (his name was changed, it's been said, to sound more 'English'). Eve had her own part in the clothing business and basically left the raising of her children to their grandmother Rose Corrie Isaacs.

Like most grandmothers, Rose spoilt the kids a little – and red-headed Malcolm, being the youngest, got the most attention; but, unlike most grandmothers, Rose had been a bohemian, a frustrated actress. She encouraged Malcolm's artistic notions – and increasingly ignored Stuart's – in the family home at 47 Carysfort Road, Stoke Newington, north-east London.[8]

---

8 It's still there and still has its decorative Vicwardian tiles in the tiny porch – the tiles show, appropriately enough, a stormy sea crashing its waves against a large blue rock. The house is now subdivided into three flats. Some of the residents there had heard of Malcolm McLaren but none seemed to be aware that he'd spent his childhood there.

After Rose's years of indulgence, young Malcolm was almost uncontrollable and was subsequently thrown out of school after school – Avignor Primary, William Patton – before a private education was paid for after the family had moved to Hendon. It was a move he resented, for the skinny, pale-faced lad had now discovered rock'n'roll and Stoke Newington and Stamford Hill were close to Tottenham, a major Teddy boy centre, with its vast nightclubs and dance halls. These areas, particularly the first two, were also one of the birthplaces of Mod, the movement that started as well-dressed Modern Jazz fanatics (it was perhaps the social mix of working- and lower middle class that made the area such a style crucible – that and a surplus of eager Jewish tailors).

Top Mod Mark Feld, later Marc Bolan of T. Rex fame, was a Stamford Hill–Newington boy, while a regular visitor was actor Brian Croucher. Both teenagers modelled clothes for Vince Man in Carnaby Street, then an obscure backstreet. 'I didn't really know it was a bit of a gay hang-out,' says Croucher now. 'It was a more innocent age then, though I suppose I should have been suspicious when they kept asking me to model shorts and tight t-shirts.'

McLaren was a modernist too – though he still loved early rockers such as the leather-clad Gene Vincent and Britain's own Billy Fury, with his immaculate looks and suave, passionate voice. The 'scene' – clothes, records, coffee bars – was soon all that counted and, as McLaren 'commuted' down to London's West End at every opportunity, his other big love, football, was soon forgotten (even though he had, by now, been offered a trial for Tottenham Hotspurs' youth team).

The teenage Malcolm left school with only two O levels and rejected the vintner's job he started after realising he'd have to work for much of the time in Spain. This would have involved too long an absence from the bohemian playground of Soho. The beatnik and modernist worlds, both with their own little codes, uniforms and snobberies, appealed to Malcolm Edwards, and Soho had become the heart of it all, but just being there wasn't a living or career in itself.

In 1964 he attended Harrow Art School, the start of almost

seven years in art colleges. There he made friends with a northern-er named Gordon Swire and his pal Fred Vermorel, the latter the son of a French Resistance fighter. Vermorel and Swire, and Swire's forthright sister Vivienne, were soon to become crucial fixtures in Malcolm Edward's life. It was during a flat share with them that McLaren bedded Westwood, allegedly pretending to be ill in order to get into her bed. Others say she was the relationship's initiator.

Some said Westwood found him immature – she was five years older, had been married and had a young child – but he was also undeniably intense and imaginative. At the expense of many other things, including the children in her charge, they developed a relationship that was to become, for a time, a career.

To some who knew them they were a fun team, full of mischievous ideas and outrageous suggestions – perhaps the most creative couple of the 20th century, 'Mr and Mrs Andy Warhol' – with an anarchist bent. Others, probably a majority, resented their direct opinions right from the start.

After Harrow came Goldsmiths and Croydon art colleges, and a drift into 'radical fun' politics – extreme 'pranksterism' taken to its, often illogical, conclusion. The year 1968 saw a couple of McLaren's scams with the King Mob gang – burning the US flag during that October's anti-Vietnam War demo in Grosvenor Square and dressing as Santa Claus to give away Selfridges' toys to visiting children. Alarmed store detectives starting snatching the toys back but only succeeded in part; the fuss from the children and their parents was too great and the store lost thousands of pounds as well as the goodwill of those present who *didn't* get any free gifts (this action of McLaren's was, perhaps, a dig at Clore, the owner of Selfridges, who had been romantically linked with his mother).

King Mob was a London-based organisation modelled on the French Situationists, their allies and mentors. They were then dominated by Guy Debord, author of the dense 1962 tome *The Society of the Spectacle* (this was a numbered treatise that claimed that modern society was dominated by pseudo-culture and pseudo-events – 'the spectacle'). Fakery – widespread fakery – kept people in soul-destroying dead-end jobs. Only by creating provocations, 'situations', could real revolutionaries hope to inspire a reaction, a backlash that would reveal the nation state's true, repressive, nature. This was the way to crusade against the new 20th-century disease, 'banalisation'.

This was all very well and, in some ways, accurate. But for someone advocating indiscipline, Debord was a particularly strict taskmaster. Any situationist accepting work Debord deemed unacceptable – designing a church, say, or associating with the soft, or even the hard, left – was subject to instant expulsion from the Situationist International (London's King Mobsters were themselves former members who'd been expelled – it's said because their alleged boast of having 60 trained guerrillas was proved blatantly false by a surprise visit from a French delegation who found a handful of skint ex-students clustered around a crate of cider). But, as more than one former associate has since said, if Debord had ever gained real power then 'people would have died – in numbers'.

While more of a humanitarian than Debord, McLaren too had a ruthless streak. As fellow Goldsmiths art student and future sculptor Malcolm Poynter was to find out in 1967. 'I was an ex-mod who'd been through about thirty jobs in six or seven years. Been a messenger boy who shot around on a scooter – that was when I first saw trouble with the ton-up boys, the rockers – before I went to Goldsmiths. Malcolm McLaren, well he was actually called Malcolm Edwards back then, was in the same year as me there, in 1967, and I was to see him around, on and off, for most of the next three years. He was part of the Maoist gang, was essentially their leader – they all had their little red books and took that Chinese stuff very seriously.'

Poynter knew McLaren-Edwards was already going out with Vivienne Westwood but he didn't realise how much the agitprop couple were already feared – in some cases hated – until he too had a girlfriend called Vivienne. 'If ever I phoned anyone and said, "Hi, it's Malcolm, is it OK if me and Vivienne come over?" people would slam the phone down. So I'd ring back and say, "Hey, it's me, Malcolm, what's goin' on?" And then they'd say, "Malcolm Poynter? Oh, thank God it's you, we thought it was the other Malcolm and Vivienne, Edwards and Westwood . . ." '

'The fact that Westwood and McLaren were together a lot, often alone, was kind of important,' says writer Paul Gorman. 'It meant that for three years or so they hot-housed together. They were often virtually penniless and forced to entertain themselves. Almost like Joe Orton and Kenneth Halliwell when they started out.'[9]

'I was practically a virgin,' McLaren was to say later. 'I slept with Vivienne and she became pregnant and my entire life changed. There I was, just nineteen years of age, not a pot to piss in and my new girlfriend's pregnant. A girlfriend who was a little older than me and already with a kid of her own. I was a bit stunned by it all. So my grandmother said Vivienne should have an abortion and stumped up £100. We walked up and down Harley Street a few times and Vivienne suddenly said, "No! I've changed my mind, I'm keeping the baby! Think I'll spend this hundred pound on a skirt suit." And so she went off and bought some cashmere twin-set thing instead.'

McLaren returned to Goldsmiths as a parent – and threw himself into the student turmoil of the day. 'We were the first generation to actually question the set-up,' Poynter recalled decades later. 'Before that, your working-class students were too grateful to ask any awkward questions. Anyway, we'd join the students' union and demand to know why certain lecturers had three-hour lunches in the pub and all that. Malcolm [McLaren] joined in and went further – him and his group smeared dogshit all over the principal's front door, put up Maoist banners everywhere. I remember his final year's work – it was four great big portraits of Marx, Trotsky, Lenin and Chairman Mao Tse Tung, that was it. I found most of his

---

9 Orton and Halliwell were lovers and playwrights – although Orton was to get all the credit – who had stormed the West End with the anarchic, camp humour of plays such as *Loot*, *Ruffian On The Stair* and *Entertaining Mr Sloan*. A jealous Halliwell killed Orton, and then himself, in August 1967.

stunts vaguely amusing but I think those of us from working-class backgrounds thought his gang were just kids being crazy.'

McLaren's active extremism was not diluted but, instead, actively encouraged by primary school teacher Westwood. As a child, Westwood was reduced to tears after the crucifixion was explained to her. Yet, by the time she was living with McLaren, she was the one who would sometimes resort to violence first if she felt slighted.

'I felt she was the real boss, the real power,' says former Westwood–McLaren employee Alan Jones, a gay trendy who worked part time in the Portobello Hotel. 'What she wanted usually happened. She was also the one who helped pioneer saying outrageous things just to see if she could get away it, to see if anyone would dare defy her. It became something a lot of people, a lot of their friends, began to do and it led to people saying some stupidly extreme things.' Or, as one near contemporary put it, 'Vivienne was Robespierre to Malcolm's Danton . . . '

Although he was later said to have been present during the Situationist-inspired May '68 disturbances that shook Paris, McLaren was actually in London throughout this time. He had, though, seen Situationist books in Camden's Compendium Books, usually texts that Bernard Rhodes had recommended. 'In those days they had this eye test there,' says McLaren now. 'You'd ask for a certain book by the Lettrists or the the lot that followed them, the Situationists, and the guy behind the counter would just stare at you, look you right in the eye. If you could hold his stare long enough then he'd decide you weren't a plainclothes cop and he'd fish the book out from under the counter.'

McLaren would struggle with the French texts and now admits that he'd often 'mainly looked at them for the pictures, you know, not the theory'. The Paris '68 slogans were mostly Situationist – 'Never Work!', 'Under the Pavement Lies the Beach!', 'Screw Coca-Cola!', 'Imagination is Seizing Power!', 'Forbidding is Forbidden!'. He'd seen photos and found them similarly inspiring, 'they were just so damned big and heroic'. One particular slogan, 'Come in the Cobblestones!', was prophetic, for it combined sexual liberty and revolutionary zeal.

In one yellowing magazine he found out about Buenaventura Durruti,[10] 'a fantastic character', in McLaren's own words. Despite recent claims – most noticeably in Claire Wilcox's 2004 biography *Vivienne Westwood* – that Durruti was an Italian fascist, he was, in fact, a Spanish anarchist. He was more than that, being an armed revolutionary who, as McLaren puts it, 'had this anarchist Black Hand Gang back in the Thirties. They'd go around Spain blowing up banks and churches and they'd always leave this smouldering black glove in the ruins. He came out with all these great quotes, "We are not in the least bit afraid of ruins", stuff like that. I discovered a bit about him.'

McLaren and Westwood both actually read quite a lot on Durruti, including Abel Paz's definitive biography *Durruti: The People Armed*, and the Spaniard's slogans were later to turn up on both t-shirts and Westwood's most notorious item of clothing, the anarchy shirt.

Durruti had actually been a metal worker and organiser in the Spanish workers' union, the CNT – a syndicalist formation. His oldest friend, Ascaso, was a baker and former waiter who had attempted to assassinate Spain's King Alphonso in 1921 before killing Madrid's leading lace-maker, a society lady accused of beating her young girl employees. In those days, Spain was a monarchist police state where employers and their *pistoleros* could freely attack union men, such as the popular organiser Salvador Segui, who died of his wounds after a particularly nasty beating.

Segui's killing had been paid for by the corrupt Archbishop of Saragossa, a man said to hold regular secret orgies within his quarters, orgies in which novice nuns were assaulted and raped. Sexual abuse stories are now investigated with rigour by most branches of the Catholic Church but back then, in Spain, Saragossa's reactionary Archbishop Soldevila was untouchable – right up until the moment Durruti and his gang forced the prelate's limousine off the road and shot him dead in front of his sister. A black glove was

---

10 Durutti Column were later to mis-spell the name they adopted.

accidentally left on the floor of the limo and the legend of the Black Hand Gang was born.

After going on the run – a worldwide spree of shooting fascists and robbing – Durruti returned to Spain in 1936 as the new Republic's first democratic elections gave power to the centre-left. But within weeks General Franco, backed by Hitler and Mussolini, had launched a coup and the Spanish Civil War had begun. Durruti was among those who prevented a fascist takeover of Barcelona, temporarily creating an anarchist state in Catalonia. Here beards and breasts were the only things that separated the sexes as everyone wore overalls and work jeans. Magazines were allowed to print pictures of semi-nude women; banned books and plays were reprinted; and those churches belonging to priests judged 'fascistic' were occupied or blown up. Pleasure was no longer just a secret vice of the upper classes but the right of Everyman. Culturally – and sartorially – it was, in many ways, the world of the Situationist late sixties come three decades too early.

But as the Nazis continued to aid Franco, the Spanish Republic and its anarchist allies began to crumble. In November 1936 Durruti was killed during the Battle of Madrid. Durruti's funeral saw the biggest gathering of human beings that Spain had ever witnessed – a crowd of over 300,000.

In April 1939 the Republic fell and by the late forties, Durruti – although hailed as a 'character out of Dostoevsky' by blue-chip historians such as Hugh Thomas – had been more or less written out of most accounts of the Spanish conflict. Some books didn't even mention the anarchists any more. In mainland Europe in general, and Spain in particular, Durruti was a non-person for almost half a century.

Another half-forgotten character McLaren rediscovered was the 19th-century nobleman Lord Gordon – the chief protagonist of the Christopher Hibbert *King Mob* book from which McLaren's radical friends had taken their name. Lord Gordon was a dazzling paradox – a red-haired Scottish dandy who was also an MP and ex-naval officer, an opinionated only son of privilege who'd applauded the American Revolution and campaigned hard against the evils of capital punishment and slavery (such notions of liberty were considered 'insane' by the mainstream press of the time). But he was also, despite all his genuine idealism, an opportunist. The Protestant Association, formed in 1779 to repeal the Catholic Relief Act, gave Gordon the opportunity he craved. The Protestant Association's petition had been signed by tens of thousands and a decision was taken for 'a peaceful protest march upon the honourable Houses of Parliament for the purpose of delivering said petition'.

The date set was 2 June 1780. Even before the handbills were printed it was obvious the government was rattled – Gordon was offered a sea captaincy, something that had once been his dream, but which he now promptly rejected. Gordon's brother was then offered a sinecure worth £1,000 a year (over £60,000 today) if he would persuade his brother to leave the Protestant Association. But he couldn't, and on a hot Friday, crowds of protesters began to gather at St George's Fields, the area just south of London's Waterloo station.

Although some there were genuinely concerned about the religious implications of the Relief Act, most were only worried because the new wave of immigrant Irish labourers – nearly all Catholic – had undercut the wages of unskilled and semi-skilled Londoners. And many of the 65,000-strong crowd were up for trouble: the underpaid apprentices, delivery boys, foot-pads, pickpockets, beggars, malcontents and radicals – the hungry and ignored, the underclass of their day.

By noon the marchers had completely filled Parliament Street and Westminster. When the MPs started to arrive, those known to be hostile to the appeal were dragged from their carriages and manhandled. Armed cavalry were called out but the numbers were too great and Parliament Street still could not be cleared. Gordon's petition was eventually presented but his repeal bill was voted down by a defiant House of Commons.

After much window-smashing and stone-throwing, the huge mob slowly dispersed. And that, the establishment assumed, was that. But they were wrong – over the weekend rioting spread throughout the city as the houses of wealthy Catholics were pulled down and foreign chapels burned. Local magistrates, called out supposedly to read the Riot Act and order military action, were intimidated by locals – who often knew them personally – and swiftly found excuses to do nothing.

For the next week the mob ruled: Irish shanty towns were attacked, the hated Newgate Prison was put to the torch and its inmates freed as hundreds of bars, restaurants and gin distilleries were looted. Towards the end of the week, the actions became more political – the Catholics were forgotten as the guns were, quite literally, turned on the establishment. An armed raid shook Downing Street, the Bank of England came under siege and there were even rumours of an attempt to put King George on trial. There was also much street talk – not all of it drunken – about the possibility of making Lord Gordon Prime Minister or King or perhaps both.

But Gordon himself was torn in two, unsure of whether to calm the storm he'd whipped up or ride it to the very top and damn the consequences. As he equivocated, the army moved in with General Amhurst under strict instructions to re-establish law and order no matter what. Amhurst used his troops with a vengeance. The mob, in a week of rioting, had killed comparatively few – estimates vary from 9 to 13. Amhurst's soldiers killed over 800 in less than two days, some say over 850 – the exact figure will never be known. The dead were men, women and children, some mere passers-by caught in the army's deadly crossfire. Many were hung from lampposts as a warning to the populace (and it was a bloody warning that worked – the East End would not rise again until the masses blocked Oswald Moseley's blackshirt march down Cable Street over a century and a half later).

Oxford Street, the then crooked but crucial spine of a whole warren of central London streets, had been pivotal in the riots. It was an important road, a major trade route that led from St Giles's Circus in the east to Tyburn, the place of popular public executions, in the west. The fact that rioters could, and often did, disappear around Oxford Street's many bends and corners made widening the avenue a priority for the authorities after the riots. In the end it was widened only a little but it was also straightened – to make it easier for soldiers to fire down.

Gordon himself died in Newgate, of 'jail fever' (typhoid) on 1 November 1793. Within a lifetime, both of Gordon's big 'insane' ideas were adopted by the state: capital punishment for petty theft was abolished as was the slave trade within the British Empire. Gordon received no credit for either move.

But this only added to his appeal for McLaren; for here, at the margins, swept under the carpet, lied about and slandered, here surely were the real precious truths of history. The real heroes. One or two men – like Gordon, like Durruti – could have a huge impact. And if they had to hustle, exploit, exaggerate and even embrace the threat of violence to get somewhere, then so be it.

Fired with revolutionary enthusiasm McLaren-Edwards organised Goldsmiths' end-of-term summer event, which was to be a free festival for that year of 1969. King Crimson were the only name band who actually made it. The other star acts, 'awaiting confirmation' according to Edwards's poster, included Pink Floyd, the Stones, and Beatle superstar, John Lennon.

On the day of the festival over 20,000 people turned up – some 15,000 more than expected – flooding Goldsmiths' corridors, classrooms, toilets and grounds. Many of the crowd were soon angry at the non-appearance of their various heroes and the police were called after noise complaints during the sound check – the volume was so loud that some of the moans had actually come from the next borough. One witness described it as 'complete, utter and absolute bedlam'.

But, despite some trouble and a fair bit of theft, the few bands present did eventually play and there was no riot. Not that Malcolm would have seen it anyway – he'd waltzed off with a crate of drink that same morning.

Although disappointed that there hadn't been more fuss at the 'Goldsmiths fest', Malcolm was pleased that his hype had worked. The carefully worded handbills had drawn many times the expected number. He'd rightly deduced that most young people were bored – most of the time – and so the right words, the right attitude could easily lure them out of their classrooms, backrooms and bed-sits. If those words were said, those attitudes struck – with the right degree of belief. As the radical saying of the time went, 'in the modern world we are all of us wading through petrol, no one knows which cigarette end could spark the blaze . . .'

The next year McLaren set about making a film using Goldsmiths' only movie camera, an ageing but expensive 16mm Bolex. His film crew consisted of fellow art students Jamie Reid and Helen Mininberg, a pretty bottle blonde from South African who happened to be a dwarf. The film was not completed and the camera disappeared. Malcolm innocently claimed he'd lost it on the tube somewhere, much to the annoyance of Goldsmiths.

After toying with the idea of another sit-in, McLaren finally dropped out of the art school system and also dropped the name Edwards. He and Westwood then took over the back half of a shop at 430 King's Road, Chelsea, in 1971. It was in the area known as World's End – a suitably apocalyptic location.

The move into 430, perhaps funded by the lost Bolex, was a bit of a long shot. According to Westwood, the 'only real stock we had was twelve pairs of Lurex drainpipe trousers that I'd stitched together and a big pile of Malcolm's 78 rock'n'roll records. We were actually only looking for a market stall – that was all we could really afford at the time – but then we were invited to take over the back half of Paradise Garage at 430 King's Road.' Paradise Garage sold denim dungarees, arty t-shirts and jeans. Its main point of note was the American sports car that was often parked outside, complete with flocked velvet stripes on the bodywork, zebra-style. Within a few months Paradise Garage had given up and, in Vivienne's words, 'we just came to take it all over'. McLaren later claimed that the then owner 'was this gay black Teddy boy, which was a pretty rare breed back then I can tell you, he just gave the keys to me one day and said, "I'll be back next week" and then he never returned, I mean we literally never saw him again'.

'I remember meeting Westwood and McLaren at the beginning of the seventies,' said top rock'n'roll DJ Fifties Flash back in 1984, 'when they were just getting into the rockin' scene. And Vivienne

Westwood came into the pub and she was really sweating with this bread and milk in her hand. I asked her if she was alright and she said, "Yeah, yeah, I hate to pay for food when the Tories are in power . . ." And I thought then, "Blimey, what planet are you on?" '

It was partly the Teds' violent reputation that had attracted McLaren and Westwood as the sixties blurred into the seventies. Not because either one of them was particularly into violence for violence's sake, but because the Ted lifestyle seemed a way out of the impotent apathy that the 'love'n'peace' hippies were drifting into. Woodstock Festival photos used in Levi adverts, long hair and flared jeans becoming acceptable to the liberal trades, advertising and the arts bureaucracies – all these seemed of a piece to McLaren and Westwood: the corporate co-opting of the failed sixties revolution.

Malcolm McLaren's nomadic days of bumming round art colleges, the south coast or the French Riviera were finally over. He had found a place in Clapham with Vivienne and, more importantly, he had also taken over his King's Road power base. Now, he just had to build it up. 'The Beatles' music producer Chris Thomas came in my shop,' McLaren noted some 30 years later. 'Bowie came in and eventually became a client. Bryan Ferry came in but was quite snobby and never really bought anything. But Iggy Pop was a client, even though I'd initially thrown him out for having a long hair. I thought he was a hippy at first, y'know? The New York Dolls were clients too as were Motorhead, Ringo Starr, Chris Spedding, etc. We had the new rebel outlaw look.'

And they did, even though then, despite the odd original t-shirt or heavily chained mini-skirt, Let It Rock's clothes were almost all fifties originals or lovingly made repros. Many of the original clothes were in fact bought from future rival Steph Raynor, a stylish ex-mod from Leicester. Steph was named after violin virtuoso Stephan Grappelli (local legend had it Raynor was his godson). He'd been buying up classic old stock for a couple of years, stock he'd bought discounted from crumbling out-of-town warehouses.[11]

'Malcolm got most of his old stock from me,' Raynor says now. 'Jackets with piping, the cowboy stuff, the Tommy Steele and Billy Fury jackets, the fleck jackets. I later became co-owner of Acme Attractions and it always amused me when people said, "Oh, you Acme guys are just copying Malcolm and Vivienne" – I supplied those two with clothes in the first place! I must admit though that Let It Rock was great fun for a time – there'd always be dwarves and Teddy boys or Iggy Pop or someone hanging around. It was a laugh. Malcolm could be a laugh. He had some nice ideas too. It only got depressing in there when Vivienne became more involved.'

It was a view of the couple that Let It Rock staffer Alan Jones seems to concur with. 'I thought that Malcolm was always the one creatively 'cos Vivienne was very much behind the scenes at that point and Vivienne really only came into the fore on the cusp of Too Fast To Live and then moving into SEX. I knew she was around but, to be honest with you, I always thought that Malcolm did most of the clothes at that time.'

The fifties clothes, fashionable again in some circles, were supported by some interesting displays; apart from the classic 1957 Rock-Ola jukebox pumping out Eddie Cochran or Joe Meek gems like 'Monster In Black Tights' or 'Jack The Ripper', there were also piles of shrink-wrapped valve radios and original cheesecake mags featuring pouting photos of Shirley Ann Field, Marilyn Monroe and Brigitte Bardot.

Let It Rock was intriguing to many, especially the more cutting-edge media folk, and the Westwood–McLaren clothes began to crop up in the odd British feature film, either tight t-shirts for randy teenagers in soft-core porno comedies or leather, swastika'd mini-skirts for one of the climactic scenes in Ken Russell's *Mahler*.[12]

Malcolm had given up on the idea of his Oxford Street movie but he was, for a time, interested in making a documentary about Billy

11 He'd found the funds to launch this venture while working on a sewage farm in the Midlands, when he came across an abandoned box of original art deco Mickey Mouses.
12 This was for a musical section concerning the composer Mahler's abandonment of Judaism for career reasons – it wasn't enlivened by great lyrics, the somewhat superficial song rhyming 'true boy' with 'Jew boy'.

Fury, one of the more stylish rockers from the stable of near-legendary British pop manager Larry Parnes ('Parnes, shillings and pence' as he was known in the tabloid press during his early sixties heyday). McLaren seemed obsessed by the Billy Fury idea but his approach was hardly realistic. Although a few minutes were shot in and around the shop, no film funding organisations were approached formally and he seems to have made no serious attempt to sketch the project out with Fury himself (the latter was then still alive).

What McLaren needed now was some regular retail income since his longest-running benefactor, Rose Corrie Isaacs, was going through a crisis of her own. Within 18 months of McLaren's moves – commercially to 430 King's Road and domestically, with Westwood and children, to Clapham – Rose received the reward of most over-indulgent grandparents: she was increasingly ignored. In Rose's case the results were more serious that is usual for ageing relatives. With her own husband now dead, the frail Rose was living just a few minutes' walk from the new McLaren–Westwood house. It was expected that the couple would take care of her but he was busier and busier, and Westwood barely seemed to have time for her own dependants, let alone anyone else's.

Finally, in December 1972, McLaren strolled round to see Rose with a large bag of food in his hand and was stunned to find her sitting alone, naked, quite dead. She'd been in this state for so long she was stiff with rigor mortis. (McLaren could not face the agony of going to the funeral and he has not – at time of writing – spoken to his mother or stepfather since.)

The years 1972 and 1973 had also seen the rise and fall of two other strange and disparate phenomena that were both to have some impact on those at 430 – the Angry Brigade and Ziggy Stardust.

The Angry Brigade were Britain's answer to the urban guerrilla Baader–Meinhof Gang, the SLA and the Weathermen. Ironically, they mostly lived in and around Amhurst Road – the street in Stoke Newington, five minutes' drive from McLaren's childhood home that had been named after General Amhurst, the man who'd ended the Gordon Riots. 'I used to have tea with the Angry Brigade lot – well, actually, I had tea with friends of theirs; they were people in the corner I didn't know that well,' Sophie Richmond, a friend of Jamie Reid, said years later. 'Their sort of extreme activism seemed normal university stuff then. Well, not the bombs, but everything else: radical opinions, demos, pickets, sit-ins. It was such an exciting time then, it really did seem possible that the system of things could be changed, that we could do something.'

The Angry Brigade was busted in Amhurst Road in 1972, caught red-handed with the heavy-duty machine gun that had shot up a side wall at the US embassy.[13] The Brigade had also detonated a small bomb in a car outside the home of the new Tory Home Secretary Robert Carr as well as at the Biba boutique in Kensington (only one person was injured in the carefully timed blasts). But what attracted almost as much attention – at least in radical circles – was their slick communiqués, which flowed or snapped like rock lyrics. Or like the Situationists' '68 slogans. Or perhaps the Brigade's words could be compared with advertising slogans – except these slogans were designed to sell subversion: 'Bogside – Clydeside – Join the Angry Side!', 'We Are Getting Closer', 'The Angry Brigade Are The Man On The Bus Next To You, The Woman In The Bank Queue', 'We Have Guns In Our Pockets and Anger In Our Hearts', 'Capitalism Doesn't Work – Kick It 'Till It Breaks!'. Unlike the Weathermen, SLA and Black Panthers, the Angry Brigade killed no one, but some were still jailed for 15 years

---

13 This was a night-time attack – both to avoid casualties and detection. They were too successful in this: no one in sleepy London town – least of all the US security staff snoozing through their night-shift – noticed the bullet holes for some three days afterwards.

after rattling Whitehall's cage with a bit too much force. Most of those imprisoned served at least ten years.

As the Angry Brigade began their jail sentences, David Bowie was preparing for the retirement of his alter ego Ziggy Stardust.

In his increasingly desperate search for fame, Bowie had tried dozens of different avenues by 1970: mime artist, post-Dylan singer-songwriter, Anthony Newley-style crooner, music hall artiste, hippie folkie, psychedelic rocker, occult lyricist, heavy rocker . . . But, that same year, his friend, folk photographer Ray Stevenson, had given him a germ of an idea: 'Observe the trend and do the opposite.' Since the trend was sloppy rock stars in unisex flared jeans trying to look like they weren't millionaires, the opposite must be to dress 'as a superhero, to get out there and tell the people it's a hype. To be honest.' Bowie tried the idea too quickly – the band was even called The Hype – and using the same songs he'd been singing for the last 18 months. But in 1971 the Ziggy Stardust concept – the Hype plus new songs sung by a Bowie *playing the part* of a rock star – finally began to gel. Bowie started 1972 by telling *Melody Maker*, then Britain's biggest-selling music paper, that he was 'gay' (although the full story, and various follow-up pieces, later refined this to 'bisexual'). With his make-up and spiky blond hair – lifted, depending on who you believe, either from Japanese designers or Vivienne Westwood, who'd been wearing the same style and colour for months – Bowie did indeed look like some twisted superhero. Or like some 'gay vandal' from the 22nd century. Aided by his Spiders from Mars backing band, led by the brilliant rock guitarist Mick Ronson, Bowie started gigging to support his new album *The Rise And Fall Of Ziggy Stardust And The Spiders From Mars* (a collection of songs, some sexually threatening, which narrated a *fictional* rock star's journey from rags to bitches to early decline – all played out with a dozen edgy guitar tunes and 'nadsat' words borrowed from the new *Clockwork*

Orange film). This was the intelligent end of the chart-obsessed Glam rock.

Stevenson attended the early shows – it was, after all, partly his concept – and even took a few snaps. But Bowie had already decided to reject his old friend in favour of New York photographer Mick Rock, the latter swiftly becoming responsible for most of Bowie's PR shots. As Bowie's live set – augmented by the Spiders, mime acts, dancers and a stunning light show – began to garner rave reviews, a disappointed Stevenson gave up rock photography in disgust. 'I was making no money at all. And so I got some work driving a cab, one of the worst jobs I've ever had, before finally getting a job in the BBC dark room . . .'

By the summer of 1972, *Ziggy Stardust* was well on its way to selling a million; in fact, sales were so fast that RCA used demand for the album as an excuse to introduce the 'new dynaflex' LP (basically a 12-inch flexi-disc that used 30 per cent less vinyl than a normal album). More importantly, Bowie was being hailed as the first serious music sensation of the seventies, his 'onstage acting', his glamorous clothes and his 'bisexuality' the subject of endless Sunday supplement discussions. Like The New York Dolls in Manhattan later that same year, Bowie instantly became a stylistic magnet for any fashionables who were camp or daring. His followers ranged from art school graduates to gay disco regulars to smart casuals from building sites, offices and factories. As 1973 drew to a close, a heavily pressurised Bowie – pencil thin after almost two years on the road in the UK and US – 'retired' Ziggy forever. He was, by now, busy working on a new image – 1959 modernist 'bum-freezer' jackets with Oxford bag trousers – and a new retro album, *Pin Ups*. This latest set comprised sixties covers – 'Rosalyn', 'I Wish You Would', 'Don't Bring Me Down' – from his Mod adolescence, mostly played a little faster and wilder than the originals.

One fan of *Pin Ups* was the new Saturday boy at 430 King's Road, would-be bassist Glen Matlock who'd first entered the shop when he was 15. 'Malcolm's place, before it became SEX, was basically a Teddy boy shop. For me it was like walking into my nan's front room. I was lucky enough to be born in the fifties and sort of caught the tail end of the rock'n'roll thing. My uncle was a bit of a Teddy boy and he gave me and my mum and dad these old 78s, so when I was five years old I was listening to 'Whole Lotta Shakin' Goin' On' and Little Richard. Stuff that had a real raw power about it. Then I got a little bit older and it coincided with the beat boom and pirate radio, so all these fantastic bands were coming through and I'm suddenly excited by it.'

Sport beckoned briefly – 'I got involved with football and stuff' – but it was perhaps too organised for Matlock, who was already something of a non-comformist. 'There was this silly record I got hold of somewhere, this Pete Seeger record – he was a pretty left-wing folk kind of guy who did the "Little Boxes" [song] – but he did this one song called "The Goofing Off Suite" and it was about kind of getting away from everything you were supposed to do. When I was at school I was no brainiac but I just kind of got my head down and got through it. But I'd kinda come to the conclusion that it's really hard to be good at maths and learn the guitar at the same time. But, from listening to "The Goofing Off Suite" . . . I was "Goofing Off" and learning the guitar. I thought that was more important really, so you know it's not a big political statement but I decided that I wanted to do what I wanted to do and not what other people wanted me to do.'

With the Vietnam War still raging, sparking demonstrations in London, Washington and Paris, this was a time of big political statements and a little of it did permeate into Matlock's world. 'Also you soon become aware of gross injustices and you kind of cope with it in your own particular way . . . I was always more interested in more left-field artists than *Top of the Pops* people. I started listening to music again and started going out having a drink and seeing birds and stuff.'

Matlock's new-found passion for nightlife was initially fuelled by part-time jobs, first at the Whiteleys store in Bayswater then, of course, at the McLaren–Westwood shop, Let It Rock, in the King's Road. Matlock's move to 430 coincided with the heyday of Rod Stewart's band The Faces. The latter were lovable rock yobs born of the ashes of the post-Marriott Small Faces. 'The Faces then came along and there was something about them that was totally different from anybody else. I'd already got into the Small Faces 'cos I'd seen them on *Ready Steady Go*. Their "Itchycoo Park" was on the transistor radio in the Morris Minor when we was going down to the seaside when I was 11 or 12. And The Faces was my link with Steve Jones and Paul Cook as they were big fans too.'

Steve Jones, an itinerant young street thief from a broken west London home, had illusions of becoming a younger, hipper Rod Stewart. School pal Paul Cook , a would-be drummer who worked as an apprentice carpenter at Watney's brewery, seemed like he might be able to help with this rock dream as did a friend – well, acquaintance – called Warwick 'Wally' Nightingale. 'Wally used to go to our school,' explained Jones some quarter of a century later. 'When I left home at fifteen and was living with my mate Stephen Hayes, who lived across the Westway, Wally lived around the corner. His dad worked at Lee Electrics and me him and Glen used to go round his house.'

Wally's role as a fence came into play at this point. 'I nicked him a guitar,' admits Jones, 'and he could play a bit and he'd sit up in the bedroom, playing Faces songs. We had the idea of putting a band together and I'd be the singer. He was like a nerdy guy, Wally. He used to nick all the stuff and we'd dress up in all the satin and go down the King's Road posing, like we were rock stars. "Yeah we've got a band together, were gonna do this, that and the other blah blah." There was this other guy called Jim Makin who played keyboards, Stephen Hayes was the bass player, Paul would play drums and Wally was on guitar. But slowly they fizzled away 'cos they weren't into it but Wally stuck around and that's how we got the rehearsal space at the BBC, 'cos his dad had the keys to it.'

Feelings and fashion came into play at this point. 'I didn't really like Wally, he bugged me,' confessed Jones. 'He was a bully even though he looked like a right wanker. He was always a strange guy, although he got me motivated, one way or the other, I owe him that. He steered me in some direction to want to be in a band. We did one show and I was f—ing terrified. I didn't like being a front man – I remember getting out there and I took a couple of

Patti Smith –
Keith Richards meets
Rimbaud, live in
London, 1976
(Ray Stevenson)

Max's Kansas City:
the legendary NYC
punk venue that was
once the haunt of
dukes and senators
(Ray Stevenson)

Tom Verlaine, frontman of Television, the New York
art-punk band that also launched Richard Hell
(Redferns)

The Sex Pistols lurk around Soho, early summer '76. Their offstage clothes were still thought wildly outrageous at the time (Ray Stevenson)

The Ramones in typical pose – guitars slung low as 'hip nerd' Joey leans on the mic (while the crowd check out each other) (Redferns)

The 100 Club's beer-soaked stage after another quiet Sex Pistols gig (Ray Stevenson)

'I thought they were terrible.' One of Ray Stevenson's classic shots of the Sex Pistols taken at the first gig he attended, St Albans Art School, January '76

Pistols' John Lydon, Glen Matlock and Steve Jones top the bill at the 100 Club 'fest'
(Ray Stevenson)

The Sex Pistols on stage at 4 a.m. for the Midnight Special at Islington's Screen on the Green
(Ray Stevenson)

Sex Pistols manager Malcolm McLaren works the phones at his Glitterbest office, Dryden Chambers, late '76 (Ray Stevenson)

OPPOSITE PAGE
Top Rotten and erstwhile friend, producer Dave Goodman on the Anarchy tour (Ray Stevenson)

Bottom Out of the woods – Steve Jones and a tipsy Vivienne Westwood, a few hours before the Pistols' Parisian debut in the Bois De Vincennes (Ray Stevenson)

A doll-like Debbie Harry onstage with Blondie, wowing young Londoners in 1977 (Ray Stevenson)

quaaludes for that and I couldn't remember the lyrics. I was just standing there and it wasn't for me, to be a front man, and at that point McLaren said, "You should play guitar, mate, and you should look for a singer and another guitar player as well." '

But, though his voice wasn't bad, he seemed too shy and so in McLaren's similar version: 'We gave him a guitar as a prop and he began to learn to play it for something to do.'

So Wally was out but he had given Cook'n'Jones one of his own best songs to kick around, the rockist but doggedly exciting twelve-bar workout that was 'Did You No Wrong' ('A bog is no place to remember your face!'). It led him, understandably perhaps, to believe he was a founding Pistol. As Matlock recalls now, 'Wally fitted the bill totally – he had this house in East Acton where he lived with his parents but it kind of seemed to me, as the outsider, that it was just the centre of operations for Steve's nefarious activities. Wally was like a young version of Noel Coward in that *Italian Job* film and he reckoned he gave Steve the idea of – instead of nicking this and that – nicking guitars so they could then form a band. Steve, Paul and Wally would come in the shop. I used to see it as my job to stop them nicking stuff.'

The would-be band finally jettisoned Wally – partly on McLaren's advice – and adopted the name QT Jones and the Sex Pistols. The latter name again coming from McLaren: 'I was reading this old-style porno magazine, *Continental*, I think it was, and it had a keyhole design on the cover. And I thought well, if the keyhole is the feminine symbol, what's the masculine? A key? The Sex Keys sounded too boring. And then I thought Sex *Pistols*, that's it, Sex Pistols, young sexy assassins . . .'

By now Malcolm had renewed his friendship with another ex-mod radical, Bernard Rhodes, who was running a Renault repair garage in Camden as well as a small silk screen printing business (useful for McLaren, who needed a printer for his Gene Vincent and Let It Rock t-shirts).

The gruff but well-read Bernie, the self-educated son of a Russian immigrant seamstress, was both amused and bemused by McLaren: 'I could never work out why Malcolm would try and talk pinky posh most of the time.' But Rhodes admired the energy and extremism of 430. And, after his own stall in Antiquarius market had failed, he respected McLaren's ability to keep the World's End shop going. The latter also gave Rhodes an outlet for his own, occasional, t-shirt designs, most noticeably the slash neck us-or-them t-shirt 'You're Gonna Wake Up One Morning And Know Which Side of The Bed You've Been Lying On'. Its headline slogan divided the world into two camps – two camps that were represented by two typed columns. One column, the 'negative' side, had the House of Lords, Elton John and 'good fun entertainment that's not good and funny'. The other, 'positive', side had Gene Vincent, the Angry Brigade, coffee bars that 'sold whisky under the counter' and 'QT Jones & His Sex Pistols'. . . The latter had made it onto a t-shirt before they'd played a proper gig. Before they even really existed . . .

In 1974, McLaren decided that it was time for a radical change and Let It Rock, and its leather boy, ton-up child Too Fast To Live, Too Young To Die, were gone, replaced by a new concept called SEX, complete with four-foot plastic letters spelling out the name.[14] McLaren says now the idea came because the flaunting of sex was the one thing that was to 'bound' to upset British notions of good taste and propriety.

'Then they [McLaren and Westwood] turned the shop into SEX and started selling the rapist t-shirts and the nude boy t-shirts,' says Matlock, 'and those kind of bondage masks and things hanging up, you know. There are things like that almost everywhere nowadays but they weren't back then, and there were certainly some horrible characters hanging around. Some of it was tongue-in-cheek as far as Malcolm was concerned but Vivienne was very po-faced about

14 This notion was almost certainly sparked off by the title of the West End farce *No Sex Please, We're British*, which Cliff Owen had turned into a film in 1973 – with Let It Rock providing some fringed rocker mini-skirts for the movie's 'dolly birds'.

it. I've never met a more humourless person in my life. Some of the stuff that they were bringing in seemed a bit over the top. I remember talking to my art teacher at school and he said, "What's going on down at this place?" And I said, "I'm not sure about some of this stuff." And he said, "Well, you don't have to work there, you know." ' But Matlock did have to work there, 'Because I kind of thought to myself, "Well I *don't* have to be there . . . but I *do* 'cos its kind of my exit from the straight world." It was a doorway into a whole other thing.'

The 'whole other thing' also, now, had other aspects. Steph Raynor had joined writer and retro jukebox dealer John Krivine and moved the small Acme Attractions stall into the larger Antiquarius basement (now that Rhodes had left, Acme was the only Antiquarius shop selling post-war pre-hippy clothes). Soon the ancient paintwork below ground was being flaked off the wall by manager Don Letts's dub reggae tapes, music that intrigued most of the customers who heard it. Joints would sometimes be rolled and green smoke spilled over Krivine and Raynor's amazing array of jukeboxes, fleck jackets and peg trousers. Letts was one of the first men with dreadlocks in London and that, plus the fact that his girlfriend Jeannette Lee, a fellow Acme staffer, was breathtakingly beautiful, added to Acme's attraction. It was a half-hidden ganja-scented world just a few feet from the expensive tat and parking meters of the King's Road.

Another factor in Acme's success was the fact that there were those who found the clothes in SEX too expensive – and 430's atmosphere too darkly perverse. 'Malcolm and Vivienne were selling the pegs, the zoot suit trousers, for £16 to £20 a pair or more,' Letts says now, 'while we were doing 'em for £12 – that was a big difference back then. Also the vibe in Acme was more multicultural, more open I guess.' Acme's clientele came from a broad range: young electricians, bricklayers, window-dressers and art students who were later joined by real reggae 'stars' like Bob Marley and Peter Tosh.

One customer was John Ritchie, later to be known as Sid Vicious. 'He was always getting in these stupid arguments with me,' according to Letts, 'and he'd lose them but he wouldn't let it go. On the way out he'd suddenly stick his head back round the corner and say, "And another thing . . . " It was a bit hard work sometimes. I'll give him one thing, though – he was always curious. He had this insatiable thirst for ideas and was always asking questions. It seems strange but, in another time and place, he could have been an academic.'

Originally, John Simon Beverley, aka Ritchie, he was born on 10 May 1957. His mother was one Anne Beverley, a former RAF cadet whose first serious boyfriend was Sid's father. He did a runner then later joined the redcoats outside Buckingham Palace.

In 1959 the apparently doting father had sent Anne and the baby John on to Ibiza, promising to send some cash and come after them himself later. 'The money didn't turn up,' Anne said, 'and when the money doesn't turn up you sure as hell know the man isn't going to.'

Heartbroken, she bought a little *kif* (hashish), selling some to jaded tourists to make ends meet before mother and child drifted back to London in the mid-sixties. Back then the fastest way to get subsidised accommodation was by being, or pretending to be, a junkie. Hard-drug addicts only numbered in the low hundreds in those pre-Thatcher days, and those with children could get allocated a council house with garden within a few weeks.

Anne Beverley played the part, got the house and found herself with neighbours who were serious addicts – mostly harmless, she thought. Within weeks she was putting her Spanish experience to good use by selling those same neighbours hash, then speed, then heroin. Within months she was taking heroin herself. Her various failed relationships, and the mounting pile of red final bills, were forgotten in those moments of blissed-out semi-death.

She tried to 'go straight' a couple of times but it didn't work out. A job as cleaner at Ronnie Scott's jazz club didn't help; plenty of jazzers, from Miles Davis down, were heroin addicts who could sniff out a fellow abuser within seconds. Anne was still fairly young and attractive, as well as being both a good talker and listener. She dated Ray Davis of The Kinks for a time. Some claim the singer-songwriter would even occasionally babysit her quiet and lonely only child John. The boy had an idealistic streak, probably based on those early sunshine years in the Med when he was the apple of his mother's pre-addiction eye and dad was believed to be *en route* with plenty of toys and money. Paradoxically, those early years often served to depress Sid more later – the contrast was too great . . .

Back in London Anne Beverley's heroin dependency grew worse, of course, and she was in a heroin haze the night that 12-year-old Sid killed his first cat, a desperate and bloody attempt to get his stoned mother's attention. It was an ominous sign – nearly all those who mutilate or kill pet animals go on to mutilate or kill human beings. Or, occasionally, themselves . . .

By the time he was in his mid-teens John/Sid was also a huge Roxy Music follower, prone to hanging around near Bryan Ferry's west London apartment. 'He was a big fan of Roxy,' according to Jah Wobble, 'liked most of their stuff. Went to see 'em live and all that.' And Sid was indeed at the last Roxy Music gigs before their 1976–78 'retirement', wearing a glitter drape jacket that he'd bought cheap off Westwood – she'd taken a shine to him – a jacket which had, on its lapel, a guitar-shaped badge he'd bought in Acme. A badge commemorating the biggest pop group ever – The Beatles. *Honey* magazine was so impressed by his outfit they even took colour slides of him, along with several other Roxy fans, and reproduced his minimal answers to their questions about his name and occupation: 'I'm John. I do nothing . . . '

Rotten called him Sid – after his pet hamster and after Pink Floyd's acid casualty founder Syd Barrett – and, when the word 'Vicious' was added, it stuck.

'Glam rock people got their clothes in the King's Road,' Matlock confirms now, 'although Glam had been and gone a bit by that time, and Anthony Price and Bryan Ferry were always swanking up and down. Malcolm kind of laughed at them so we did too. Especially the hairy old Prog rocker types. Now all these people were already millionaires but we'd just laugh at them. We didn't have a pot to piss in but we'd go in the Roebuck pub and go "Oi!

Wanker!" So it gave us a good attitude. We thought "F— you, we're where it's at" even before we had the band.'

And those from the fringes of the music biz continued to visit 430 – more interested than ever in the curious turn things had taken – as did a new group of shoppers, divided equally between middle-aged perverts and the young people McLaren now describes as 'disenchanted Bowie and Roxy Music freaks, disenchanted because they didn't get to see those people often any more – those acts had got too big – and now they only heard those tracks in discotheques. It had all got a bit too anonymous for people who really wanted to look individual – that's why they'd come to my shop in the first place.'

After McLaren's 1974–75 stint in New York, with the dying Dolls, he returned to London. In his absence, Vivienne had started her amazing anarchy shirt: a dyed, bleach-striped garment[15] with large red and black oblong patches which were themselves splashed with italic bleached-out writing, usually quotes from the Situationists and/or 1968 – 'À Bas Le Coca-Cola!' ('Screw Coca-Cola!') – plus the odd Durruti saying, 'We are not in the least afraid of ruins!'[16]

These anarchy shirts also had fabric-paint stripes and a large stencilled phrase – industrial-style – over one breast, either 'Only Anarchists Are Pretty' or the slightly more acceptable 'Dangerously Close To Love'. Down one arm was the slogan 'Try Subversion, It's Fun', while the other arm bore a red armband with five white letters spelling out the word 'CHAOS'. These shirts were rounded off with one of McLaren's suggestions: embroidered silk patches of Karl Marx's face, which McLaren had originally bought from Red China's Guanghwa trading centre in Newport Place, Soho, and which were topped with a Nazi eagle, upside down to show the wearer was actually an *anti*-fascist.

---

15 Initially, these were 1950s Wemblex shirts, bought in bulk at 50 pence each from a Portsmouth warehouse.

16 The idea of the black patches may have been taken from those worn by followers of the 19th-century Islamic leader known as the Mahdi. He blessed each of these patches, which, his followers believed, made them bullet-proof.

They were – are – stunning shirts, something that might have explained their £25 price tag – around £200 or more in today's money. But their stripes also evoked the inmate uniforms of Nazi death camps and the fact that the swastika eagle was inverted was a subtlety lost on most who saw the shirt, a fact compounded by the way Westwood later began to make them with Nazi armbands towards the end of '76, visible evidence of 430's inability to resist even the most unpleasant of extremes. Yet these shirts, together with Rhodes's 'You're Gonna Wake Up One Morning . . .' t-shirt, were some kind of way forward and McLaren was hip enough to know it.

'All I needed now was a way of mounting them on a public platform, a way of presenting the look of the music and the sound of the clothes – our clothes. I needed a group.'

For McLaren had indeed become intrigued by rock'n'roll management during his short but shocking stint as The New York Dolls' unofficial manager. Despite their platform boots and late-sixties haircuts, he'd still been impressed by the Dolls, and by Johnny Thunders's no-nonsense attitude, when they'd stumbled into Let It Rock during their first visit to London in November 1972. The Rock'n'Roll Special at Wembley a few months before hadn't featured the Dolls, but had given McLaren one of his first tastes of just how reactionary many of his Teddy boy clientele really were – they'd solidly booed The MC5 throughout their entire set as McLaren was handing out the naive Letraset flyers that advertised Let It Rock ('Open Sundays! Teddy Boys Forever! Silk Toshers 50 pence, Drape Jackets £25 . . . ').

Moving beyond nostalgia politically and sartorially wasn't enough; post-Wembley, Malcolm knew that any new band that wanted to be relevant would have to threaten musically as well.

Going over to New York in 1973 and '74, mainly to peddle the increasingly sexual clothes he and Westwood were making: rubber mini-skirts, high-heeled shoes, leather drainpipes, McLaren had watched the 'new band' scene grow and was fascinated by both Thunders and the safety-pinned Richard Hell of Television, with his messy, short hair.

When the Dolls' second album flopped and they appeared manager-less, Malcolm moved in. After weeks of dazzling them with his outrageous notions and fashions, the Dolls acquiesced. On the last day of February 1975 McLaren re-launched them at the Little Hippodrome on Manhattan's East 57th Street. Hand-outs plugging the gig were headlined 'What is the Politics of Boredom? Better Red Than Dead', and claimed, perhaps only half jokingly, that the event was in 'co-ordination' with the Red Guard and the People's Republic of China. (It was also, we were told in the fine print, a programme organised by 'Sex Originals of London'.)

The venue was two-thirds full, a pretty good turnout, and speculation over the flyer was rife. Would the Dolls really be wearing some Chinese communist clothing?

And then the Dolls came on, with a couple of new songs, all clad in red patent leather, playing before a huge red hammer and sickle flag (the platform shoes, long hair and midriff-revealing waistbands were something McLaren couldn't talk the Dolls out of abandoning). They looked more camp than socialistic but there was still visual impact as well as the 'overtones'. The first of their four weekend shows was, eyewitnesses have said, sensational. But the Dolls could sometimes do that live; what they were being judged on at the Hippodrome was the new attitude – and the new look. And the judges – the Big Apple's music press as led by Lisa Robinson of *Rolling Stone* – had only one question: why all the dumb commie shit? After the gig only Thunders would defend the new look backstage. An incensed McLaren decided to get them out of town – 'off-Broadway' – both to tighten their new angle, and to get them away from the heroin-flavoured fleshpots of New York. (McLaren's brief disillusionment with the city had begun about this time; partly because half the Dolls were junkies with massage parlour girlfriends, partly because he was shocked to find two of the first three women he slept with in Manhattan had VD.)

A much-bootlegged mini-tour of the South was hastily put together after McLaren had, according to Bob Gruen, saved the lives of at least two smack-addicted Dolls by forcing them into rehab. But the mini-tour became a major disaster anyway after the group split in half. On a long drive to New Orleans McLaren then persuaded Sylvain to get his guitar, amplifier and piano over to London. Britain was the place where, McLaren said, he could easily get a tight backing band together for Sylvain and another, stronger, Dolls-like group could be launched to superstardom. The Londoner was thinking of the group his Saturday boy Matlock was slowly pulling into shape with Cook and Jones. With Wally now out of the way, here was a group who, while admittedly raw, had energy and enthusiasm on their side. With Sylvain just days from booking a ticket to Heathrow, Gruen received a series of phone calls from Japan – if the Dolls, or any gang of Doll-lookalikes, could be slung behind Johansen and Sylvain, then a $50,000 tour of Japan could be arranged. With such an incentive it didn't take long for Johansen and Sylvain to get a new Thunders-less group together, leaving Malcolm quietly fuming.

As the big New York Dolls tour of Japan dragged on, McLaren became increasingly of the opinion that a British band should maybe have a British singer anyway. When contact with Sylvain had dribbled down to a short phone call every few weeks, McLaren shifted the 'maybe' to 'definitely' – his band needed an English singer. Period.

But none of the existing Pistols seemed like a great front man. Steve Jones had blown his one serious stab at singing and was, anyway, playing guitar. Paul Cook was too shy and Glen Matlock was too unsure about his own voice, so who would be the lead vocalist? Bernie Rhodes and McLaren were up in Glasgow to buy more retro clothing in July (necessary now that Steph Raynor was co-running Acme Attractions), when they saw Jim 'Midge' Ure walking down the street (he got the nickname, which was 'Jim' backwards, to differentiate himself from his father Jim Ure Senior). McLaren and Rhodes approached him, impressed by his arcane clothes and short, stylised hair. They were amazed, and pleased too, to find that, yes, Midge liked rock'n'roll and, yes, he really could sing too. But unfortunately Ure was in a new Scottish pop group called Slik who were due to sign to Bell Records, original home of the million-selling Bay City Rollers, that very week. Ure thus decided, after a few King's Road phone calls, that an unsigned band called the Sex Pistols with their potentially damaging name – could it ever even be said on radio? – was not for him.

Kevin Rowland, later of Dexy's Midnight Runners, had auditioned and seemingly impressed Matlock. But nobody else liked him enough. A blond boy in the King's Road, name long forgotten, was seen and then rejected. A black guy from south London was ruled out from the start (for his refusal to travel far) and things were looking a bit grim when it came to finding the right singer for the fledgling Pistols. And by now Doctor Feelgood had started enlivening London's live rock circuit as well as issuing their first records on United Artists, a fact that McLaren and Rhodes were all too aware of.

In a fit of growing desperation McLaren made some expensive phone calls to Richard Hell in New York. But Hell, wary of McLaren's comparative lack of success with The New York Dolls, said 'no' to the role of Pistols' singer as well. He had his own stuff going on in New York and was convinced that one of the majors would yet pick up on 'Blank Generation' and give the song the audience it deserved.

McLaren himself then took singing lessons with the highly rated vocal coach Tona de Brett and briefly considered himself for the band's front man position, but decided that at the ripe old age of 29, he was too old. The same, eventually, applied to *NME* hack and competent guitarist Nick Kent, whose growing flirtation with heroin also irritated McLaren.

Advance publicity shots of Midge Ure's Slik were showing them with short hair – ears and collars showing – the first time a popular music group had dared to do this for almost a decade. Although Slik were pretty solidly aimed at the young teenybopper market, the pressure was now immense on McLaren and his boys, the danger being that QT Jones and his Pistols, who'd been so far ahead for so long image-wise, would now begin to look dated by the time they actually started doing some proper gigs – if they could even find a singer to gig with them. By now McLaren and Rhodes, sometimes with Nick Kent in tow, were reduced to approaching random teenagers at parties, discos and bar mitzvahs. Few were interested, none truly fitted the bill.

At this point McLaren and Westwood's first brush with the newspapers and the courts occurred, except that they weren't the ones actually charged. That honour fell to Alan Jones, who discovered for himself just how inclusive and persuasive the 430 playpen was – and yet how different, and how distant, from 'real', ordinary life. 'My friend Moose and I went to Vivienne's and she was just literally unpacking the Cambridge Rapist t-shirt and the naked cowboy t-shirt as we arrived. I said "fab" – I loved the way they tied on the corner, that was totally new, and the way they cut off at the arms. I loved them, bought them straight away, put the cowboy one on and put the Cambridge Rapist one in the bag. It was a beautiful day and I said, "Let's walk to the West End." I knew some friends at the Hard Rock. They were like, "What the f— are you wearing?" and everybody was looking at the t-shirt. Walked along to Piccadilly Circus and that's when the two guys grabbed us, the two detectives. The night before the documentary about rent boys in Piccadilly had been on TV and so this was seen as a very bad thing. And I was dragged off to Vine Street police station and literally given the third degree, "Why are you wearing this?" etc.'

Alan Jones, though, as a plant partially raised in the McLaren–Westwood hothouse, just couldn't understand what all the fuss was about. 'To me it was absolutely nothing special. I thought it was a great, it was me, the cowboys, it was funny. Vivienne had been doing this porno imagery anyway, we all had the SCUM [Society for Cutting Up Men] manifesto stuff all done as the lettering. So when the police charged me I was so shocked and still, to this day, it's a very odd feeling, it was actually going to court that made me realise how serious it actually was because I didn't really expect that. To be charged with gross indecency. For me gross indecency was getting my dick out in a toilet. And it was about time they caught me for doing that! But not for wearing a t-shirt? I phoned Malcolm straight away and he said "Oh Alan, how disgusting, terrible, terrible, we'll make sure we do something," and of course that was the last I ever heard of it.' Jones went to court – alone – and was fined £50.

But it was a story that was picked up by several tabloids, who ran it small on inside pages, as well as the more serious broadsheet *Guardian* newspaper, which used it as a front-page story. It showed that what McLaren and Westwood, and their staff and associates, considered normal could have large-scale repercussions elsewhere. But to McLaren, it also demonstrated that there were still headlines to be wrung out of the moral 'outrage' that he considered so out-dated.

In July, The Ramones, Blondie, Television, The Heartbreakers and Talking Heads all took part, along with over 30 other groups, in CBGB's Festival of the Top 40 New York Rock Bands. This three-day event had been the brainchild of Hilly Kristal. It had attracted dozens of journalists and A&Rs, and eventually led to The Ramones getting their first record deal. McLaren, who only heard snippets about it via friends, gossip and the UK music press, became more determined to push 'his' group into action. He just needed that elusive singer . . .

'Vivienne did keep going on about this guy John who came in the shop now and again,' says McLaren now, 'saying he'd make a great singer. I knew she'd spent a bit of time talking with some young guy called John when I was in New York so I thought, "Yeah, why the hell not? Let's try him." But there was no phone number for him so we just had to sit and wait for him to turn up. And then this guy, looking very different with very spiky hair, came strolling into the shop one afternoon. He had a good walk to him, you could see he had attitude just in that walk.'

The 'guy' was one John Lydon, then washing dishes at Cranks, the wholefood restaurant in Marshall Street, some 50 yards from Carnaby Street. He was 19 years old in 1975, a skinny London Irish Catholic who was one of four brothers from the rough Benwell council estate near Finsbury Park in the north of the city. He got on well with his devout and devoted mother and for the rest of her life would return home for one of her Sunday dinners when-ever he was in London, but he argued frequently with his father, whom his friends saw as something of a harsh, tough-guy dad.

Before he'd reached his mid-teens, the young Lydon had almost died from meningitis. He was rushed to hospital where he remained for months. Only his mother, and one of his brothers, bothered to visit him regularly, his father allegedly staying away throughout. The damage inflicted by the near fatal disease meant Lydon spent hours staring at trees, bushes, patches of grass, just trying to remember, trying to comprehend. It was something he even did in school. 'He had to start again,' the Pistols' first serious music producer, Dave Goodman, later said, 'and it must have been hard work, learning to walk, almost learning to talk again. But it's like taking an exam, it's a lot easier the second time round. And, of course, the teachers did give him a tiny bit of space though he always told me they continued to shove the Catholic orthodoxy down his throat. But I think that, in the end, all that beginning again, all that medical trouble actually made him quicker, cleverer, different . . . '

By the time he was in his late teens, Lydon was smart and, perhaps because of his relationship with his father, bitterly sarcastic. A big fan of musical outsiders – Lou Reed, Captain Beefheart and Steve Harley – Lydon was also something of an outsider himself. It was not quite true that Lydon was – as Jon Savage claimed in the engaging *England's Dreaming* – intelligent in a working-class culture that didn't rate intelligence. Intelligence *was* rated but to be truly applauded it *had* to be practical, it had to bring some tangible reward. Lydon's pinched face was unique; it was not unattractive but he was never going to make money being a male model. He had presence and was obviously clever, yet it was a cleverness that seemed to have no short- or even long-term benefit. His smart-arse snide remarks only got him into the occasional fight, verbal and sometimes physical – struggles that he didn't always win. There seemed to be no prospect that his biting jokes and hardcore street couture style would ever get him anything other than a few black eyes, the occasional prison sentence and, at best, the odd one-night stand.

During August 1975, McLaren finally saw John Lydon in the shop. 'This guy was looking at a pair of my white brothel-creeper shoes and someone he was with suddenly called him John. I thought that this just had to be the guy Vivienne had talked about so I asked him if he'd ever thought about becoming a singer. He came back straight away, very cheeky, with "No, no, I prefer the violin, that's all I play, why do you ask?" But I persisted and I said he really ought to come to an audition we were having. He hummed and hawed and didn't exactly look the reliable type so I said, "Look, you can have these white shoes free, for nothing, but you've got to come to the Roebuck pub later on and you've gotta audition for this new band." And he finally nodded and agreed and I quickly started ringing round, getting the group together.'

But even though Bernard Rhodes raved about Lydon and his 'I Hate Pink Floyd' t-shirt – which was then, like his green hair, something incredibly rare – the other Pistols were not, at first, greatly impressed. 'Steve came over after John had been with 'em in the pub for twenty minutes and said, "He's all wrong, Mal, he's all f—ing wrong! He's hardly spoken to us." Meanwhile Lydon was at the bar, staring straight ahead, drinking the drinks they'd reluctantly bought him. So I said, "Wait, Steve, let's just see." So we dragged Lydon to the shop, where he demands a mic before he'll audition. It's a clothes shop not a PA place but I find a shower nozzle and say, "Right, there you go, pretend that's the mic." And Lydon sneers a bit and Alice Cooper's 'I'm Eighteen' gets put on the jukebox. And then Jones suddenly said, raising this fist, "And you'd better f—ing try, mate! You'd better not muck around or you're f—ing gonna cop it!" '

Lydon had asked for trouble, had asked for pressure, as always. And now he'd got it, in spades. But encouraged by his friend, the quiet, witty John Gray, Lydon then performed a bizarre mewling, puking, hunchback-cringing version of 'I'm Eighteen'. The group were speechless, unsure of what to make of it but McLaren was convinced. 'There was vulnerability there, and there was this total shyness, and I thought this could work somehow.' Once word spread, people in the King's Road, even those outside the still-far-from-convinced group, were shocked. The few who knew Lydon knew him as a sneering, sarcastic troublemaker whose brothers and friends were, allegedly, 'boot boys and yobs, some were well dressed but they were football hooligans, people you probably wanted to avoid . . . '

Glen Matlock had mixed feelings about Lydon and his little ad hoc gang, partly because he, Matlock, now had a song he'd written, a song he wasn't ashamed of: 'Pretty Vacant'. It was, in many ways, the UK's first real song of the seventies. Matlock had seen Richard Hell's 'Blank Generation' poster and been chided by McLaren – why don't you write a song like that?

The lyrics of 'Pretty Vacant' were dedicated, according to author Matlock, to 'people like Vivienne Westwood, people who might not be bright academically, but who didn't care about that. They had their own intelligence, their own way of seeing things.'

The end backing vocals – 'We're pretty! Pretty vacant!' – brought out the song's full and partly camp irony (especially when delivered live by a drunken Steve Jones).

'Vacant' has a rare combination of swaggering musical and lyrical power with humour at once basic and subtle. Musically, Matlock began 'Vacant' by borrowing part of the chorus from Abba's, then current, pop smash 'SOS'. According to McLaren, 'The other Pistols borrowed from bands they liked and that limited them, of course. Glen, perhaps because he was a little better educated, perhaps because he was an art student at St Martin's by then, was able to borrow from bands he didn't like, was able to take the unfashionable and make it fashionable.'

This 'unfashionable' Abba steal became the first half of the 'Vacant' chorus, the verses spinning off from it were Matlock's own invention and the intro was also his own, a two-chord double strum of beautiful, dynamic idiocy (with, maybe, the faintest echo of Iggy and the Stooges' 'No Fun' arrangement). There was no real middle eight or guitar solo, in itself a daring move for 1975.

Once in the band and rehearsing (after a few angry false starts when the others didn't turn up), Lydon strengthened a couple of 'Vacant's lines, partly by removing the increasingly inappropriate 'saves on friction' words. (What were the Pistols, in PR terms, if they weren't about obnoxious friction?) Typically, he also changed some of the verses' general 'we's into the personal 'I's.

Yet the song as a whole remains Matlock's, a positive start without which Lydon's nihilism would have been anchorless. It remains the sound of the Sex Pistols in 1975 and '76: different and aloof, humorous and exciting, elitist yet predominantly working class. The band's career was gathering pace as their confidence visibly mushroomed.

McLaren finally had his British – English (and Irish) – London band. And they finally had a great original song. Now he just needed more – more songs and more bands – so that, like the Dolls in New York, the Sex Pistols could be seen as the vanguard of a whole new movement . . .

LESSER FREE TRADE HALL – Anarchy in the UK

Would-be Glam guitarist Mick Jones had auditioned for the Sex Pistols in 1975, in the Denmark Street rehearsal rooms where Steve Jones (no relation) now lived, but Mick's long hair had ruled him out from the start. As well as a fading succession of glittery post-Dolls bands, the 20-year-old west Londoner was also involved with a group called London SS. Although some would later claim the name stood for London Social Security – and then, in 1977, the more revolutionary 'Street Soldiers' – in '75 everyone understood it had direct Nazi connotations (not because anyone was remotely fascistic but because it was a tag so outrageous as to eclipse The New York Dolls' name – hence the echoing use of 'London').

Although Mick Jones had just squeezed into Hammersmith School of Art and Building – at the same time as Matlock was entering St Martin's – he was not a typical art student. Jones was a comprehensive kid who came from a broken home and who'd been raised, some said spoilt, by his grandmother (they lived together in her tower block flat overlooking the Westway motorway). He found art school, which he'd fondly imagined to be full of jamming musicians, as in the sixties, to be a major disappointment. 'I even took my guitar in, slung over my shoulder, on that first day. But I only ever saw one other guy with a guitar there and he turned out to be a right arsehole.'

Other members of the London SS were typically atypical – the future speed freak Keith Levene, a skinny but brilliant guitar player from Jewish north London, Brunel maths graduate – and Dolls fan – Tony James. It was James who had run into Bernard Rhodes when out at Dingwalls nightclub with Jones. Rhodes had initiated the conversation because James was wearing one of his, Rhodes's, insurrectionary 'You're Gonna Wake Up . . . ' t-shirts.

During the resultant conversation, James happened to let slip that he and Jones were in a group called London SS – which was enough to rouse Bernard's interest. His first act as manager was to find the group a base beneath a café in Praed Street in Paddington, where they could begin auditioning for singers and drummers (including future Clash sticks man Nicky 'Topper' Headon). 'Bernie made us understand that, in order to succeed, you've got to have a base, a place where you can hang out,' James said later. 'When we said that we both lived in Paddington, he said we should meet up in Praed Street, because that's where the hookers go.'

It was through the auditions for singers that Paul Simonon first made contact. He'd gone along to Praed Street to offer moral support to a drummer buddy and found himself being cajoled into trying out as a singer. Simonon's singing voice left a lot to be desired, but Bernie was impressed by the gap-toothed reggae-loving rogue and took note of his name for future reference.

Another soon-to-be-famous punk tub-thumper who auditioned for London SS was Chris Millar, swiftly redubbed Rat Scabies after he told Simonon that he was suffering from a bout of the contagious skin infection. The 'Rat' part came later that day, when Simonon spotted a rodent scurrying across the rehearsal room floor, which bore an uncanny resemblance to the ginger-haired drummer. Although Bernie, Mick and Tony were amused by the drummer's new name they were less enthused by his percussion ability. When they elected to pass him over, however, another of the fledgling group's prospective candidates, guitarist Brian James, went off with Rat to form the band who would swiftly become known as The Damned (helped by proto-Goth vocalist Dave Vanian and bass Ray 'Captain Sensible' Burns). Although London SS would never play a single paying gig, according to Tony James, they did record the odd rehearsal session. Rhodes persuaded them to drop the SS monicker, partly by dumping a bag full of Nazi war relics before them and telling them this was what they would have to deal with, day in, day out, if they kept the SS name. And then one of the original members left, Tony James departing a few weeks before a new, semi-permanent drummer could arrive.

'They didn't have a name when I first auditioned for them but they had an attitude,' Terry Chimes asserts now. 'They were the first band I'd drummed for, auditioned for, who were really serious about making it. They looked like they were a gang and when they walked down the street they kinda stood out, people looked – they were determined to get up there.'

Rhodes called Simonon back in and Jones and Levene began to teach him the basics of bass playing. The Jones–Simonon–Levene–Chimes line-up was completed by 'a guy called Billy Watts who was doing all the lead vocals then – he had a pretty good voice and was friendly and I quite liked him,' Chimes asserts. 'The others seemed to get on with him as well. He seemed to be, like, nineteen or eighteen then, as we all were. But I went off and then later got the call to confirm that I was in – and to tell me they had a new lead singer. Who I didn't like at first – he was like twenty-two or twenty-three or something that seemed "old" to me then. And he had these retro clothes and this croaky voice – and he wasn't polite to me. He seemed so wrong at first.' But Joe Strummer was exactly what the Clash needed; his voice – by turns barking, hectoring, howling and passionate – was the perfect counterbalance to Jones' clever, occasionally overwrought, guitar. Even Strummer's very accent – part west London geezer, part public school drop-out, part Jamaican hustler – caught the Notting Hill–Westway mood that The Clash represented. Ironically, though, they were always practising in Rhodes's rambling Rehearsal Rehearsals warehouse-garage in Camden, several miles from Notting Hill. It was to become their home, too, before the summer was out.

Joe Strummer had been born John Mellors in Ankara, Turkey, not because he was Turkish but because his father was a low-ranking British diplomat with the Foreign Office. When, after returning to the UK, Mellors Senior was given further overseas postings, John was dumped, along with his occult-obsessed older brother, in a minor boarding school south of London. Although the Mellors were hardly wealthy, the 'public schoolboy' tag was to return to haunt their youngest son (as was his age, a ripe old 23 in the early summer of '76). After dropping out of various colleges – and after his brother had committed suicide – John Mellors became Woody Strummer, folk singer-songwriter. After the brief Wembley-inspired rock revival of 1972–73, Strummer had formed The 101ers group along with Nick Cash, who'd been in Ian Dury's Kilburn and The Highroads (Dury was an intense Cockney singer, 'half-crippled by polio' as one contemporary observer put it, whose sweet-and-sour voice, and hunched, manic delivery, was unforgettable). The 101ers played R'n'B flavoured pub rock, or Strummer's version of it, 'doodly squat rock' as he called it. The band had been named after both the group's squat address, 101 Walterton Road in West London *and* the torture room in Orwell's doomy *Nineteen Eighty-Four* novel – as the latter explanation showed, The 101ers had radical political views which, in Strummer's case, went with a quiff and zoot suit trousers (a look that mirrored McLaren's outfits of a few months before, though neither man then knew it).

In the early spring of 1976 after – in Strummer's words – 'a thousand dogshit gigs', The 101ers seemed on the brink of breaking through, for they'd already recorded their debut single for London's first indie label, Chiswick Records. This outfit had been started by Ted Carroll, owner of the infamous Rock On shop in Camden and record stall in Soho market (now a car park on the east side of London's Chinatown). Carroll had already pressed up several thousand copies of The 101ers' 'Keys To Your Heart' 45. Everything seemed on target for a mini-tour across the south to support the release – and the first steps towards nationwide fame and success (a distinct possibility now that *Melody Maker* journos like Allan Jones were hardcore fans).

But, unfortunately for Carroll, Strummer was about to have his life changed forever by an unknown support band . . .

After August 1975, the Sex Pistols had Johnny Rotten on nasal vocals, a voice that presented a whine to open your skull, and a new stage name which came together because of his Irish ancestry and his initial reluctance to clean his teeth. 'They were green, John's teeth, they were really rotten,' Steve Jones said later, 'so I used to say to him, "You're rotten, you are, you're f—ing rotten!"'[17]

Rehearsals had a shaky start when no one except angry new boy John showed up. 'And,' he later told Caroline Coon, 'they used to call me a c— when I was out of the room, I know 'cos I used to listen quietly . . . ' The rehearsal room was above the Crunchie Frog pub in Rotherhithe, a venue that had been part of the old 1968 'alternative' circuit and which was still run on collective 'hippy' lines. After Malcolm had shifted operations to 6 Denmark Street – in the crumbling rooms where Beatles' faves Badfinger had rehearsed before their depressed guitarist Pete Ham hung himself – the Pistols' repertoire began to come together. As well as the 'Pretty Vacant' original and Wally's shit-kicking 'Did You No Wrong' there were several covers including Iggy's 'No Fun', three Small Faces' numbers, 'Understanding', 'Wham Bam, Thank You Ma'am' and their aggressive mod anthem 'Whatcha Gonna Do About It?'. The latter became a crowd favourite that appeared, sporadically, in their live set until early 1977.

Despite the blatant distrust and antagonism there was obviously some kind of creative chemistry within the Pistols – even their covers sounded roughly innovative, none were mere note-for-note copies. But Jonathan Richman's 'Roadrunner' was swiftly dropped

17 McLaren, perhaps to ape the Dolls, was still looking for a second guitarist and – even during the summer of 1976 – was informally auditioning guitar players like Gary Lammin of East End band Cocksparrer.

from their set when his rerecording of that driving classic – he'd been signed by new US indie Beserkley – began to get daytime airplay from Capital Radio's Nicky Horne. But though Richman's recut powered along as smartly as the original (and though it was coupled with a cover of The Standells' 'It Will Stand', an increasingly apposite testimony to the emotional power of rock'n'roll), it failed to reach even the fringes of the charts. Most record buyers were now so seemingly bleached out by the blandness of mainstream pop that they were unable to hear a solid rock song, even when it was presented to them on a (drive time) plate. It didn't bode well for McLaren's dream of a subversive group that could outsell the Bay City Rollers.

The Pistols made their debut at St Martin's the day after Guy Fawkes Night 1975. 'I thought it was great them gigging at Saint Martin's,' McLaren said years later. 'Glen would be able to get lots of gigs at St Martin's, we all thought, and then the group wouldn't even need a van, they could just wheel their equipment round the corner. Of course, in the end Glen could only get one gig at St Martin's so they still needed to beg, steal or borrow vans . . . '

The 6 November St Martin's gig saw the Pistols supporting Bazooka Joe, one of whom was Stuart 'Adam Ant' Goddard. It was a debut that made waves but it was a minor disaster for Rotten. He lost a bitter argument with McLaren over the band's name. 'John wanted to call the group Sex, the same as the shop, I said, "What do you wanna be? A brand?" The name Pistols stayed.'

Then a few moments of Rotten taking the mickey out of one of the Bazooka Joe boys ended unexpectedly when Danny Kleinman, the target of Rotten's sarcasm, leapt onstage and pinned the Pistols' front man to the back wall. Neither Matlock nor Cook nor Jones, the toughest Pistol, did anything to help, still unsure about how they felt about Rotten. Rotten mumbled a half-hearted apology to Kleinman and the group continued for another few minutes before, after barely four songs, the PA was switched off. Most of the crowd had walked out, or away, before the last song anyway, although one art student, a trendy called Simon Barker, was impressed with their racket and made a note of their name. He'd also recognised their clothes from the SEX shop where he was already an occasional customer – not that the Pistols only wore McLaren–Westwood creations. Although they bought clothes at 430 at cost price (i.e. with 60 per cent off) and were each given several items free, usually t-shirts, they also had their own style. As befits fans of the (Small) Faces, Jones, Cook and Matlock often wore mod-influenced trousers and shirts – the latter with paint-splattered Jackson Pollock-type jeans.

Rotten – infamous in one or two parts of the pre-Pistols King's Road for ripping up suits and putting them back together again with safety pins – would often write on his clothes and also continued to use safety pins well into 1977.

Clothing was so important then, part of the street theatre of the Cold War years, especially to those who were working class (who, like much of the lower middle class, felt that how they looked was, basically, all they had; it meant style, humour, wit and innovation, and now, with many of the McLaren–Westwood creations, it also meant explicit radical politics). Youths really did leave their old flared jeans behind in the Acme changing rooms once they'd bought their new pegs or drainpipes. As Strummer later said, 'like trousers, like brain'. The new look the band were pioneering could be copied, and extended, by spending mere pennies in a charity shop or paint yard. A boy could wear a battered pair of old, narrow Levis and be cool, a girl could, if she dared, wear a black t-shirt over stockings and suspenders and be high chic. The Pistols, and later The Clash, and their immediate contemporaries had a look that was not necessarily tied in with high-priced couture chic.

Despite the many subsequent remarks about punk's expensive 'King's Road fashions', people did initially have choices within 'the new look'. You could create your own variations and, ultimately, it did not just depend on cash. Anti-fashion, now the new high fashion, could cost virtually nothing. The fans in the audience in 1976 were all designers of a sort themselves – or, at the very least, stylists; they too were an active part of the cultural revolution. They didn't need to 'consume' anything new, they only needed old clothes, a few pence worth of metal and a bit of imagination. This was an anti-consumerist notion which was, in itself, subversive.

Malcolm's experience of 'manipulating student unions in the sixties' led him to conclude that art colleges would be the easiest places to get his new group gigs (gigs that, since the band were dressed in the SEX clothes, would – he hoped – lead to increased sales at the shop).

But it wasn't the sixties any more and 'many of these student union people found the very name Sex Pistols to be sexist and disgusting,' McLaren claims. 'So, in the end, I'd just ring up and say the group *were* the support act, friends of the main band. Just tell me when the sound check is and I'll make sure they're there.'

But it was a trick that could only be played a few times before both the venues' and the band's resentment became uncontrollable. The alternative arts' circuit yielded a gig at the Alternative Miss World party of camp artist Andrew Logan. On hearing that there were music press reporters present, McLaren persuaded 430 staffer Jordan, she of the twisted beehive hair, to strip onstage. She did so while being half-heartedly groped by a acid-ravaged Rotten. The gig ended with the glassy-eyed singer on the floor as director Derek Jarman filmed him and the band with his tiny 8 mm cine camera. In spite of all the fuss, no reviews were ever printed.

But a support slot at the Marquee in February '76 – with mutated pub rockers Eddie and the Hot Rods headlining – led to a Neil Spencer live review in *NME* that broke the media silence. It was printed in a music weekly that then sold over 200,000 copies a week – 'Don't Look Over Your Shoulder But The Sex Pistols Are Coming!'. It was a perfect piece from the band's point of view, ignoring the Pistols' headlining rivals Eddie and the Hot-Rods, an above-average bluesy pub band, while mentioning the chair-throwing and dancing girls and applauding the Pistol's energy and attitude: an attitude that reflected their indifference to sterile musical standards ('You lot can't play!' 'So what?') and their embracing of a whole new schtick – 'We ain't into music . . . we're really into chaos . . .'

There was even a photo of Rotten's face, wide-eyed and snarling as he menaced the mic. It was barely a quarter of a page but it was a good start and a three-line piece in the London *Evening Standard*'s gossip column kept up the faint but growing flicker of press interest – 'New group the Sex Pistols startled onlookers with semi-naked girls and songs like "I'm So Pretty Vacant".'

The same day the *NME* piece appeared, the Stevenson brothers – designer Nils (real name Ralf) and photographer Ray – saw the Pistols play live for the first time, at Hertfordshire College of Design in St Albans. 'I had a stall in a market on the King's Road,' said Nils, the younger of the two, in 1999, 'and I was cashing in on the revivals of the time, you know the fifties and sixties, just as we were coming out of the Glam thing. I used to drink at the Roebuck and I was going out with June Child – Marc Bolan's ex-wife – who worked at Blackhill Enterprises. They managed Pink Floyd, Marc Bolan and others. I got to know Malcolm through her – he was always asking her about the music biz – and also through a friend, Alan Jones, who I'd known through the Glam era. Alan had started to work in Malcolm's shop and he dragged me in there.'

And then Nils, ever the ladies' man, developed an infatuation with Westwood. 'And bit by bit I started hanging about with them and less with the obvious Chelsea crowd. My stall was doing badly and Malcolm suggested we start a club together. Then, as an afterthought, he mentioned this band he was trying to manage, who he reckoned were going to be the new Bay City Rollers. I met Paul and Steve in the Roebuck and thought, "Well, they don't look like the f—ing Bay City Rollers!" So I went off to watch them one day, him and Boogie and Chrissie Hynde [then a 430 staffer] came to pick me up and we went off to St Albans.'

Brother Ray had dug his 35 mm SLR out and took a few snaps, even though he wasn't too impressed with the Pistols. 'It was just a room, no stage or anything, the band were just playing in a corner. They sounded pretty poor to me. There were no stage lights or anything, obviously, and I didn't have any flash with me so I had to turn the room's ceiling light to face the band – but Rotten, who didn't know who I was, kept turning it away.'

Despite the restrictions, and his own initial lack of enthusiasm, Ray Stevenson produced some great images that night. The coarse grain of the photos, partly caused by the need to push the unlit film to its limit, only added to the stark black and white power of the shots: Rotten singing with his hands behind his neck as Jones looks on; Rotten sharing a mic with a bellowing Matlock; the latter trooping away at the end, guitar down as Rotten blows his nose into a grey hanky . . .

But while Ray was 'unsure' of the Pistols and whether he really wanted the 'gig' of regularly snapping them, Nils was hooked. 'I thought this is nothing like the Rollers, it's absolutely brilliant! I was determined to get involved – so I quit the stall and started working permanently on the Pistols. It was meant to be a business partnership [with Malcolm McLaren] and I explained all that to Rotten – I was tighter with him than anyone else; on tour Rotten would always stay in a room with me 'cos he was just too weird for everyone to deal with. Much as I love Steve and Paul, they were much more laddy. Rotten was an aspiring intellectual and he'd try and pick my brains. I explained my [management] situation with Malcolm to Rotten and he said, "If Malcolm ever gives you any gyp, I'll quit the band," so I felt quite secure.'

Three others affected by the Pistols the day Spencer's write-up appeared were Mancunian art students Howard 'Devoto' Trafford and Pete Shelley, and their pal Richard Boone, who'd been toying with the idea of getting a band together and who'd been intrigued by the *NME* piece.

The next week the trio drove for almost five hours in order to catch the Pistols at Buckinghamshire College of Higher Education, High Wycombe. There the band was supporting Screaming Lord Sutch, whose vintage amps were damaged by a manic Rotten. A minor riot broke out after Rotten's baiting of the crowd exploded into a brawl. The place was littered with Pistols' handouts afterwards – the arty A4 sides put together by Stevenson, McLaren and McLaren's old art school friend Helen Wellington-Lloyd, formerly Helen Mininberg.[18]

Devoto and Shelley were suitably impressed with both the music and visuals on display – and all the surrounding fuss. They drove back to Manchester determined to bring the Pistols north and more serious than ever about forming their own band.

Also in the crowd was the man who booked the 100 Club's rock nights, Ron Watts who found McLaren's boys a breath of fresh air after endless nights of second-rate Prog and Metal acts (pre-punk, most Metal had slowed down to a ponderous, pedestrian pace). Watts agreed to get the band into the Oxford Street venue.

With the continuing, if unsteady, flow of gigs being supported by several press reviews, and with Ron Watts's 100 Club now involved – Dai Davis's Albion Agency agreed to handle a couple of Pistols' gigs, and it did turn out to be just two – the first of which was to be at the Nashville Rooms pub in West Kensington replacing, with another group, a bizarre pair of cancellations – The Stranglers and Vivian Stanshall, the former founder of the comic rock group the Bonzo Dog Doo-Dah Band.

The Pistols would have to pay some cash – under £20 – for the PA, which they would then have to share with the headliners, Joe Strummer's 101ers. At the gig, the DJ intrigued a few present by playing a couple of tracks from a forthcoming album by The Ramones. 'Everybody went up three gears the day they got that first Ramones album,' Tony James claimed in 2005. 'Punk rock – that rama-lama super fast stuff – is totally down to The Ramones. Bands were just playing in an MC5 groove until then.'

The Pistols' gig at the Nashville on 23rd March was to be pivotal in

18 According to McLaren, it was Helen who first used the blackmail/kidnap style of lettering on Pistols' flyers – mainly because she couldn't be bothered to buy Letraset and opted instead for the cheaper, lazier option of hacking the letters out of old newspapers. The style was then used by Jamie Reid for the Sex Pistols' logo and track titles.

many other ways. Acme Attractions' manager Don Letts came along and checked out the band with girlfriend Jeannette Lee who'd already seen them at Andrew Logan's Shad Thames bash. Ray Stevenson snapped the band for the first time in London and The 101ers' Joe Strummer saw the Pistols live on stage for the first time. Amazed and enthralled by the energy and anti-showbiz attitude of Rotten and the rest, Strummer later said, 'Yesterday I was a crud, but then I saw the Sex Pistols and became a king – and moved into the future.'

But, for the Pistols, the most important connection made that night came right at the very end when the two long-hairs at the mixing desk came storming into the changing room after the Pistols had played. They were in their mid-twenties and they were Dave Goodman and his PA partner Kim Thraves. Goodman had been in bands himself: The Frinton Bassett Blues, Orange Rainbow and Polecat. With the latter two bands Goodman, then a funky bass-player, had toured the UK and Europe backing various international stars. But since the three-day week and black-out of 1973, the demand for live acts had fallen a little and Goodman had decided to get involved into the PA hire business.

At the sight of Thraves's shoulder-length ringlets and Goodman's mullet, both McLaren and the band were expecting to be either insulted or patronised by some standard 'music biz hippies'. The group were to be surprised, however.

'Dave Goodman was the first music business professional to actually come along and say, "Hey! You guys are really, really good!",' says McLaren now. 'No one had ever said that before, let alone someone with years and years of experience behind them. And Steve and Glen got on with Dave – and him and Kim had offered to do some more gigs for us so it seemed perfect timing. I didn't like the way they looked, of course, but then again they were gonna be more or less out of sight behind the mixing console most of the time – and we did have a few northern gigs looming, plus the 100 Club residency, so the timing was great. Later on Dave helped them work on songs and spent a lot of time on the road with them. He made them more confident, gave them the nerve to go and create ever bigger, better disasters!'

It was a key meeting for Goodman's experience was vital at that stage – apart from his playing, and occasional recording work, he'd also seen The Who, The Kinks, Hendrix and Pink Floyd at their sixties' height. And, in McLaren's words, 'He effectively became part of the Sex Pistols group.' He also confirmed the secret hopes of Lydon, Matlock, Cook and Jones; beneath their youthful brava-do none were really convinced of the strength of their direction until Goodman confirmed it.[19]

Within weeks of Goodman's addition to the gang, Jonh Ingham, a reporter with music weekly *Sounds*, caught the Pistols live at the El Paradiso strip club and spent half an hour babbling to his editor about it. His boss, the hard-drinking Alan Lewis, knew a good attention-grabber when he heard one and told Ingham to give the band a double-page spread for an interview. Advance word of the interview was enough to encourage McLaren to reprint the picture-less black-and-white publicity sheets he'd prepared for the Pistols; these consisted of a single paragraph which spoke of the Pistols being 'four teenagers' whose strident new lyrics, music and spon-taneity 'threatens all the pre-packaged pop' currently cluttering up the charts. Jones and Lydon were no longer actually teenagers but the rest of it – the important part – was true enough. After several false starts (more McLaren mind games), the Ingham-Pistols inter-view finally took place upstairs in the Cambridge Arms pub on Cambridge Circus, the south-eastern boundary of Soho. It appeared in print on Thursday 22 April and was, basically, a two-page advert for the new British music that, so far, only the Pistols were playing; it was also the big (music) press break that McLaren had been hoping for since November.

19 It was Goodman, too, who first noticed the fact that the chords in the most famous, and arguably most important, classical music composed in Western Europe between the late-18th and mid-19th century – that of Mozart, Beethoven, etc. – reoccurred in fifties rock'n'roll and then again, 20 years on, in punk rock and the songs of the Pistols.

'I wanna change things so that there's more bands like us,' exclaimed Rotten who'd earlier gone into an intense anti-hippy, anti-complacency rant at the moustachioed Ingham. 'I hate hippies and all they stand for. '

'At least the rest of us can see the Pistols,' wrote Ingham before Jones mournfully ad libbed, 'Yeah, I wish I could see us . . . '

Lydon also slagged off the miming that dominated the BBC's *Top of the Pops* music show – then the only regular pop show on UK television – as Ingham concluded that the band and McLaren wanted a 'rumbling anarchic' group scene such as had obtained 'during the mid-sixties'. It was a telling remark – from autumn '75 onwards, Acme Attractions had been selling more and more pre-1969 Sta-Prest, along with skinny ties, both new and originals, and small-collared shirts that were not fifties jobs but, instead, from London's 1963–67 fashion heyday.[20] As the year progressed the design team's ideas took on more attitude – 'riot' t-shirts mixed with plastic shirts, PVC pegs and rubber-yoked shirts with a single sleeve dyed a different colour.

One of the more poignant lines in the *Sounds*' Pistols piece concerns not clothes but drugs. It comes from Jones, 'There's no drugs in this band,' he'd said proudly – perhaps to contrast the band's attitudes with what he'd learned from McLaren about the New York scene. Of course what Jones actually then meant was that there were no *hard* drugs used by the Pistols, discounting Rotten's occasional use of borderline chemicals such as speed and acid. Sadly, the group's relatively mild intake was not a state of affairs that was to last.

20 In spring 1976, the author became part of an informal Acme design team – which included both the imaginative Raynor and the talented Helen Robinson – which began to work on 'updated' sixties Mod imagery for shirts and t-shirts. This sixties-based look is sometimes, mistakenly, thought to have been copied from the Anglophile New York scene and the new groups such as Blondie that were slowly getting record deals together – but almost no one in the UK knew what the Blondie band or anyone else in NYC looked like in early 1976; only a couple of blurred shots of the Ramones had appeared at this point – and with their long hair, ripped jeans and bike jackets they were hardly the epitome of UK mod styling circa 1964.

The next Pistols' gig at the Nashville ended in a huge fight when Vivienne Westwood had returned to her seat to find a young girl occupying it. She ordered her out but the girl refused to move, so Westwood slapped her until her long-haired boyfriend intervened, violently pushing the older woman away. He was promptly beaten senseless by a mob that included Sid Vicious and, according to eye witness Neil Tennant, the band's 'El Dementoid' – John Rotten.

The Sex Pistols played Manchester's Lesser Free Trade Hall on 4 June, a gig arranged by Devoto and Shelley. Despite the latter's enthusiasm, the gig was hardly a sell out. 'There were only twenty people there,' says McLaren now, 'thirty at the very most. Barely two sets of hands you could count them on. I don't even know if Tony Wilson was there in June. So when people say to me, "Oh, I was there the first time the Pistols played Manchester," I normally say, "Well, you couldn't have been, the place was three-quarters empty." I ended up drifting around the local pubs before the band went on, seeing if I could talk any likely looking people into coming down to the gig. I saw that guy who later started The Fall – Mark E. Smith – I said, "There's this group playing over the road that you really ought to see." He said, 'Why the f— would I wanna do that?" I said they're really good, they're from London and he said, "Why the f— would I wanna see a band from f—ing London?" So I told him they were the Sex Pistols and he said, "Oh yeah, I've heard a bit about them . . . they sound f—ing shite!" I think he did actually turn up later, looking all beery-eyed . . . but it was seriously uphill getting people in.'

Among the less than two dozen present at the first Lesser Free Trade Hall were Bernard Dickens and Peter Hook, later to be members of the group known as The Stiff Kittens.

One man present who wasn't supposed to be there was Steve Diggle, then a young bassist looking to meet a guitar player who was into starting a band to do 'fast, three-minute songs'. A mix-up led Diggle to Shelley and Devoto and the Pistols' gig. The subsequent 'almighty racket was f—ing loud but also f—ing brilliant, I was completely transfixed,' Diggle says now. Within minutes he knew he 'wanted to get in a group like that,' and so accepted Shelley's offer to join The Buzzcocks.[21]

The month before the Manchester gig Nick Kent had stormed angrily into SEX. Kent was a smack addict at the time and he was annoyed with his American girlfriend Chrissie Hynde. He therefore decided to teach her a lesson – publicly. Before McLaren and Westwood's disbelieving eyes Kent took off his heavy leather belt and beat Hynde senseless. Then, to the even greater horror of Westwood, Kent also knocked over a window display.

Kent had been hanging out with the Sex Pistols for months by this time, albeit on an irregular basis, at one point even offering to take over the group (much to McLaren's annoyance). But he hadn't used his exalted *NME* position to write about the band, even months after Neil Spencer's seminal review.

At the 100 Club in mid-June '76 came the chance for revenge. Kent took Howard Thomson of Island Records, and went to the front, near the stage. Kent by this time was carrying a flick knife every other day and was even continually clicking it open and closed at *NME* staff meetings, until a more senior hack had told him to 'put it away or use it'. Kent put the knife away but continued to carry it. But there is, of course, a huge gulf between violence as a pose and violence for real. When Vicious – with Wobble at his side – stood directly in front of Kent at the 100 Club, Kent objected, asking them to move in terms that were perhaps intended to show Thomson that he, Kent, could handle the natives with the right degree of firmness.

'Move out the f—ing way, will you?' was not the kind of thing most 100 Club regulars would have said to Vicious or Wobble. When the latter replied, in an angry snarl, 'F—ing move yourself!', Kent was still too naive, or too stoned, to see the danger signs.

21 The strangely topical name had been found by Devoto in a battered copy of London's *Time Out* magazine, in an article about the TV show *Rock Follies*, the piece ending with the punchline, 'Get a buzz, cock!'.

'Think you're tough, do you?' Kent was said to have asked. 'Guess what?' snapped back Wobble. 'I f—in' am.' Before Kent could open his mouth again, Wobble had pushed him and produced a knife – though he didn't use it. Vicious knew about Chrissie Hynde's beating at 430 – though Wobble maintains that he was unaware of it – and he suddenly moved Wobble aside and wrapped a big greasy bike chain around Kent's head. Blood pouring from his scalp, the journalist staggered from the club. Westwood materialised by his side on the way out and, according to Kent, assured him that Sid was 'just some crazy, he won't be coming to any more Pistols' gigs I promise you'.

This turned out to be untrue, of course, but Vicious did miss some gigs while cementing his position in a new band called Flowers of Romance. They took their name from the Pistols' noisy sound-check 'song' and the only semi-regular members were bass player Vicious, rhythm guitarist Albertine and blond lead guitarist Levene moonlighting from the fledgling Clash. Like Vicious, Levene was another friend of John Rotten's who'd visited Rotten's Highgate squat. And, like Vicious, Levene was, by this stage, a regular injector of amphetamine sulphate, 'speed'.

During that blisteringly hot summer of 1976, Vicious had played along with The Ramones' debut LP non-stop for 12- and 18-hour sessions. With Levene's help he became a competent, if unexceptional, punk rock bassist. He wasn't a McCartney or a Matlock, of course, but he could hold a straightforward song – despite the future myths about his inability to play. He was still taking too much speed – for some people, perhaps most, a little is more than enough – and acting the fool in ways both pleasant and unpleasant. 'Sid used to do things at Linda Ashby's,' Nils admitted later. 'One of the things he did was go to the phone book and look up people with Pakistani names and phone up and call 'em "dirty f—ing Paki bastards" and he said he was going to come round and kill them – he thought that was really funny.' His sick sense of humour aside, though, in any serious discussion Vicious would always passionately attack racist organisations such as the National Front.

Within weeks, the competition for the Pistols' uneasy leadership of this unnamed movement had hotted up way beyond Sid's Flowers of Romance: The Damned played their first gigs (four secret events at a gay club and one backing the Pistols at the 100 Club) and The Clash launched into full-scale rehearsals.

Meanwhile The Ramones had flown in from the States for their 4 July Roundhouse gig with The Stranglers and the headlining sixties-style band The Flamin' Groovies – a seminal night for many of the 2,000 punters, including Sid Vicious, who started off the evening handing out Pistols' flyers outside (anyone who refused one was tripped up by Vicious, whose hair was so short at that time that Andy Blade of schoolboy band Eater thought he must be involved with some 'religious cult or something').

The Pistols themselves were playing Sheffield's large Black Swan pub that evening, supported by The Clash as they made their public debut, Dave Goodman allegedly helping Levene tune his guitar before Levene helped Simonon tune his bass. Both bands were back in town the next night to see The Ramones in Camden Lock's Dingwalls club (the Pistols were involved in a few scuffles and The Stranglers' Jean-Jacques Burnel got into a fight with Simonon).

McLaren felt a movement was happening – more in London than New York, despite the queues and rave reviews for the Ramones – and that anything was now possible. More specifically, he now believed that a serious record deal might be on the cards. But neither he nor the band were really happy with the demos that session guitarist Chris Spedding had recently recorded for them. 'They sounded like they'd been cut in an aircraft hangar,' according to Goodman and/or McLaren, and virtually no one gets a recording contract without decent demos. So, when Goodman himself offered to record the band in Denmark Street, for expenses only, all concerned leapt at the chance.

'I'd learned enough to know that I could get a decent sound with my old Teac four-track,' Goodman said years later, 'though I also knew we'd have to bounce it onto an eight-channel system later and add a few overdubs if we were gonna mix it all properly.' So with his four-track, a small mixing desk and a handful of mics, Goodman moved into 6 Denmark Street on 13 July '76 to record the Sex Pistols. For a period of between five to eight days – no one seems sure any longer – he spent endless hours trying to capture the band's on-stage excitement.

And he succeeded, mostly. 'If The Beatles had Abbey Road and George Martin,' said Ray Morrissey of the Sex Pistols website in 2004, 'then the Pistols have Denmark Street and Dave Goodman. He was absolutely crucial.'

From the start, Goodman used the limitations of time, space and equipment to the group's advantage – simply overloading the desk input led to the OTT distortion that gave 'I Wanna Be Me' exactly the right jagged feel, while bouncing the guitar's feedback type drone between the channels produced a dynamic wall-of-sound feel during the verses of 'No Feeling'. There's no question that these versions of the above songs are the definitive ones (in fact, the former was later to appear on the group's EMI debut disc, while the latter was put on the flip of the group's unreleased A&M single).

Also recorded that week in Denmark Street were the first versions of a new song 'Anarchy In The UK' – far slower than any since recorded – as well as 'Pretty Vacant', 'Satellite', 'Seventeen' and 'Sub Mission'. The last track was cut in one painfully slow instrumental version and one far niftier take that has Goodman 'playing' the studio kettle in order to get the right bubbling intro – it goes well with the lip-mic music, a sort of electric kazoo drone, that Rotten used as a solo (all put down over a beat that is almost reggae-like with its rolling, staccato feel).

The song itself is a bona fide gem – what started out as a Rotten–Matlock mickey-take of McLaren's request for a bondage anthem became something else entirely. A mysterious epic about the submarine pursuit of a female, a woman whose 'watery love' could not be explained (perhaps she was the silent demi-mermaid Marina, the female lead of TV's *Stingray!* puppet series, watched by both Matlock and Lydon during their primary school days). The finale, with its echoing chorus and wild yelps, truly sounds like the punk barbarians breaching the gates of Prog's po-faced citadel.

Before the final mixdown of tracks – started at Decibel in Stoke Newington and finished at Chiswick's Riverside Studios – the Sex

Pistols had to play their second Manchester gig. By now McLaren had his own artwork 'department' for the Pistols. Initially this had consisted of himself, Nils and Jordan giving a few words of assistance to Helen Wellington-Lloyd, who had created some of the more memorable of the early Pistols' flyers, all with her own unique wit and compositional panache (one flyer for the Nashville perversely dedicated most of its space to advertising television's Foreman versus Frazier boxing match, another spoke of 'sartorial correctness' and featured the band's signatures, stars already).

But in the summer McLaren decided to raise the stakes even further – he called in one of his old art school pals, Jamie Reid, who, with his equally radical girlfriend Sophie Richmond, had been running *Surburban Press*, a libertarian magazine and print shop based in Croydon. But the *Press* had run out of both cash and distributors and Jamie Reid was now free.

It was Reid who, taking the cue from Wellington-Lloyd's artfully chaotic posters, created the infamous Pistols' logo. It was the perfect complement to McLaren's view that the Pistols should be 'young, sexy assassins', young people seemingly outside the law. For the second Manchester gig, in late July, however, there was a hotch-potch of posters – the post-Glam group Slaughter and the Dogs, who were also on the bill supporting the Pistols, and the much-talked about Devoto–Shelley band, The Buzzcocks, cheekily produced their own posters portraying themselves as the headliners.

The gig was on Tuesday 20 July as none of the groups was big enough to warrant, or afford, a Friday or a Saturday night at the hall, but it finally did see the live debut of The Buzzcocks in their own city (after a mere half-dozen rehearsals with 16-year-old schoolboy drummer John Maher at Devoto's flat at 364 Lower Broughton Road – rehearsals interrupted by Devoto's hissing monitor lizard). 'The adrenalin and anger was incredible when we went on,' Diggle declared later. 'Our amps and guitar stuff was all cheap and tacky and sounded terrible. But it was all so fast and loud it had a kind of terrible beauty too.' Shelley was playing a Woolworths' guitar that had been deliberately snapped in half. Despite such self-inflicted snags, The Buzzcocks fizzed and roared and instantly became local heroes, a status they confirmed at the end of their set by abandoning their screaming guitars and casually plunging into the audience and strolling up to the bar. 'Before the Pistols we were blagging into stadiums to see some spoilt brats playing with lots of ten-thousand-pound synthesisers,' Diggle said later, 'with punk all that changed, the barrier between ordinary kids and the musicians on stage came right down.'

Also present were the future Stiff Kittens–Warsaw–Joy Division crew, Fall co-founder Mark E. Smith, Steven Morrissey, Bernard Sumner, Mick Hucknall, student Paul Morley and film undergraduate Julien Temple, who'd been following The Clash around since just after their very first rehearsals and now seemed to be about to 'switch sides'. Morley, and others, got drunk and started a few half-hearted scuffles, usually between the Mancs and those few Londoners who had made the long haul north, but the Pistols silenced them all.

After the Dogs' and The Buzzcocks' tense energetic sets, it seemed the headlining London group would have their work cut out. But the endless rehearsals, and recording sessions, with Goodman, had worked their magic. With Jones, Matlock and Cook tighter than ever, Rotten had the perfect backdrop over which to spit his sneering tirades. Many in the crowd were initially speechless but there were wild shouts and screams by the end as, for an encore, Rotten tore up his shirt. This second Manchester gig has now entered north-eastern folklore and the city's post-'76 cultural renaissance is said by many to have started there. Before this event – or, rather, what it eventually inspired – Manchester had merely been another northern industrial city slipping slowly into decline. Such was the impact of the July gig there are both television documentaries and books – most noticeably David Nolan's *I Swear I Was There!* – about that single night when the Pistols, Buzzcocks and Dogs played at the Lesser Free Trade Hall.

The Jonh Ingham *Sounds* review of the Manchester event was head-lined 'Anarchy In The UK' – the gig was, effectively, the song's live debut – and 'anarchy' was now the battle cry. *Sniffin' Glue* – the Mark Perry–Danny Baker DIY fanzine – had launched in sunny Deptford, south-east London, the week before and, within a few issues, it would accuse the Pistols of writing 'Anarchy . . .' merely to peddle the new £25 shirts in SEX.[22]

But the song 'Anarchy In The UK' had a more tangled history than that of a shirt commercial. Jamie Reid was later 'accused' of writing it (and the lines that sneer at 'shopping schemes' and stop-ping 'traffic lines' certainly ring of his sub-Lettrist-Situationist mag-azine *Suburban Press*). But when asked directly if he'd written the song in 1979, Reid had said that ' "Anarchy In The UK" was more Jordan's idea than mine,' while McLaren now says, 'It was a mar-riage of a lot of people.' The words themselves spoke of wanting to eliminate the passer-by. It was us-or-them rhetoric, a time-to-take-sides stance that was the logical extension of Bernie Rhodes's 18-month-old manifesto t-shirt.

In the song 'Anarchy In The UK', the personal 'sick joke' violence of Lydon songs like 'No Feeling' – which spoke of kicking people in the head, of beating them black and blue – was now made general, was now delivered widescreen, for, seemingly, political reasons.

Matlock undoubtedly wrote virtually all of the 'Anarchy' tune – 'I was going for a kind of marching song, an anthem' – and Rotten certainly came up with the opening and closing few lines. These included the 'D-e-s-t-r-o-y!' finale – possibly borrowed from Steve Harley's 1974 track 'Psychomodo' – and, in the first line, Rotten's notorious claiming of the title 'anti-Christ'. This latter move was initially resisted by Matlock, not particularly for moral reasons, though they may have been there too, but mainly because they

---

22 The first, cheaply photocopied *Sniffin' Glue*, though it at last provided a British answer to New York's *Punk* magazine, was hardly ultra-hip or even London-friendly, as it concen-trated wholly on American acts such as The Ramones, Flamin' Groovies and the ageing Blue Oyster Cult. Even London's comparatively 'straight' Eddie and The Hot Rods were only deemed worthy of a one-line mention.

made the rhyme with 'anarchist' impossible (Rotten got round this in performance by pronouncing the word 'anar-kyste').

The song's first producer, Dave Goodman, accepted such words without hesitation "cos I thought its sentiments weren't really anti-Christ as such, I thought it was just part of John's whole stance, which seemed to be against Catholicism, against any organised religion. It was just part of that song, which was a very heavy song.' But that doesn't explain Lydon's several poses – captured on film – where he deliberately mocked the crucifixion.

And it was Goodman, among others, who were invited by Lydon to meet 'his friends in Highgate, who visited the cemetery there'. These friends, according to Goodman, were the people who Rotten later said he 'took acid with, before talking about the devil, trying to see him, stuff like that'. Goodman never went and it may all have been some kind of elaborate wind-up on Rotten's part. But, during many hundreds of hours on the road, and in various cheap hotels, Goodman spent more time with Rotten-Lydon than anyone else around the Pistols in 1976, and he seemed to think Rotten's invitation was serious.

'I heard something about Highgate too, about weird goings-on there,' said Clash roadie Roadent decades later. 'There was a weird hippy side to John [Lydon], a secret side – just like his going-to-football side, and his Sunday-dinners-with-mum side and his Sex Pistols side, etc.'

'Most of the great front men, the big stars, have a secret life, a really private life,' Wobble repeated in 2005, 'and I do remember many strange things happening around John. There was this squat in Barnet where all the windows and doors kept opening and slamming shut – all by themselves. Real poltergeist stuff. That was a bit f—ing freaky. And then there was the time – either in that squat or the one near Tottenham – when John [Lydon] was on the stairs. He turned and smiled back at me and continued on upstairs. And then I walk straight into the downstairs kitchen and he's in there too! Which was impossible, logically speaking. That was really, really strange – he didn't seem to be aware of causing it himself but who knows? I knew John was a bit interested in that occult stuff, but it was still a shock, still very weird. It's not something I can explain. I did used to drink a bit in those days but on the occasions I'm talking about I was completely straight – they *did* happen. It was all a bit dark and strange . . . '

There was a 'darkness' at 430 too, in the inverted crucifix earrings, the witchcraft jewellery and the Nazi accessories (such as the pagan wedding rings used by the SS, items that were collected and occasionally sold in SEX).

And the only time Jones, Cook and Nils seriously claimed to have seen a UFO was when they were with Rotten.

It was almost as if his sheer presence was enough to cause some kind of psychic disturbance (even if, in most cases, the events only took place in the imagination of those present).

All of the above may have been, indeed probably were, coincidences, or have some other totally rational explanation, but Rotten was undoubtedly the most shocking, most unforgettable, performer of his generation. To Neil Tennant he was 'El Dementoid', to Giovanni Dadomo, the 'nastiest' front man ever, to many others he seemed on the brink of insanity (Rotten even admitted as much during interviews in late '76: 'If I hadn't got in the Pistols I'd have been quietly put away, classified as insane . . . '). On-stage this all gave him a power that seemed to go beyond that of a mere rock'n'roll singer. It was a tenuous yet real power that Rotten alternately shied away from and revelled in . . .

One man convinced of Rotten's uniqueness as a front man was Granada TV's twenty-something presenter Tony Wilson. Although, despite McLaren's memories of the event, Wilson *had* been present at the first Lesser Free Trade hall gig, he'd missed the second as he'd been on holiday. One viewing was enough, though: 'They [the Sex Pistols] were so powerful. Even though they couldn't play that well, they could kick enough to be powerful. And their front man, John Rotten-Lydon, was just so charismatic.'

Afterwards, Wilson spoke to McLaren. 'Someone must have told him I was running the *So It Goes* rock show because he came over and said, "What do you think, Mister Wilson?" I answered that I thought the guitarist would have to drop his Pete Townshend impersonation – because Steve Jones had been doing these Who-type windmill poses all night. McLaren hurriedly said, "Yes, yes, we're dealing with that." And then he went off as I began to scheme ways of getting the Pistols onto *So It Goes* – I could see I'd have a fight on my hands.'

And Wilson was right. The Pistols weren't local nor were they a household name nor did they even have a recording contract. Worse still, there were ugly rumours about violence, while other hacks had moaned about the group's apparent inability to play their instruments. Wilson kept arguing but he was only allowed to put the Pistols on during the last five minutes of the last *So It Goes* of the series – and even this could only go ahead after Granada researcher Malcolm Clark had witnessed this group in action and reported back to head office.

'I think I spoke to Boogie, John Tiberi, who was working in Malcolm's office and he said they were playing Walthamstow's Assembly Hall in a couple of days' time,' Wilson relates now, 'so we drove down during another incredibly bright, sunny day – that whole summer was so amazing – and found ourselves in this huge, dark empty hall with the group almost lost down one end of it. Everyone was standing back in a semi-circle about fifteen foot wide, just out of John's gobbing range. But they were great, of course, and Malcolm Clark could see that virtually straight away and that was it. The Pistols were gonna be on *So It Goes*.'

What Wilson didn't see that night was the confrontation between McLaren and Ian Dury – the latter playing a reunion/farewell gig as a goodbye to the Kilburn and The Highroads band he'd started half a dozen years before. The Pistols were supporting the Highroads and the aggressive Stranglers, a band combining post-pub rock with touches of punky garage band psychedelia – they even had a Seeds style keyboard in their line-up as well as powerful melodies. After watching the hunched, snarling Rotten in action, Dury had turned to McLaren and said, 'So when did you and your boy decide to nick my act then?' The Pistols' manager laughed it off with an embarrassed shrug, but there was an undoubted similarity between the two frontmen and their on-stage attitudes. To be fair to Rotten, though, his unique act had also been influenced by Iggy Pop, Wilko Johnson, Mick Jagger and several others.

The television debut of punk rock was recorded on Wednesday 1 September 1976. The Sex Pistols drove up to Granada TV's Manchester studio with McLaren, Goodman, Nils Stevenson and Jordan all in attendance – and all eight of them were to play their full part in the spectacle that was to unfold that evening.

Wilson greeted the band and the others wearing a satin suit jacket and clogs, and he irritated some of those present by still arguing the worth of bands such as Steely Dan. 'Tony Wilson was OK, he'd at least booked the band for telly, months before anyone else dared to, but he was still hedging his bets a bit,' the late Dave Goodman claimed in 2001. 'As well as talking about all these older bands, he'd also put us on last during the last show of the series. The Pistols were going to be just one of three unsigned groups – and we were only going to be allowed to do one number before Tony stood in front and signed the series off.'

Or that, at least, had been the Granada plan. McLaren was determined things were not going to go quite that smoothly. 'We should take it easy, play really laid-back during the run-through. And then, when they're doing it for real, make a bit of real noise,' he told 'his boys'. The band agreed and ran through a subdued 'Anarchy . . . ' as the camera and lighting crew 'marked up' the main stage.[23]

As the band started drinking, McLaren urgently pulled them to

23 'Marking up' involves taping 'X' marks to the floor where guests are supposed to stand – it made life a lot easier for the crew, editor and director, especially in an age when TV cameras were more than twice the size and weight of similar modern cameras.

one side: 'I'd ignore those crosses on the floor if I were you, boys – stand where you want, run where you want, move around a bit, let's make those cameramen work for a living!' Moments later, a huge row erupted. Members of the two other unsigned bands, Gentlemen and The Bowles Brothers, were now outraged that the scruffy short-haired 'Sex Punks' were being offered the main stage when they – proper musicians with matching silk shirts and expensive synthesisers – were merely being offered a side stage. The Pistols were not prepared to swap places.

By now those who had watched the run-through wondered why Jordan, who was going to 'shoulder dance' by the edge of the stage, was still wearing her Nazi armband. When told she'd have to take it off before the videotape recording could begin, Jordan refused. Having smoked enough Thai sticks to be moderators, Goodman and Thraves convinced Jordan to allow the armband's swastika to be covered with a small circle of paper, upon which Thraves had carefully written the word 'Censored'.

Australian comedian and *So It Goes* warm-up man Clive James was witness to all this and began taking the mickey out of the group's appearance in general, and Rotten's in particular. But, after months of dealing with drunken hecklers and bikers, James was easy meat, with Rotten and Jordan outwitting and out-insulting the man they called a 'baldy old Sheila, Bruce'. An irritated James was finally reduced to an angry silence.

With the studio's 300 seats full and the performance just minutes away, the band demanded the right to have Jordan announce them. It was bad enough having to be signed off by a representative of the station, to be introduced by him as well would be too much of an insult. Jordan was game since getting on mic would draw more attention to both her extreme but careful make-up and the word 'censored' on her armband.

Expectation crackled in the air as the cameras did their last-minute run-through, a mock tracking of the few moves they'd been told the band would make. This, in turn, was watched by an annoyed Granada sound mixer – annoyed because of Goodman's nerve in asking for the chance to mix the sound high up in the main control room (accessible only by a steep metal staircase).

McLaren's last, hoarsely whispered pep talk ensured that things were going to end explosively. 'When it comes to the end of "Anarchy", if I were you I wouldn't stop, I'd just keep going, do "Problems" and "Pretty Vacant". Just don't let him sign you off!'

As Wilson started his intro, Goodman climbed into the control room to 'assist' Granada's sound mixer. Halfway through Wilson's words came a shout from Jones. Finally, the host gave in and cued the band. Jordan made her intro. She spoke with demure sarcasm: 'The Sex Pistols are, if possible, even better than the lovely Joni Mitchell . . . '

A second of puzzled silence is followed by the thundering opening chords of 'Anarchy' as Rotten screams, 'Get off your arses!' The band explode into life, moving back and forth – everywhere, it seems, except to their stage markers – as Nils and Jordan chuck chairs on stage. Rotten and Matlock briefly pogo as Jordan scrambles around, as energetic as the camera crew whose lens desperately chases the band. Johnny gives the camera the finger and slams the mic stand back and forth. Jones continually flicks between melody and discordant pure rock noise, striking poses with such speed that they are scarcely believable. He is no longer Pete Townshend Junior – the fake has become real. Up in the control room, Goodman has pushed the sound, and his luck, to the limit by grabbing the hands of Granada's soundman and then pushing the volume levels up with his feet. The middle-aged soundman naturally objects and a struggle ensues. In normal circumstances Goodman would be instantly ejected from the control room for such a blatant breach of televisual protocol – but these are not normal circumstances since everyone else in the room, including Wilson, is staring, stunned, at the monitors. As 'Anarchy . . .' grinds to its 'destroy' ending, the relief in the control room is palpable – but short-lived. The Pistols refuse to stop, instantly launching into a raw version of 'Pretty Vacant'. In the control room an enraged producer – one Chris Pie – bellows 'Cut! Cut now!' to be contradicted by Wilson and Goodman, 'No! No! Let it roll – ' 'I Said Cut!' 'No!'

The three Pistols' numbers end with a withering Rotten stare of insane intensity as Matlock kicks over a mic stand and Jones trashes a guitar and amp. Behind them, Nils and Jordan start to demolish the main stage's carefully crafted set . . .

For the first and last time in Granada's history, a musical group finish their act to be greeted with complete and utter silence.

The audience – mainly consisting, according to Wilson, of 'Chorleton hippies from the worst part of hippy Manchester' – sit frozen, motionless in a daze of shock and disgust.

'Afterwards,' said Matlock later, 'this old guy who was one of the cleaners said, "That was great, lad, really great, liveliest thing I've seen since the Yardbirds played here over ten year ago." But he was the only one, the only guy there who seemed to like it.'

'The only sound after they'd stopped playing,' Wilson recalled a quarter of a century later, 'was the slap, slap, slap of Chris Pie's shoes on the stairs as he came storming down looking for someone to hit – he was that furious at all that had happened . . . '

Once Chris Pie had finally calmed down, there were postmortem drinks in the Granada bar. Seminal comedian Peter Cook was there, having caught some of the Pistols' performance. Cook, there to see Clive James, was intrigued by it all and spent several drinks talking enthusiastically to both McLaren and Rotten. But Cook was very much alone that night. Punk and the Pistols were to divide fans and critics alike as no genre or act has done, before or since. Even those pundits who were swiftly to become fans – Mark P of *Sniffin' Glue*, Charles Shaar Murray of *NME*, Allan Jones of *Melody Maker* – were initially hostile, Jones to a shocking degree.

Former drug worker Caroline Coon, also of *Melody Maker*, had to rave about the Pistols for a staggering six months before senior staff finally, reluctantly, allowed her to write a feature about either the band or the new 'whole new scene' that was erupting around them.

It was like a self-fulfilling prophecy: the more industry figures ignored or attacked the new bands, the more their aggressive stance seemed justified.

The next day, the rest of the band drove back to London, while Matlock opted to stay and hang out with Shelley and Devoto for a day or so. It was a decision that annoyed Rotten, who made several sarcastic remarks about it.

Rotten seems to have distrusted Matlock's musical ability and songwriting prowess from day one. The fact that Matlock was better educated, conventionally handsome and came from a slightly wealthier background only added to the tension.

At one of the early 100 Club gigs, Rotten had tried to pick a fight with Matlock mid-set and, at the very start of the *So It Goes* appearance, the Pistols' front man can even be seen trying to kick his bass player. The most unusual – and one of the most promising – songwriting teams in rock history was already under great pressure . . .

NO.6

DENMARK STREET –
Fagin's Lair

The month preceding the Pistols' visit to Granada had been one of intense and increasing activity among rock'n'roll's new prime movers – and not just in England. On 3 August, New York's camp Wayne County issued his 'Max's Kansas City' single on the Max's label – the song, seemingly dedicated to the eponymous venue, name-checked Manhattan's rising stars; The Ramones, Johnny Thunders's post-Dolls group The Heartbreakers, Mong, Fuse, Blondie, Patti Smith, Mink DeVille, Richard Hell, Pere Ubu, Cherry Vanilla, etc. – while, in France, final confirmations were made for the 'Euro Punk Rock Festival' in the southern town of Mont de Morsan. The most promising Brits in the line-up were The Damned, the only vaguely punk group on the list, a group now managed by Acme's accountant Andy Czezowski. There were other UK acts, including The Hot Rods, Roogalator, Nick Lowe, Mick Farren's Pink Fairies and Jesse Hector's Gorillas.[26]

---

26 Formerly The Hammersmith Gorillas, they were Mod-suedeheads with the mutton-chop sideburns that Hector's Crushed Butler band had pioneered back at the turn of the decade. The Gorillas also had a neat line in tight Small Faces/Kinks covers but, like The Pink Fairies and Nick Lowe, they had been playing the circuit in one form or another since the late sixties . . .

The Pistols' own invitation to Mont de Morsan had been swiftly withdrawn after the bewildered organisers claimed the band's demands for top billing and some entourage accommodation went 'much too far. Who the hell do they think they are, the Rolling Stones?'

Back in London, Caroline Coon was now finally allowed to her write a two-page *Melody Maker* feature on the Pistols *et al.* under the ambiguous 7 August headline: 'Punk Rock: Crucial Or Phoney?' While the story dominated the front page – with Joe Stevens's photo of April's Nashville fight – there was little actual lay-out space given to the Sex Pistols or The Clash (and Bruce Springsteen's tenuously connected name was even bandied around).

Coon's assertion that punk 'would inspire a fourth generation of rockers' was brave, though that too was undermined by Allan Jones who, on the very same page, attacked the 'nihilistic' new groups. He ended with the words that were to come back to haunt him – 'if the Pistols or Patti Smith really are the new rock then I am going into the air-raid shelter with Granny until it all blows over . . .'

Three days after *Melody Maker*'s 'punk debate' issue, the Chris Spedding-inspired group The Vibrators – all in their mid- to late twenties, bandwagon-jumpers albeit with a touch of musical style – backed the Pistols at the 100 Club where the crowds were now regularly squeezing past the hundred mark. This was not a huge attendance considering that the band's on-off residency at the basement jazz club had begun way back in March . . . but it was still a respectable showing for a Tuesday night, especially as Britain was enduring its hottest summer for over half a century, with a constant stream of water shortages, standpipes and 'Phew! What A Scorcher!' headlines as the temperature regularly topped 82°F (28°C).

A junior A&R man – Mike Thorne – was also present that steamy night, there to check out the group that the music press had begun to pay increasing attention to (with the exception of *NME*, which had changed direction and virtually ignored the band after the Sid Vicious attack on Nick Kent).

Other A&Rs had looked at the band before – Dave Dee and

Howard Thomson among them – but Thorne was the first from the mighty EMI, the richest label in the world and the home to fifties MOR veterans such as Cliff Richard as well as younger pop Prog acts such as Freddie Mercury's Queen (whose million-selling 'Bohemian Rhapsody' had been the biggest UK single of the last two years).

Thorne was suitably impressed – the negative hype, the rumours that the Pistols 'couldn't play' turned out to be false. The band could kick it live, all of them looked good and Rotten undoubtedly had a bizarre charisma all his own. The next day Thorne was telling all who would listen that the Pistols had 'something'.

On 13 August, The Clash had played a 'private' Rehearsal Rehearsals gig in front of Giovanni Dadomo of *Sounds*, Caroline Coon and half a dozen friends. Dadomo's review declared The Clash to be like a 'runaway train . . . so powerful, they're the first new group to come along who can really scare the Sex Pistols shitless . . . '

His response wasn't surprising given that, according to Chimes, 'We'd rehearsed and rehearsed just so much. Bernie wouldn't even consider letting us play live 'til he thought we really had it right. So when we finally went on stage the energy just poured out of us.' Bernie's boys had their own look too: their demob jackets and narrow Oxfam trousers had the Jackson Pollock dribbled-paint effect (as borrowed from Mick Jones's mate Matlock).

The same day saw the launch of Stiff Records, the UK's first post-pub rock indie. It was the love-child of ex-Feelgoods manager Andrew 'Jake' Jakeman and Irish tough guy Dave Robinson, the manager of Graham Parker and Brinsley Schwartz. Their debut 45 was Nick Lowe's 'So It Goes', a medium-fast rocker that was then considered punky by more mainstream thinkers. The very word 'punk' was now beginning to stick, despite previous attempts by Ingham and Coon to float more imaginative tags for the mid-seventies' first genre: Mach rock, Surge rock, Dole Queue rock and even the quizzical? rock. *NME*'s Roy Carr had suggested 'New Wave', after the Truffaut–Godard French movie 'school' of the sixties, but this was only adopted the following year, usually as a term for those 'less extreme' acts – Blondie, the Hot Rods, Chrissie Hynde's Pretenders – who could grudgingly be granted a few radio and TV spots.

The day after The Clash's private gig at Rehearsals, the Pistols played Birmingham's Barbarella's Club, watched by up-and-coming singers Kevin Rowland and Simon Le Bon. Polydor A&R Chris Parry was also in the audience – no doubt tipped off by Thorne's recent appearance at the 100 Club. Contact was made later that week with McLaren, who was now beginning to realise that a major record deal was indeed possible.

He'd already taken steps to ensure August didn't see the Pistols, and friendly rivals The Clash, eclipsed by the Euro Punk Rock festival. The first event organised was an all-night extravaganza he'd arranged for the last Sunday in the month at Islington's Screen on The Green, where the Pistols and The Clash were supported by The Buzzcocks, and some old movies by 'film witch' Kenneth Anger were shown before the bands came on. It was the 'Buzzers' first London appearance.

It was quite a show, with the half-naked Siouxsie Sioux – then just Suzie Ballion – dancing on-stage with Debbie 'Juvenile' Wilson and Tracey O'Keefe as the bands played their hearts out at dawn (McLaren waking the crowd for the Pistols with a variety of smoke bombs and thunder flashes). Others who were present from the so-called Bromley Contingent – the first die-hard Pistol fans – included Suzie's boyfriend, Steve Havoc aka Steve Severin, and their mutual gay friend Berlin.

The slow trickle of music press stories had suddenly turned into a minor torrent. *NME* bowed to the inevitable and reopened their Pistols' review file, with Charles Shaar Murray giving the event a fairly positive review. He did, however, damn The Clash – partly because he felt that, with Levene, they had one guitar too many, and partly, perhaps, because Strummer and Co.'s fast

Pistols–Ramones style racket might have been a step too far for him then. When there is an emphasis on tempo, as there was then, there's a temptation for the next wave to up the ante a little. The Clash did this musically, the occasional dazzle of Levene's guitar-work hiding the fact that their layers of sound didn't always line up.

NME's leading writer also noted that the horror of many of punk's critics was more than a little misplaced; for months, years in some cases, many of them had been crying out for something new and drastic. And now they had it they felt it was too rough and nasty and threatening. Well, tough, Charlie Murray seemed to be saying, this is the future and you'd better get used to it, whether you like it or not. Suddenly a bank of expensive keyboards and a privileged background were liabilities, especially for those who were about to take 'their' music back. As Patti Smith had shouted on her feedback-drenched version of 'My Generation', released just a few weeks before: 'We created it, let's take it over. . . '

The second event McLaren had organised was the two-day 100 Club Punk 'Special' in late September – the word 'festival' was too hippy for McLaren's new Glitterbest management group and it was not printed on the original A3-sized posters. The two sessions were to feature the Pistols, The Clash, The Buzzcocks, The Damned, France's Stinky Toys, Chris Spedding and The Vibrators and Vic Godard's weeks' old Subway Sect. And – so very late in the day they only just made it onto the poster – 'Suzi' and The Banshees. The latter consisted of Siouxsie, Severin, hip young guitarist Billy Idol and Flowers of Romance bassist Sid Vicious – the latter playing not bass but drums. They were going to play a sarcastic, improv version of several well-known pop classics but, once Idol had abruptly pulled out – to be rapidly replaced by the talented Marco Pirroni – it was all narrowed down to a pounding mid-tempo version of 'The Lord's Prayer' (with occasional diversions into 'Twist And Shout' and Dylan's 'Knocking On Heaven's Door'). This dirge was to be played until the band were physically pulled off-stage. 'I just knew I had to play live on-stage before I was twenty-one,' Severin later told Jonh Ingham. 'This was the perfect chance to do it.'

But there were other adventures further afield first, including the Pistols' trip to the Chalet du Lac folly to play their first, and last, engagement in Paris. Thinking she'd have to go to extremes to match the chic denizens of the French capital, Severin's girl Siouxsie wore her Nazi armband'n'suspenders outfit and got punched and almost knifed for her audacity (it wasn't just because every Parisian they saw seemed to be wearing cheesecloth and flares – 3 September was the date of the first Chalet Du Lac gig – only 24 hours after the anniversary of the end of the Second World War, then a very emotional subject in a Paris which the Nazis had occupied for over four years).

Caroline Coon was also attacked by the locals but the band, with Rotten resplendent in the new McLaren–Westwood bondage suit, were treated as heroes that night, winning several encores from the crowd of tipsy fashionistas (Kenzo and Yves Saint Laurent were in the front row, while Philippe Stark was the Pistols' reluctant drum roadie).

The next day saw the Pistols' hit the Chalet du Lac's under-lit stage for the last time as, back in Britain, their *So It Goes* TV debut was broadcast in the London and Granada areas. No TV critics seemed to have seen it but Genesis drummer Phil Collins was swift to denounce the Pistols' television debut as displaying 'a complete lack of talent'.

Undeterred, the Pistols prepared for the 100 Club Punk 'Special' with a benefit gig at Chelmsford Prison, where a near riot erupted. Earlier Paul Cook had fallen off his drumstool, drunk after over-celebrating leaving his brewery job. A year before, he'd been about to leave the Pistols; now he was leaving legitimate 'straight' employment instead. 'I'd always wanted to avoid work – proper work,' he said. 'And we do know we're doing something that is worthwhile.' The Pistols *were* going to happen, even the most uncertain member of the band was now convinced of it.

On the opening night of the Special, there were troubles. The venue was packed with 400 sweating fans, so perhaps this wasn't surprising. There were several, in hindsight, *minor* scuffles before the Banshees played for a mere 20 minutes with Pirroni pulling some stylish strokes and Vicious keeping remarkably good time. The A&R men present, including Thorne and Parry, weren't impressed, but Nils Stevenson was. He offered to manage the band on the spot, despite Sid's parting on-stage shot, 'Thanks for nothing, Bernie, you mean old Jew . . . ' (Rhodes had refused to lend The Banshees the Rehearsals' brightly coloured PA – mainly because he didn't want Siouxsie's swastikas associated with it). Sid was, Nils soon found out, going back to the Flowers anyway. But Siouxsie and Severin were intrigued by Nils's proposal – the last thing they'd thought their on-stage farce would provoke was a management offer.

The Banshees' first live performance was watched, but not filmed, by New Zealand's *Grunt* TV show team (they were there to shoot the Pistols only, which was naïve perhaps, but they were still weeks ahead of any local TV crews). Their presence added to the glamour of it all, the feeling that something big was about to break. The Clash, minus Levene, sounded powerful and in time, but it was the Pistols who ultimately stole the show that first night. Rotten's opening announcement – 'See you at the end of the world!' – was followed by blisteringly fast'n'tight versions of 'Anarchy' and 'Submission'. The end result of that performance was three tumultuous encores, skilfully mixed by Goodman as a stunned Chris Parry sat beside him, soaking it all up. 'All the record labels were big media whores back then,' says McLaren, 'so I knew with the coverage we'd had they'd be sniffing around and they were.'

The second night of the Special was a disaster. Violence erupted during the set by The Damned, then going all out to try and out-aggro the Pistols. As they baited the audience, Sid Vicious threw a glass at the stage – it shattered on one of the club's stone pillars, its shards blinding a girl in one eye. Within minutes the police had arrived and they soon carted off a protesting Vicious, who was heavily beaten on the drive to West End Central police station.

There was an instant 100 Club ban slapped on punk acts in

general, and the Sex Pistols specifically. This was hardly fair considering the Pistols were playing in Wales that same night, but there was the faint but definite link to Vicious. The 100 Club was the fourth major music venue in the capital to officially ban the Pistols (the first three being the Marquee, Dingwalls and the Nashville Rooms).

But, overall, the effect of the Punk Special seemed to be a lot more positive than negative. *Sounds*, with a four-page spread, quoted new fans verbally abandoning their previous Prog rock heroes while TV Advert and his girlfriend Gaye were more determined than ever to push ahead with their band, even as Nils cajoled The Banshees towards their first 'proper' gig. Marion 'Poly Styrene' Elliot had seen the Pistols on Hastings Pier back in the spring, but the Punk Special made her return to her X-Ray Spex group with a burst of manic energy.

Less than three months before, there'd been only the Pistols and maybe, if you stretched the definition, The Stranglers (formerly The Guildford Stranglers). At the end of September there were nearly a dozen groups. A band had become a scene had become a genre. In record time.

The Pistols were the undoubted 'leaders' of it all, but were still without a recording contract, despite the interest that Goodman's exciting demos had stirred up. It was not a situation that could be allowed to last though; a week after the punk 'festival', the band had played the Outlook Club in Doncaster. Nick Mobbs, an EMI A&R higher up the corporate food chain than Mike Thorne, had heard about the gig with only a day's notice. He had abandoned his trip to Switzerland instantly and flown to Leeds to see if he could catch the band. He made it – after several cab journeys – and was hugely impressed with what he saw as the band's artistic power and raw honesty. Here were the new Stones, the new Who. Here, at last, was the real start of the seventies. Threatening, edgy semi-revolutionary . . .

As The Damned announced news of their debut single – the pounding post-New York Dolls 'New Rose', complete with its Shangri-Las type intro and fast, tumultuous drumming from Rat

Scabies (an effect aided by producer Nick Lowe's little trick of speeding the whole tape up) – The Stranglers entered complex negotiations with the major United Artists label (the British musical offshoot of the independent Hollywood film studio that Charlie Chaplin and Mary Pickford had started almost half a century before).

Although The Stranglers were, as far as most punk insiders were concerned, merely a pushy pub band jumping on the rolling bandwagon, they had live presence, some strong songs and, initially at least, some surprisingly international roots.

'A rhythm and blues band came over from Sweden,' explained French-born bassist Jean-Jacques Burnel decades later, 'which comprised Hugh Cornwell plus an American draft dodger and two Swedes. In London they lost one of the Swedes and got a drummer called Jet – he had lots of businesses, an ice cream shop, an off-licence.'

But Jet Black's marriage fell apart and his businesses and band followed suit – and then he met Burnel. 'One night, I used to train a lot at karate in Kingston, and I was just driving down the A3 and gave a lift to this long-haired bloke. Everyone had long hair in those days except me – people used to think I was a copper 'cos I had a short crop. This hitch-hiker was the American singer with this band. He turned up a few weeks later at my bedsit and taught me the guitar, 'cos originally I was a guitarist. He said, "My band's left me, I'm just living here, me and my drummer, Jet." And as the evening progressed it became, "Would you like to join a band?" I turned up for the first rehearsal on 30 April 1974.'

But time was running out in what was then a very young man's game – Burnel was already twenty-five years old, singer Hugh Cornwell was older still at twenty-seven – and the need for dedication was stressed to Burnel. 'They said, "You've got to burn your boats and commit to us," so I gave myself till Christmas '74, 'cos I had been planning to go to Japan to be a karate man.'

Christmas actually saw The Guildford Stranglers (the 'Guildford' was dropped within a few months) getting established on the pub rock circuit but not making a fortune. Eighteen months on and fans were still few and far between, though those that hung on in there were fanatical about the band.

'Dagenham Dave was our first fan,' says Burnel, 'a black guy from Manchester who was very bright, self-educated and he could debate Hugh and I – who'd been to uni – into the ground. He introduced me to books by de Sade and Sartre and he was fun, buying us drinks and adopting us as his personal cause, to the extent of offering us his girlfriend. And then the Finchley boys turned up and tried to frighten us off stage one night and we weren't going to have that – they'd done it to The Damned the week before – but we started taking the piss . . . and they thought, "These guys are cool," and they latched on to us.'

But the Finchley mob's presence was too provocative for at least one older fan. 'We were at the 100 Club one night and Dagenham Dave – we called him that 'cos he lived there – he was just so pissed off, he couldn't get to the front and they were pushing him about. He lost it and tried to take on about fifteen of them, and they beat the crap out of him and we didn't see him for a while.'

From the start, punk bands and those thought to be punk seemed to attract the brightest and the most intense – and the most disturbed – of the post-sixties generation. This factor, and the 'active extremism' that the current mood then encouraged, could combine to deadly effect. As Dagenham Dave's fate illustrates: 'He died a few weeks later,' recounts Burnel. 'I don't know what went on in his head but he just overdosed and jumped off London Bridge, which was really tragic . . . He did that when he knew we had the United Artists recording contract.'

The Stranglers' first 45 was due for release in New Year 1977, but the brutal post-pub rockers were not going to beat the Pistols to the punch – on 8 October 1976, having already talked Polydor's Chris Parry up to offering a generous £25,000, McLaren wound up Mobbs and his boss Leslie Hill during an all-day session of argument and counter-argument. It ended, incredibly, with EMI offering £40,000 – 'it was the sum my lawyer Stephen Fisher had told me to aim for,' McLaren says now. ' "Ask for forty grand for x number of albums. But you might have to settle for twenty-five or thirty grand . . . " But I thought, "I'm not gonna take any deductions, I want the *whole* forty . . . " and I just kept telling EMI, this is the way forward, this band . . . or are you just gonna give up and keep putting out Dean Martin singles? And, in the end, I got it, I got the whole forty. And at midnight the contract was signed – their fastest deal ever – and a picture was taken and then they cracked open a single bottle of champagne.'

EMI was a big-time label – the very biggest – and they had the clout to swiftly get a band into the fast lane. Which was all very well except that the Pistols, for all their speed, had little in the way of gears, let alone brakes . . .

REHEARSAL
REHEARSALS –
White Riot

Keith Levene had left The Clash just weeks before the Punk Festival. His growing addiction to speed made his departure inevitable, but his fuzzy guitar was also overly arty for a band aiming at creating terrace-style stomp-a-longs. The band's parting gift to him was a guitar – a quality Gibson copy (legend has it that Levene hocked it within a day . . .)

Levene returned to The Flowers of Romance, convinced that he, Sid and Viv Albertine still had a future together and also convinced – after a brief conversation with Rotten during the Screen on the Green all-nighter – that he'd one day be in a band with the Pistols' front man.

Levene's departure helped rather than hindered The Clash, at least in the short term. Throughout the late summer Mick Jones and Strummer – with some help from Bernie Rhodes – had turned ideas into serious solid songs. 'Career Opportunities' was a sarcastic, high-energy attack on the growing *lack* of opportunities; 'Janie Jones' exposed corruption and boredom at work; while the fine, floor-strutting 'Deny' spoke of betrayal – by a drug-addicted friend – at the 100 Club.

'London's Burning' showed the growing urban alienation The Clash were trying to punch through. And, as the leftish but strait-laced *New Society* magazine noticed, Strummer and Jones did it in a way that was almost Dylanesque, with their references to howling winds and running through the empty stone – 'Cos I'm All Alone!'.

As lyrics they read well, but when actually performed by Strummer's tough but strained voice to a pounding feedback-ravaged backing, such words take off with a desperate energy that goes beyond poetry, an energy that defines rock music.

Although they sometimes played the working-class-hero card early on, the fact is The Clash, like most of the rest of 1976's prime movers, were actually a blend of working class, 'the upper working class' and, in Strummer, the bona fide middle class (although Strummer's Scottish mother had herself known deprivation during her younger years). But Strummer's diplomat father, and all that that stood for, was still something that he, fuelled by Rhodes's paranoia, kept as secret as possible for as long as possible.

The big difference between punk and the post-war cults that preceded it was that some of the working-class people involved now had positions of creative influence and, in a few cases, power. Rhodes himself, for instance, had hustled his way into a position of strength that his machinist mother, a Russian immigrant, could only have dreamed of. Others – like McLaren – were 'class mutations', who had been born in one class, had perhaps flirted with another and now belonged to no easy classification. Either way, with the working class and 'lower middle class' continuing to filter through into office jobs, and art colleges, Britain's once exclusive castes were mingling as never before.

'These days, though, you've got expensive gated mews on one side and council estates with crack houses on the other – and lots of fences in between,' asserts Jah Wobble, 'but the different strata rubbed up against each other a little more in those days, in the seventies, especially when it came to a scene like punk, which was all about the dropouts and the outsiders, those that didn't fit it . . . '

With punk, the classless promise of the sixties was, at least in part, finally coming true. But it was coming true in a society that was on the brink of drastic change, and within a genre that was about to be crudely pigeon-holed, both by its critics and even by some of its insiders.

After producing the Pistols' demos that had first helped intrigue record companies, it was taken as read that Dave Goodman would produce the Pistols debut single. The fact that he wasn't an EMI hack, or even a well-travelled producer with a huge track record, added to his appeal for McLaren. The band and its management did their own composing, recording, production, photos and artwork. All EMI had to do was pay some expenses and keep out of the way. Goodman, though, was given a shockingly mean EMI advance of £200 against a production royalty of two per cent.

Still, neither Goodman nor the band had ever been only in it for the money, and thus began a tumultuous eight days unlike any other in the history of EMI recordings.

The sessions had begun at Lansdowne studio in Holland Park, a fair-sized 24-track with a solid reputation. According to Goodman, before recording 'Anarchy In The UK' had even begun, McLaren had dished out a line of cocaine to each of the band.[25] Then, with the group neatly separated by screens – separation being sonically necessary for clarity, eliminating mistakes and for overdubbing – the fun began. As the band slammed into 'Anarchy', McLaren sprayed the same word in shaving foam over the control-room window. The house engineer cringed and complained to both McLaren and Goodman. After a day, Goodman and the band had given up at Lansdowne and moved on – to Wessex studio in Highbury (they'd already tried Ray Davies's Konk but the king Kink had refused to meet them, pretending to be out).

By now, the group were already wondering what was 'wrong' with what they'd cut at Lansdowne – there seemed no obvious mistakes, why couldn't overdubs and mixdown begin immediately? Goodman

25 This was uncharacteristic. McLaren generally steered clear of drugs and drink.

put them straight – it wasn't enough to just get a listenable pass down. There had to be a really great 'performance' captured on tape before it was worth tinkering with. So the Pistols played it again, this time without vocals. And again. And again and again. Most of these were kept and EMI were astonished as Goodman continued to call for new reels of two-inch – as takes were attempted between covers from the Pistols' set, with vocals: 'Whatcha Gonna Do About It?', 'Substitute', 'Stepping Stone', 'Doncha Give Me No Lip' and a seven-minute version of 'No Fun' that ended amid much chaos and scream-ing from Lydon. 'A joke version,' Matlock later called it, though McLaren and most of the others seemed to like it.

The Pistols had demanded – and got – a thousand beers from EMI, though the drink in question was low-strength Breaker, so it took a few pints to get drunk enough to deal with the spies the label kept sending down every other day (one of whom was soaked in water by the band).

The EMI emissaries were there to ensure that 'Pretty Vacant' was recorded since, despite the band's artistic freedom clause, the label still hoped to persuade Glitterbest to issue that as a single before the more inflammatory 'Anarchy'. But 'Vacant' was deliberately *not* recorded, although much else of the set was. Goodman, though, was starting to irritate certain members of the band, Matlock specifically. 'Dave was OK in the studio but he just kept making us do "Anarchy" over and over again. And there was always this pressure for us to speed up. I think it was maybe 'cos Malcolm was over his shoulder most of the time, whispering in his ear, and Dave didn't feel he could tell him to piss off.'

But the producer still wasn't happy with the performance of 'Anarchy' and he wasn't afraid to say so; as an only son who was a former 'star session musician' himself, and who'd been with the Pistols from the very early days, Goodman felt able to stand up to the group. Things were getting volatile though: waste bins were set on fire, amps and guitars were demolished. Lydon made things worse by coming back to jeer as the band ran through yet another take of the 'Anarchy' backing track – 'The papers are bleedin' right, you lot can't f—ing play!'

The breakthrough finally came on the seventh day. Lydon was dragged in and told, at Goodman's suggestion, to sing The Creation's 'Through My Eyes' as the rest of the group played 'Roadrunner'. It didn't work as a song – Lydon only attempted it for a few seconds – but it broke the tension. After dashing through 'Johnny B. Goode' and 'Roadrunner (Again)' Goodman suggested having yet another go at 'Anarchy'. Lydon's voice was hoarse, his throat sore by now, but he was game and the band blasted straight into it. This version, which starts with the Lydon ad-lib, 'Words of Wisdom! Bible Quotation Number One!', has never been mixed down properly, even to this day, yet it remains the definitive record-ed performance of 'Anarchy In The UK'; fast without being manic, buzzy guitars, strident drums and bass jaggedly fluid as they pump along. Clear in the mix, yet deep within it too, is Lydon's breaking vocal, belting out the song at the top of his voice as if he means it. Which, of course, in many ways, he did. Goodman's EMI version of 'Anarchy In The UK' was the sound of the future, the way many recordings were to hit the ear over the next 30 years.

If Goodman's critics were to later claim that his early studio per-fectionism – the dozens of retakes of 'Anarchy' – was partly to cover up his relative lack of experience in a large 24-track studio, they are undone by the sheer power of this take (and eight days now actually seems a pretty short time to conjure up such a ver-sion). Goodman did a quick rough mix and, despite a minor row between Matlock and Lydon, everyone – from the group to Wobble to Lydon to McLaren – seemed impressed.

But, as Goodman went off to get some rest (he'd been awake and working 18 hours a day for over a week), the doubts began to set in. The EMI A&Rs thought Goodman's 'Anarchy In The UK' was far too wild. This was, however, a new genre and the label was, ulti-mately, prepared to release that version if McLaren insisted.

Yet, after several listens, and despite the affection between Goodman and McLaren, the latter now felt, 'It just doesn't sound like a hit to me, sounds too raw.' Today McLaren is mildly mysti-fied at his own caution, 'I dunno why I thought that. It seems crazy now as there was nothing wrong with Dave's version. I think it was just because I'd been in the [SEX] shop for years, listening to juke-box records that were fifteen or twenty years old . . . '

Whatever the reason, the old firm – and Glitterbest's previous let's-keep-it-in-house attitude – was fractured as a new and more experienced producer was called in; SEX customer Chris Thomas – who'd helped The Beatles complete their 1968 *White Album* before producing various Roxy Music bestsellers (he'd also engineered Pink Floyd's multi-million-selling *Dark Side Of The Moon*). Goodman was understandably hurt but McLaren's assurance that he'd still be the live sound mixer for the forthcoming tour kept an uneasy peace.

Thomas promptly took the band back to Wessex and gave a larger role to top engineer Bill Price.

With The Damned, and most post-Ramones bands speeding things up – whether with excitement, the drug 'speed' or the tape deck's vari-speed dial – Thomas and McLaren decided to take things in the opposite direction by slowing 'Anarchy' down a little. 'We wanted to make the words clear, they were important words to hear,' one Glitterbest insider insisted.

Five takes of 'Anarchy' were recorded with Thomas, none quite right. In the end, with the clock ticking for the release date, Thomas spliced together two different takes and called it a day. McLaren was quietly elated with it all but EMI shocked him – 'It's not that much different to the original, is it?'

Thomas's slightly slower, clearer take of 'Anarchy' was issued by EMI on 26 November – as talk of an Anarchy Tour with Talking Heads and The Ramones was seemingly firmed up. The first 5,000 'Anarchy' singles were in plain black sleeves but, to add insult to Goodman's injury, his name wasn't on either those thousand or the next 5,000 (even though it was Goodman's exciting version of 'I Wanna Be Me' on the B-side as recorded in Denmark Street).

This was potentially damaging for Goodman as the first couple of thousand records always contain the promotional copies that go out to journalists, publishers, artists and fellow music-biz professionals. His lack of a credit would almost certainly cost him cash. Goodman was offered no compensation whatsoever for this mistake by a dismissive EMI that had always considered him a 'mere live mixer'. He, in turn, consulted a west London solicitor and was even issued with a High Court injunction against the release of 'Anarchy'. The question was, would he serve it?

After talks with McLaren and some reassurance from a meeting at EMI – the company would, after all, offer some token compensation then place adverts announcing their error and stating publicly who had actually produced 'I Wanna Be Me' – Goodman decided to take no further action and the injunction that could have completely wrecked the release of 'Anarchy', and the career of the Sex Pistols, was halted.

But EMI had, of course, duped Goodman and his suburban lawyer, for none of the label's earnest pledges had been in writing – and when they were challenged later they completely denied ever making any such promises. So there were no adverts, no apologies and no compensation payments for Goodman. Those who had secretly heard his version of 'Anarchy' were, in the main, disappointed with Thomas's reworking – the latter, to his credit, had told McLaren and EMI right from the start that there 'is nothing wrong with Goodman's production'.

The ever dry John Peel, whose late-night Radio One show was Britain's only real platform for genuinely new music, was mildly scathing about EMI disc 2566, the new version of 'Anarchy'. What had happened to the wildness of the previous take?

EMI were going to celebrate the Pistols' first single with a gig at the exclusively expensive Talk of the Town club off Leicester Square (it is now the equally expensive Hippodrome). But the venue's managers had second thoughts when they caught a glimpse of Goodman and the band, who'd gone down for a quick look around a fortnight before the projected event, and the gig was promptly cancelled. This was probably for the best as regards the Pistols' reputation, since Rotten had purchased a long-haired wig and a full-length woman's dress, which he insisted he was going to wear 'for a laugh' at The Talk of the Town (the wig very briefly made its debut at Notre Dame Hall – it gave Sid the excuse to heckle, 'Get off, you dirty hippy!' – but Rotten's dress was never to be worn in public).

The Monday after the release date, and just 24 hours after two million people had seen Janet Street-Porter's lunchtime LWT special on the Pistols, The Clash and The Banshees, 'Anarchy' sold just over 1,700 copies. Not bad for a group that hadn't fully played the length and the breadth of the country; but these weren't world-shattering sales either – not for a group with several TV appearances and a clutch of large single reviews just behind them.[26]

Even slightly tamed on record, The Pistols were still too strong a beer for many – even those who became firm fans after two or three viewings (everyone from Ray Stevenson to Tom Robinson and, eventually, *Melody Maker*'s Allan Jones). If the Pistols were to make the crucial Top 30, where the real sales and influence lay, then they would need something completely out of the ordinary to grab the nation's attention. They knew that and they wanted it. And, for their sins, they got it.

After John Peel's half-hearted put-down of the Chris Thomas version of 'Anarchy', McLaren made noises in Manchester Square about wanting to record the track for a third time. From scratch.

An outraged EMI told him that, first, the more than generous £10,000 recording budget had virtually all gone and, second, any reworking would muck up the pre-Christmas schedules. McLaren gave way and concentrated on the forthcoming Anarchy Tour – The Ramones and Talking Heads had already dropped out in an argument over billing and expenses, while Nils's band Siouxsie and The Banshees were still rehearsing new songs and were in no fit state to gig.

Reluctantly The Damned – second on the bill as they already had a single out – and Bernard Rhodes's Clash were drafted in (the latter were bottom of the bill although they had the poster tribute 'special guests').

---

26 Caroline Coon had previously spoken of 'Anarchy', with its countdown of guerrilla and para-military groups – Angola's MPLA, Northern Ireland's IRA and UDA – as being 'frightening in its teenage vision of world disintegration' and she swiftly made the EMI 45 Single Of The Week in *MM*. Alan Lewis repeated the Single Of The Week trick in *Sounds*. *NME*, however, continued their minor feud with the band by merely making it 'Talking Point Of The Week' in a write-up that labelled the Pistols a 'third-rate Who'.

But McLaren still felt this wasn't enough – the venues for the 19-date tour were, in many cases, around 800–1,200 capacity, large for the UK. Filling them would also require an American element. Several dozen desperate phone calls to New York confirmed that Johnny Thunders's new group The Heartbreakers (also featuring Jerry Nolan) were sounding good but making little progress. If the New Yorkers were prepared to get haircuts and fly straight over, then McLaren was prepared to pay expenses and put them second on the bill. Thunders and Co., going nowhere fast in the Big Apple, needed no second invitation and were flying out within 48 hours. They bought with them some of the best songs Thunders had ever written. They also bought with them heroin addiction – and, two flights later, a groupie by the name of Nancy Spungen . . .

As the four groups began last-minute tour rehearsals in a fleapit cinema in Harlesden – all concerned trying on different clothes and attitudes as their first nationwide look at Britain drew closer – EMI press agent Eric Hall phoned McLaren. EMI band Queen had dropped out of an appearance on Thames TV's teatime *Today* show – could the Pistols' step in and replace them, chatting live with the host about punk? There was a guaranteed play for the 'Anarchy' pop video. A promo video was still something of a novelty in those days, this one being shot by Mike Mansfield as a blond Rotten sings from behind the drum kit. McLaren spoke to the group; they were tired but finally agreed if EMI would send a limousine. Some snappy dressers were rounded up – Siouxsie, Steve Severin and the black girl Simone were joined by Glitterbest part-timer Simon Barker, the man who had started the Pistols' connection with both art schools and the bright young things of the King's Road.

Curiously, *Today* host Bill Grundy, a middle-aged curmudgeon, had for years been the main newsman up at Tony Wilson's Granada before coming to his 'second home', London (he later penned a book for Quest Publications, *Grundy's London*). Curiouser still, Grundy had been one of those who'd seen the 'shocking' Yippie invasion of David Frost's LWT show in November 1970 – Jerry Rubin and a dozen other long-hairs had stormed Frost's stage, shouting revolutionary slogans and offensive words (i.e. 'shit').

Even stranger, Grundy himself had appeared in the 1974 feature film version of the popular sitcom *Man About The House* – Grundy had played himself, a Thames TV host who was faced with a studio upset live on air . . .

Grundy hadn't been especially looking forward to dealing with the fey young men of Queen, and sneering young punks the Sex Pistols seemed even more of a nightmare. His five o'clock drinks came in early – the Pistols were already knocking back beers in the limo and this continued in the hospitality Green Room, where it soon became obvious that Grundy was as drunk as they were. 'Grundy had a fairly outrageous reputation at Granada,' Tony Wilson says now. 'At least once or twice a week he'd be drunk in the canteen, saying stuff like, "Who the f— cooked this shit? Bring him out and I'll punch the bastard!" He really didn't give a shit.'

When the Pistols came on at 6.15, their first time live on TV (all their other appearances had been taped and their expletives bleeped out), everyone concerned was more than primed. And the band weren't even aware the show was live.

As Grundy began his intro spiel, the group irritated him by reading off the same autocue . . .

The Sex Pistols sat in front, left to right: Lydon, Jones, Matlock and Cook, with Barker, Severin, Siouxsie and Simone standing behind. Grundy sat to Cook's left, a sheaf of papers on his grey-suited lap.

BILL GRUNDY: Safety pins? Chains round the neck? And that's just it fellas, yeah yeah [momentarily bewildered] Eh . . . ? I mean, it is just the fellas – yeah.'

GLEN (reading Grundy's autocue): 'They are punk rockers, the new craze, they tell me.'

BG: They are punk rockers, the new craze, they tell me. Their heroes, not the nice clean Rolling Stones – you see, they are as drunk as I am. They are clean by comparison. They are a group called the Sex Pistols – and I'm surrounded now by all of them! So just let us see the Sex Pistols in action! Come on, chucks . . .

[The first 30 seconds of the Mike Mansfield pop video of 'Anarchy in the UK' is shown.]

BG: I'm told that that group have received £40,000 from a record company. Doesn't that seem slightly opposed to their anti-materialistic way of life?

GLEN: No, the more the merrier.

BG: Really?

GLEN: Oh yeah.

BG: Well, tell me more then –

STEVE: We've f—ing spent it, ain't we?

BG: I don't know, have you?

GLEN: Yep, it's all gone, down the boozer –

BG: Really? Good Lord –

GLEN: Golly gosh –

BG: Now I want to know one thing . . .

GLEN: What?

BG: Are you serious or are you just making things up?

GLEN: No, it's –

BG: Really?

GLEN: Yeah –

BG: But I mean about what you're doing?

GLEN: Oh yeah.

BG: You are serious?

GLEN: Mmm.

BG: Beethoven, Mozart, Bach and Brahms have all died –

JOHN (sneering): Oh God, they're heroes of ours, ain't they?

BG: Really? What? What are you saying, sir?

JOHN (sarcastic): They're such wonderful people –

BG: Are they?

JOHN (fake enthusiasm): Oh yes! They really turn us on.

BG: Well suppose they turn other people on –

JOHN (quietly): That's just their tough shit.

BG: It's what?

JOHN: Nothing, a rude word – next question.

BG: No, no. What was the rude word?

JOHN: Shit.

BG: Was it really? Good God, you frighten me to death.

JOHN: Oh all right, Siegfried —

BG: What about you girls behind?

GLEN: He's like yer dad, inni? This geezer —

BG: Are you worried or just enjoying yourself?

GLEN: Or yer grandad —

SIOUXSIE: Enjoying myself.

BG: Are you?

SIOUXSIE: Yeah.

BG: That's what I thought you were doing.

SIOUXSIE: I always wanted to meet you.

BG: Did you really?

SIOUXSIE: Yeah.

BG: We'll meet afterwards then, shall we?

STEVE: You dirty sod! You dirty old man!

BG: Well, keep going, chief, keep going. Go on, you've got another five seconds, say something outrageous —

STEVE: You dirty bastard!

BG: Go on, again.

STEVE: You dirty f—er!

BG: What a clever boy!

STEVE: What a f—ing rotter!

BG: Well, that's it for tonight. The other rocker Eammon —

GLEN: Eammon!

BG: I'm saying nothing else about him, will be back tomorrow. I'll be seeing you soon — (to Pistols) I hope I'm not be seeing you again. From me though, goodnight!

As the *Today* end-titles rolled over the scene, Grundy turned to his producer and wearily mouthed the words, 'Oh shit!' Paul Cook faked a yawn as Steve Jones jumped up and started doing a ridiculous bump'n'grind dance, while Barker made obscene gestures at the astonished cameramen . . .

The out-of-date words used by Jones seem strange now – though most are easily explained. The Victorian definition of a 'cad' – a 'rotter' – was almost certainly used by Jones because soft drinks firm Schweppes had recently used it in a series of TV and poster ads ('You can always tell a rotter by his total lack of Schweppes . . .').

With only one, single expletive exception, no one had sworn on live TV in Britain up to that point – the fact that there was a veritable torrent of abuse, and that it was at 6.15 p.m. when both young children and pensioners were watching, led to the Thames TV switchboard being jammed with angry complaints. Soon the overload was spilling onto the studio phones and Siouxsie and Steve answered some of the calls – 'This is Thames TV, piss off!' – until they were physically restrained from doing so.

'We've got to get you out of here,' said the EMI driver to the Pistols and the band's vehicle screeched away just as the first police vans pulled up at Thames studios. The appearance of the police in Euston Road was perhaps the first indication of how very seriously the incident was going to be taken. It was an ominous sign of all that was to unfold over the coming months . . .

The night the Pistols-Grundy 'swear-in' was broadcast, the furore it caused was mentioned on late-night current affairs programmes – with Thames offering what could be seen as a *mea culpa* after ITN's *News At Ten*. It ended, 'We very much regret the offensive interview and apologise most sincerely to all our viewers . . . '

It was to be too little, too late, but Thames TV were not themselves going to be the ones to reap the whirlwind.

After escaping from Euston Road, the Pistols returned to the rehearsals still going on at Harlesden's Coliseum cinema. By the time they'd arrived, news of the media outrage had leaked out and, according to Goodman, the band were met with a huge ironic cheer from the assembled bands and roadies. 'They asked for it, Mal,' Jones was still pleading with McLaren, 'that bloke kept pushing his luck . . . ' And, Jones and others later claimed, the group hadn't actually known the show was live. But McLaren was inconsolable; aside from the faint but real chance of the band facing criminal charges over the public use of obscene language, there was also the possibility of gigs being postponed or even cancelled. The band would lose momentum if the Anarchy Tour was reduced or aborted. The nightmare of the New York Dolls' last days flickered through McLaren's mind – a band evaporating as a difficult tour fell apart. Of course, the Pistols had a record contract with a major label . . . but then, so had the Dolls just months before they split . . .

It all depended now on how the morning papers would play it. Glitterbest, like 99 per cent of UK companies in 1976, had no telephone answering machine, so it was impossible to tell what was happening when McLaren swung by the office on the way back from Harlesden late that night. He hoped that the *Daily Mirror* might be sympathetic – they'd run a two-page punk piece the same day as the Grundy interview and, although the tone had been suitably shocked – 'It's The Punk Rock Horror Show!' – there had been a little humour as well as a hint of appreciation for the excitement of this new underground cult and its music.

But at dawn the next day a shaken McLaren knew the worst as the first editions rumbled out of Fleet Street, then still the centre for virtually every UK national newspaper. And every paper had indeed mentioned the group's 'yobbish behaviour' and Grundy's foolishness (especially his naivety in taking on a group whose recent TV appearance with Janet Street-Porter had had various swear words bleeped out).

But few of the reports were prominent and the story, and cultural history, might yet have been different if it hadn't been for the *Daily Mirror*. The staunchly Labour *Mirror* had devoted almost its entire front page to Grundy and the Pistols – 'TV FURY OVER ROCK CULT FILTH!' was the first edition headline, rapidly followed by the bigger-selling print run that went nationwide. 'THE FILTH & THE FURY!' were the, now infamous, words in 72 point. The 'fury' was the viewers' angry response, including that of James Holmes, a 42-year-old lorry driver (and father of an eight-year-old child), who'd been so disgusted by the *Today* show that he'd kicked in his 'nearly new' £380 colour TV.

Interestingly, Holmes, like most people who were initially quoted, did not blame the group for the trouble but instead blasted the *Today* host: 'I am not a violent person but I'd have liked to have gotten hold of Grundy.' The papers, however, were blaming the group as much as Grundy in reports filled with errors (the Pistols were 'a five-man group' who'd called Grundy 'a silly bastard' before 'millions of viewers').

And their readers were responding: in Stoke Newington, Matlock had already been blanked by some, previously friendly, locals, while future Chinawhite DJ Jay Strongman found himself in a similar situation at the London College of Fashion. 'It had been OK at the LCF up until that point – Boy George, Maggie Lydon and Phillip Salon used to hang out there and the models and designers tolerated my weird clothes and my interest in this weird new rock group. Some of them were even curious about it and, as head of the Student Union, I'd managed to get the Pistols and The Banshees pencilled in for a couple of New Year gigs. It was all going OK. But the day after the Grundy thing – forget it. The LCF gigs were cancelled and not one of the students would talk to me – some of the girls wouldn't even *look* at me, they were just so outraged by it all.'

As McLaren and Sophie began to field a mounting number of calls, a sheepish band trooped into the tiny room. Within the hour there were a dozen journalists waiting outside, effectively door-stepping the Glitterbest office (the outside door to the Dryden Chambers courtyard was left unlocked during office hours). Inside, the gloom had lifted a little, partly because of the band's photographer. 'The next day in the Glitterbest office it was total shell-shock at first,' Ray Stevenson says now. 'Malcolm was depressed, there was talk of cancelled gigs, EMI trouble, all of that. Everyone was very quiet and contrite, even Steve. And then I remembered years before with Jimi Hendrix – how he refused to play along with the host when he was first on TV. And all the TV guys were saying afterwards, "You're finished, mate, you've been unprofessional, you'll never be on telly again." But Chas Chandler rushed into Jimi's changing room afterwards and said, "You've made it! The parents hate you!" ' When I told him this, Malcolm began to cheer up a bit.'

By midday there were a dozen more reporters waiting and a decision was taken to lead them out for an impromptu press conference.

The boys' hangover jokes were duly noted and used against them, although McLaren's central point – '"My Boys Were Goaded" Claims Punk Boss!' – *did* eventually get printed. But the rest of the *Mirror*'s two-page spread on 3 December was dedicated to slamming the band and 'these punks'. By then the *Sun* had weighed in with a front page of its own – 'WERE THE PISTOLS LOADED? Punk Rock Group "Plied With Booze"', as had the *Daily Express*, 'PUNK? CALL IT FILTHY LUCRE!'

These three papers then sold a total of some eight million copies. They effectively *were* the popular press and the public response to their headlines mushroomed: at EMI's pressing plant in Hayes, the women packers who put the vinyl records in their sleeves refused to touch the 'Anarchy' single. The women were backed by their union, although a shop steward finally, reluctantly, did ask them to return to work after listening to the Pistols' debut 45. ('It is not really offensive,' he said later, generously adding, 'it is just rubbish.') This incident in itself became another *Mirror* front page – 'OFF! OFF! Union Bid to Ban Pistols!' – one that also featured Siouxsie Sioux ('I drank too much firewater,' she said of the night at Thames TV). The press feeding frenzy was now beginning to feed off itself and the newspaper talk of gig cancellations began to become self-fulfilling.

Side B

PUNK ROCK: GOING OVERGROUND

THE ROXY CLUB –
Bored Teenagers

Tomorrow the *News Of The World* blasts the weird world of punk rock and the Sex Pistols rock group who disgusted and enraged TV viewers with their foul behaviour! Punk Rock? We say Punk Junk! You'll be Shocked By This Report on Pop's New Heroes! Only In the *News Of The World* – Tomorrow! (*News Of The World* TV advert, Saturday 4 December 1976)

The *News Of The World*'s post-Grundy issue damned all-out pub rockers The Rockets with faint praise, but reserved its main ire for the Pistols, Judy Nylon and Patti Palladin's Snatch band, and the 'sex-obsessed' Stranglers with their 'gross' songs.

The Anarchy Tour was already under pressure and EMI were complaining bitterly, with an under-pressure Nick Mobbs now advocating caution and abandoning his straight jeans and safety pins for flares and tour jackets.

Patti Smith had said that 'art + electricity = rock'n'roll' but she hadn't said what happened when 'mass-media' entered the equation . . .

To the right-wing papers, the 'punk generation' – all 400 of them – were what happened under a weak, decadent socialistic government. To the left in the media the punks were the product of a lack of investment in the country's future, a legacy perhaps of the Tories' three-day week (and – in the *Mirror*'s case – the punks were also, perhaps, a useful distraction from the woes of a Labour government that the Treasury had just forced to go 'cap in hand' to the International Monetary Fund).

Either way, Bill Grundy was suspended for a fortnight, his director was fired and EMI said they'd try to 'control the Pistols' behaviour' as the pressure grew for a formal apology from McLaren and his group.

To some, the Bill Grundy incident finished the band and damaged the whole punk scene.

'It [punk] should have grown at a slower rate,' future Clash PR Kosmo Vinyl says now. 'The Grundy thing made it all happen way too fast, made it too public, too early. No one was quite ready.' It also made the bands appear more yobbish than they really were – the sexual ambiguity, the design nuances, the underground arts vibe, all these factors were undoubtedly lost or weakened.

There was, however, at least one early fan who thought differently. 'The swear-in was great in a way,' said ex-mod record dealer Don Hughes years later. 'It was like The Beatles conquering America or The Who smashing their PA on *Top of the Pops* or the Stones saying, "We piss anywhere, man." It got pop back on the front page, made it big and threatening again, a real talking point. It made it like the sixties again.'

Although McLaren, perhaps rightly, blamed Grundy – 'My boys were goaded!' – he now insisted that there were no regrets. The refusal to formally apologise sent the nationals into a further frenzy. As the Anarchy Tour bus took off, there were literally dozens of journalists and photographers in pursuit.

The tour bus would have been combustible enough as it was; any moving vehicle containing the Sex Pistols, The Clash, The Damned, Dave Goodman, Johnny Thunders's Heartbreakers *and* Malcolm McLaren and Bernie Rhodes was always going to attract attention. Factor in the post-Grundy British press – and quite a few from mainland Europe – and it became a circus on wheels. McLaren had wanted a 'rumbling anarchic' scene according to the *Sounds* interview in April '76, but he hadn't expected it to be a mobile feast pursued by the national media – and with each forthcoming gig being cancelled.

Norwich University – the first gig on the tour, scheduled for 3 December – was called off by the college authorities despite an angry last-minute sit-in by students trying to save the gig. Then at Derby's Kings Hall, the next day, bands were told they could only play if the Pistols agreed to perform in the afternoon for the council – so the local politicians could decide if the band was obscene in itself. (There was already wildly exaggerated talk in the nationals of how the band regularly swore, spat 'and vomited' on stage – the fact that most groups of all genres occasionally swore on stage was ignored.)

'That whole thing made me so cynical about the press,' Ray Stevenson said in 2005, 'because if they can't get a story, especially the tabloid guys, then they'll just make one up, make it up completely, total fiction . . . '

The Pistols seemingly agreed to the Derby council's plan and the PA was set up, but then, at Goodman's suggestion, the band refused to appear – driving off at the last minute, with the coach changing directions several times to try and lose the Fleet Street posse. The next gig was Newcastle's City Hall, but that had already been cancelled, so the coach headed for Leeds Polytechnic where a performance finally took place, despite a Yorkshire TV crew putting the Poly's chancellor on the spot, demanding to know why this 'offensive group was playing in Leeds tonight when they've been banned virtually everywhere else'?

At Leeds, the omens were not good. The openers were the bottom of the bill Clash, who won over some of those who'd come to jeer, but who were not the centre of attention (half the crowd were still in the bar). The Damned played a lacklustre set, perhaps because of the friction caused by their offer to play Derby without the Pistols, an act of 'betrayal' that had already been the subject of discussion and meant their days on the tour were to end shortly after Leeds.[27]

---

27 After the violence at the second night of the 100 Club festival, the apolitical Damned had anyway shifted their persona – less the pushy punks trying to out-provoke the Pistols, more the fun-loving jokers. Captain Sensible even borrowed one of Goodman's fancy dress outfits – a nurse's uniform – and wore it regularly on stage.

The Heartbreakers went on to a scattering of applause and Thunders's loaded, ominous, question to the audience, 'Don't you have any junkies in Leeds?' A blatant appeal for smack that occurred because none of the Americans had found a connection during the afternoon. Despite some half-hearted assurances to friends and managers about their new, cleaner act, Thunders and co. were already desperate to score.

When the Pistols finally went on, they were met with a hail of spit and jeers. There was a little laughter when Rotten said, 'You're not wrecking the place enough, the *News Of The World* will be disappointed!', but the mood was overwhelmingly hostile and halfway through, the spit became a wave of glasses, bottles and rotten fruit. The mass of students and locals present had come to sneer at the freaks, the new 'public enemy number one' and nothing would persuade them to seriously listen, let alone keep an open mind. On tapes of the Leeds concert there can be heard, between songs, the crunch of broken glass as the band try and walk over an uneven sea of shattered pint mugs. Those few concertgoers who were into the band found themselves pushed and jostled.

The group, and the movement, which had split the music press were now busy dividing not just a generation but an entire country . . .

Only four venues remained open on the tour as one cancellation followed another (the Pistols were actually banned from physically entering the towns of Glasgow and Aylesbury, bans that would nowadays contradict the European Convention on Human Rights).

At Manchester, where two gigs were played, Tony Wilson found the situation incredible. His employers, Granada, refused to give him the promised TV crew to interview the Pistols, so he had to set out in a taxi, now merely to have a chat with the Pistols on his own. But, at the first two hotels he found the Anarchy Tour had already been expelled and at the third he had to get out and walk the last

800 yards as the road was, 'completely blocked by two ambulances, two fire engines and five police cars. It was like ebola, that was the Pistols' impact, it really was like ebola!'

The Manchester gigs were riotous in themselves. At the Electric Circus, Thunders had to knock football yobs back with his guitar and the Pistols had to be rescued afterwards by a limo sent to a side-door fire exit – the limo screeched away under a tide of bricks and bottles with the laggardly Paul Cook being forced to jump into the car's boot as it began to speed away.

After virtually closing the Welsh town of Caerphilly for one gig – all the bars and cafés closed down for over 24 hours – the Anarchy Tour bands managed to play but then found themselves facing a strange alliance: in the streets immediately outside the cinema venue, a gang of Hell's Angels had been joined by 200 protesting carol singers ('God can forgive anyone,' the local priest was quoted as saying, 'anyone except punk rockers, for they are the devil's children!').

The very last dates on the ill-fated tour took place just before Christmas 1976, twice in a row at Plymouth's Wood Centre. The Buzzcocks had by now replaced the 'traitorous' Damned and McLaren had, wisely, fled back to London along with a dwindling group of journalists (Bernard Rhodes, who stayed, found his bed being used as a toilet by those road crew and band members who'd become tired of his dictatorial ways).

The venue hadn't had a chance to advertise the second gig and only a handful of London punkies and a dozen bikers were there – 'Wankers the lot of you!' the latter shouted encouragingly at the bands. Goodman and his business partner Caruso Fuller took advantage of the last night mayhem to heckle and sing choruses through the PA's mixing desk mic. The hotel was then trashed – the bar, swimming pool and sauna were broken into, Steve Jones exposed himself and Roadent had be hospitalised after diving head first into the pool's shallow end. The damages bill ran into four figures but the hotel manager was naive enough to believe Fuller was McLaren and accepted an unsigned cheque.

An invoice went to EMI who initially disputed it, for they were no longer supporting the tour or the Pistols. Newspaper headlines had begun to target EMI chairman Sir John Read – 'So Comfortable, The Mansion Of The Man Who Makes Money From Punk!' – and the label had finally had enough. So had Matlock. Lydon's continual jeers and insults – 'Drop dead, Glen!' – had finally worn him down. More importantly, he felt that Jones and Cook were now always siding with Rotten, allowing the front man to completely dominate the band. In Holland there were a couple of dates in early January '77 at the Paradiso Club, all that remained of an EMI European tour that would have embraced France, Belgium, Denmark and Germany. The Pistols, still technically on the world's largest record label, were reduced to selling copies of 'Anarchy' at the door in the Amsterdam venue. Emotionally, things within the group came to a head even as EMI were drafting their 'mutually agreed' termination of their contract with the Pistols.

'When you're abroad, surrounded by strangers,' Matlock said later, 'you need to get on with your bandmates, you've got to be friends. And we weren't any more. There was John – and Steve and Paul – and me. That's when I decided I should get out.'

EMI deleted the 'Anarchy' single across all territories as McLaren threatened to sue the label: 'Legally we're still on EMI. How can they say "mutual agreement"? We haven't mutually agreed anything!'

The first day of the New Year saw The Clash's triumphant opening of Andy Czezowski's Roxy Club in Neal Street, Covent Garden. The founder of the Rastafarian religion, Marcus Garvey, had foretold of tumultuous change in the year when the 'two sevens clashed' – a prophecy that was already the subject of a reggae classic by the vocal group Culture – but when Joe Strummer took to the Roxy stage on New Year's Day with '1977' emblazoned across the front of his shirt, he was not merely plugging the name of one of his songs ('No Elvis, Beatles and No Rolling Stones in 1977'), he was also giving forewarning that The Clash were intent on making it their year. A passionate version of a new Strummer–Jones song 'I'm So Bored with the USA' – a bone of contention with US acts later on – was another high point. Among those watching were the Pistols, Matlock and Lydon standing ten feet away from each other and not exchanging a word the whole night. This was an ominous sign in itself, though Matlock insisted the band would be 'putting out "No Future" as soon as we've got a label behind us . . . ' They were still signed to EMI, technically, but anyone who was anyone knew it couldn't last . . .

The Roxy itself had a small, upstairs bar area and a room below that was not much larger – 40 foot square. It was in a semi-derelict area (the fruit and veg market had left the vicinity just months after Hitchcock had immortalised it in his 1972 thriller *Frenzy*), but it was still within a stone's throw of both Denmark Street and Soho. It was a magical deserted place for young punks to wander around alone at two or three in the morning. Within a few months, though, London would become far too dangerous for such activities.

Gene October's Chelsea was the support band for the Roxy's opening night – back in the autumn they'd played the Institute of Contemporary Art's Prostitution show.[28] A month after the ICA gig, Bromley Contingent star Billy Idol, London SS veteran Tony James and drummer John Towe all left October's Chelsea to form Generation X, citing disagreements over politics and musical arrangements. To the hard-nosed October, real name John O'Hara, this was only a minor setback, and he'd recruited replacements within days. After a delayed, false start the seventies had finally got a sound of its own – and no hip young musician wanted to miss out. The seventies had a new politically edged sound. The post-idol/James Chelsea group went political – 'Right To Work' was their first single – and their music had enough melody and raw sing-along energy to typify the early football 'terrace roar' of much pre-eighties punk.

28 This ICA show featured Genesis P. Orridge's S&M parodies, an event that itself led to the *Daily Mail* headline: 'These People Are The Wreckers of Civilization!' next to a photo of Siouxsie, Steve and Debbie. The quote was from Tory MP Nicholas Fairbairn.

It was October who had first told wheeler-dealer Czezowski about the small gay club Shagoramas – the owners were sick of ever dwindling bar receipts and were looking to let it out. They weren't frightened of controversy, otherwise they'd never have allowed the venue to get a gay reputation, and so, by offering several hundred pounds cash per week, Czezowski was able to launch the UK's first punk venue. It only lasted 100 days, however, under the management of Czezowski and his girlfriend Sue Carrington – a designer and make-up expert who, post-Grundy, had been fired from her cosmetics job for featuring the Bromley Contingent in an advert.

But before the avaricious owners had seized it back, the Roxy became the shabby, chic centre of London punk and, in its first two months, it saw a huge parade of the talented – and the talentless.

The Banshees – Siouxsie and Steve – finally had a guitarist and drummer to help them (P.T. Fenton and Kenny Morris respectively) and, at the Roxy, they were to prove a competent, tough outfit, Siouxsie stylishly barking out their handful of stark originals plus incongruous covers that took in everything from The Beatles' dark 'Helter Skelter' to the theme from the sixties kids' show Captain Scarlett. By then, other bands that had played the Roxy hot-house included The Adverts – singer TV Advert bringing some biting wit to songs such as 'Gary Gilmore's Eyes' just as his girlfriend, bassist Gaye, brought some much-needed glamour to the new scene – and melodic Chelsea spin-offs Generation X, with Billy Idol now a full-time singer. Sting's new band The Police put in an appearance – backed by Step Forward, the label launched by Miles Copeland, the son of a CIA insider. But Copeland's talented brother Stewart, The Police's drummer, had been in bands way back in the sixties and so, to most Roxy regulars, the group were old-stagers whose pretty mediocre mix of punk and metal had little appeal. It wasn't until nationwide tours with Jah Wobble as roadie, when they picked up on the many obscure reggae cassettes he was always playing, that The Police began to formulate a more original sound (though their successful flirtations with reggae had already been sketched out – on one level at least – by The Clash).

Conversely, the youngest band to play in Neal Street were Eater, the energetic schoolboy band of Finchley teenager Andy Blade and his 13-year-old drummer Roger 'Dee Generate' Bullen. They'd started to gig in the summer, penniless school kids playing stolen guitars in 'divorced houses' in suburbia, initially unaware of what the Pistols and Clash were up to. Then a Jonh Ingham piece in *Sounds* alerted them to the new beat, and the names and look of these new groups were intriguing – as were the photos of scantily clad female fans. But it wasn't until 15-year-old front man Blade read that punk rockers didn't have to play that well that the connection was made. 'I thought, "we play fast and we can't play that well – we must be punk rockers!" And so we called Jonh Ingham and he saw us rehearse and confirmed it all – we were indeed punk rockers. And then we talked a teacher at our school into doing a gig and The Damned and Slaughter and the Dogs played with us, and Joe Strummer was in the audience – and that was it. We were off. The only problem was getting our guitarist to stop wearing flared jeans . . . '

At the Roxy, the personable Blade swiftly found himself surrounded by groupies, while the barely adolescent Bullen was targeted by every predator on the block – but both of them, aided by their new producer Dave Goodman, seemed able to handle the attention with youthful aplomb (or so it appeared in the short term). Beside those with something to offer, there was also a succession of supporting no-hopers, the loud and talentless who were merely trying to ape, and even increase, the thrash tempo of The Ramones, just as their ragged clothes self-consciously aped the Pistols, Clash *et al.* The tabloid press coverage that had finally launched punk into the media stratosphere had a big drawback – it was angled to attract the worst of the gutter and, in terms of music at least, it partially succeeded.

By the end of the Roxy's opening night, half the white roof tiles in the low ceiling had been ripped out – by the end of the first week they'd all gone – and that, together with the tacky beer-stained floor, graffiti'd walls and crumbling toilets, gave the whole club the aura of a post-apocalyptic youth club on a particularly bad council estate. The fact that, on any given night, the new stars mingled with the curious old legends – everyone from Led Zeppelin's Robert Plant to T. Rex's Marc Bolan and Radio One's John Peel – and a crowd of trendies, runaways, self-mutilators and speed freaks, made it an even more bizarre venue.

Just as important as the audience and those flailing away on stage were the sounds spinning through the PA between sets. Although these sometimes featured the few punk recordings then available – The Ramones' LP, the Pistols' EMI 45, The Damned's Stiff single – the core of the records spun were either reggae or its innovative offshoot, dub – spacious, shuddering recordings by Big Youth, Lee Perry and Augustus Pablo.

The DJ was Don Letts, who was still then Acme's manager – his dreadlocks and dark shades, a rare look back then, swiftly became a trademark, as did his Super 8 camera. The latter was first wielded almost as a prop; later it became the means by which he put together the first serious punk movie. No one noticed the irony at the time but here was the first chronicler of punk – a black youth in his twenties who, on a scholarship, had gone to grammar school and who had also had doubts about the new groups. 'I'd first heard about the Pistols from my girlfriend, Jeanette Lee, who ran Acme Attractions with me,' says Letts now. 'I'd been king of my block at Acme – it was Steph Raynor and John Krivine's shop, of course, and they'd provided most of the clothes and jukeboxes and all that. But I'd shaken the place with all this heavy dub and I had various friends and contacts there. It was a really nice vibe, it was the best time of my life, to be honest. Basically I turned it into my living room, a place to hang out and smoke and talk.'

Among those hanging out were Nick Lowe, Chrissie Hynde, Sid Vicious, Bob Marley, Billy Idol, Keith Levene, Joe Strummer and Jah Wobble (the latter already a firm reggae roots fan from way back) and, briefly, John 'Rotten' Lydon.

'So when the Pistols came along and I first heard these rumours about these early gigs I felt that they were kinda stealing some of my thunder,' Letts smiles, 'which was crazy but, anyway, I finally saw 'em play live after Jeanette persuaded me to, saw there was something going on, and when Andy [Czezowski] asked me to DJ the Roxy I leapt at the chance. Not that I'd ever DJ'd before, but that was the spirit of it . . . the filming came about because just playing records wasn't enough for me – everyone was picking up guitars and forming bands and I wanted to pick something up and be creative. And so when I got given a Super 8 movie camera, that was it, I started filming, shooting stuff almost every day – as often as I could afford to.'

Letts's films – of Lydon smoking and joking, of Roxy faces chatting, of The Clash and Slits barnstorming on tour – are almost the only recordings of a long-lost world; the crude grain, uneven colours and answer-phone sound perfectly capturing the flavour of the times. By the end of 1977 he would have hacked these reels, literally editing with scissors and a light bulb, into his *Punk Rock Movie*, the first insider documentary of this curious new age.

QUEEN ELIZABETH PLEASURE LAUNCH – God Save Windolene!

God save the Queen
God save Windolene!

McLaren was upset by the Sex Pistols' January 1977 expulsion from EMI and the band's seeming 'pariah' status in the industry – but he did get some phone calls from Virgin's Richard Branson, which he more or less ignored, and from A&M's London boss Derek Green, which he returned.

As the Pistols made their last-ever recordings with Goodman and Matlock – at Chinatown's Goosberry studios, partially filmed by a crew from America's NBC network – both Rotten and then McLaren contacted Vivienne's old favourite, John Simon Beverley aka John Ritchie aka Sid Vicious, the man whose style and violent attitude made him the personification of post-Grundy.

John Lydon wanted Sid in the band, said Malcolm later, as Westwood always had, but did Sid want to leave The Flowers of Romance and join the Pistols? The answer had to be 'yes' and, after a couple of days, it was. A few secret rehearsals with Sid took place before Matlock got wind of the moves going on behind his back and he finally told Malcolm he wanted out. They parted in a fairly amicable manner, although the £3,000 pay-off was less than Matlock expected after all the deals that had gone on, including the £10,000 songwriting money from EMI publishing. 'But I needed the money, so I signed and took it,' he said later. Although, on one level, Matlock had wanted out for weeks – and EMI were already interested in whatever he did next – when the axe actually fell it was still a blow. Although, at the very last minute, McLaren had told Matlock he didn't *have* to leave and should instead fight for his place in the band, the group's main tunesmith didn't want to stay where he wasn't wanted. 'Glen looked really pissed off when he came into my shop that day,' Lloyd Johnson said later. 'He was looking at these purple raincoats we had but there was obviously something wrong. When I asked what's up he said, "They've kicked me out, the band have kicked me out . . ." '

At the same time producer Dave Goodman was sidelined – any future recordings were to be by Thomas although the Goodman wall-of-sound version of 'No Feeling' was to be the next Pistols B-side, just as his 'No Fun' was to be the flip of the third release 'Pretty Vacant'. Goodman made one other serious suggestion before temporarily departing the Pistols scene – that the group 'go independent' and issue 'No Future' and 'Anarchy' alongside the seven-minute 'No Fun'. All these were to be slapped on one of those new 12-inch platters and issued by Goodman's record company The Label or a Pistols subsidiary of it. It would be the first rock 12-inch, the first punk 12-inch, the first Pistols 12-inch, the first seven-minute B-side.

The Buzzcocks' dynamic *Spiral Scratch* EP had already shown the way, a self-financed record with tracks like 'Boredom' that bubbled with fuzzy energy – and a short, two-note guitar solo. This 'New Hormones' label release of January '77 had shown that going 'indie' was possible and even, in the medium term, financially viable. McLaren was intrigued for a while, but the idea of going DIY seemed, after the bigger splash with EMI, to be a retreat.

And besides, other factors in Goodman's plan seemed problematic – 12-inch vinyl cost more than the usual seven-inch and fresh cash advances were needed, not fresh deductions. The Glitterbest money stash had been reduced by the Anarchy Tour, the cost of demos and the growing demands of 'staff' wages – £25 per week for Reid, Richmond, Tiberi and the band (upped to £40 and then £50 as the year progressed). The decision was taken – the Pistols would have to sign to a major label. Again. And they did.

But the Pistols' A&M signing – at Rondor music, then restaged the next day outside Buckingham Palace – backfired massively, even as it added to the legend.

Despite the huge interest in the band – and a drunken press conference at the Regent Palace Hotel – there were no big stories in the national press, although the *Sounds* front page was a nice consolation ('PISTOLS SIGN FOR A&M FOR £150,000!').

By the time the *Sounds* headline appeared though, some six days later, the headline was technically incorrect. The band were no longer on A&M. Derek Green was to receive several surprises the day of the Pistols' public signing ceremony. One was that the news that Sid had replaced tunesmith Matlock. The second came with the behaviour of the band. After the press conference, the vodka-fuelled Pistols sped over to the New King's Road, staggered out of their already wrecked limo and set about upsetting the A&M office staff. As Lydon baited the long-hairs with insults, Jones wandered into the ladies toilet and groped whoever he could find. Not to be outdone, Sid kicked in a toilet bowl, cutting his foot badly, and then swayed around the office trailing blood over the expensive carpets.

After throwing some potted plants out of the washroom windows, Sid sank into a near catatonic state as, upstairs, Green listened to the Pistols' tapes with McLaren. Dave Goodman's seminal take of 'No Feeling' was confirmed as the flipside for 'God Save The Queen' and there were supposed to be discussions about the follow-up 45 and its artwork.

But, as news of the mayhem happening below them filtered through, Green asked McLaren for an adjournment. Meanwhile, the tapes were rushed off for mastering *en route* to the pressing plant.

Green was already shocked by Matlock's expulsion, as well as by the nature of Matlock's 'firing'. McLaren's telegram to *NME* didn't talk about 'mutual agreement' but stated instead that Glen had been fired for liking EMI and The Beatles.

The 'firing' telegram also boasted of Sid getting the Pistols' bass job as a reward for giving 'Nick Kent what he deserved at the 100 Club'. Kent may not have been Mister Innocent, but justice delivered with a rusty bike chain is hardly ideal . . . Green changed his mind after a night of soul-searching on Brighton beach and – after his offer to resign had been rejected by A&M supremos Herb Alpert and Jerry Moss – he told a stunned McLaren his band had been fired. Despite later claims of elation, that was to be a dark hour at Glitterbest – McLaren was shell-shocked when he took calls that night, manning the phones himself in a daze as he repeated the bad news over and over again.

The 25,000 A&M copies of GSTQ were recycled via pulping – fewer than 50 escaped the furnaces – and A&M 'sacked' the band with a £75,000 pay-off (which momentarily lifted McLaren's mood).

With the Jubilee now just three months away, McLaren knew he had to move fast if anything was to be salvaged from all the recent troubles – he bit the bullet and phoned Richard Branson at Virgin. The latter was more than ready, having ordered his staff not to be offended by anything the punk kings came up with. Branson was determined that his would be the first record label to actually make a genuine profit on the Pistols and GSTQ finally had a label (and a new flip, a dogged take on Wally's 'Did You No Wrong').

Musically GSTQ was created 'as a marching song, an anthem', in Matlock's own words. 'Wig Wam Bam' by Sweet, as played by The Faces on a dark and angry night. It's call-and-response structure was old-style in many ways, but the stuttering bass throb, the dynamism of that opening roller-coaster riff combined with Jones's space-age rework of Chuck Berry – noticeable but brilliant in the guitar solo – took it to another level. Lyrically, it was, perhaps, Lydon's finest hour, a song which, according to John Peel, 'showed how society dehumanised people, from the top down'. Between the sarcastic serenades of the monarch – 'tourists are money!' – people were told not to be told what they wanted, a line that manages to be cynical and idealistic simultaneously.

The 'God Save The Queen' title was something McLaren had insisted upon – Royal Jubilees only come round every quarter of a century – but there were days of argument before Lydon agreed. The move seems obvious now and was more so then – the national anthem was played by 99 per cent of cinemas after the last movie and by BBC TV and radio before they closed down for the night. The original 'God Save The Queen' – and hence possibly anything else with that same title – thus had a resonance far beyond mere music.

McLaren also wanted the 'God Save Windolene' line taken out too. Lydon made less of a fuss about this, though he was possibly entitled to make more. Windolene, a British window-cleaning fluid sold in pink plastic bottles, was the perfect materialist *non sequitur* to throw into such a song, especially as it came just before the line about saving 'human beings' (the reference remains in the four-and-a-half-minute funkier version Dave Goodman recorded at Gooseberry Studios, Chinatown in January '77, complete with an unstoppable bluesier take on the guitar riff, and a feel which makes it almost hypnotic). McLaren didn't dislike the Windolene rhyme, he just suspected that the mention of a commercial product would be used by the state broadcaster, the BBC, as an excuse to ban the record for non-political reasons. If GSTQ was going to be banned – and it surely was – then the mainstream media should be forced to admit that it was for reasons of state.

The band's EMI debut 'Anarchy In The UK' had caused some offence with its references to the anti-Christ, destruction and 'getting pissed', but Capital Radio and BBC Radio One had given it a few plays, mainly through John Peel, of course. Its delayed release, Chris Thomas's unexpectedly mild production and its failure to make the Top 30 – partly due to EMI's staged withdrawal – diluted its impact. The Pistols were banned from playing live almost everywhere by mid-December 1976, but this was because of the swear-in on the Bill Grundy show and the band's refusal to make a full apology, not because of the 'Anarchy' single.

It was different with 'God Save The Queen', aka 'No Future', aka 'No Hope, No Glory' (the latter title dropped almost immediately because, in Sophie Richmond's words, 'you can't say there's

"No Hope", there's always hope'). The lyrics spoke of a 'fascist regime' and lines like 'made you a moron' could be taken as directly referring to the nation's monarch (although they were aimed at the listener, as is fairly obvious when it's heard with music).

The song was first performed, shambolically, with Rotten reading the words from a sheet of paper, at Lancaster Polytechnic on 29 November with the 'Anarchy' single just two days old. The song grew in relevance after the Grundy debacle, when, at Leeds University, Rotten dedicated it – amid much swearing – to the Queen.

Jamie Reid's artwork, of Her Majesty with swastika eyes, was rejected by Virgin although the follow-up they accepted was hardly tame – the Queen's face with the 'God Save The Queen' words over her eyes, like a kidnap blindfold, and the 'Sex Pistols' logo covering her mouth. The t-shirt was even more shocking – Her Majesty with safety-pinned lips and Pistols' logo, plus the notorious, and mostly misinterpreted, line 'She Ain't No Human Being!'. These t-shirts were to provoke the classic *Sunday People* letter headline, frothing with Cold War outrage as it referred to the Pistols: 'THEY MUST BE RUSSIANS!'

The *Sunday People* headline was only a small part of a massive press overreaction. Labour MP Willie Hamilton had been sniping at the Royals for years – over their 'tax avoidance', their distance, their cost to the nation – and he'd never received anything more than a few dozen angry letters, even though British public approval of the Royal family was then running at over 80 per cent of the electorate. By using music – and, more explosively, by using rock'n'roll – the Pistols had upped the ante. They had attacked at an emotional level – and the response would come at an emotional level. And, as Peter York said at the time, they did it in a song that spoke of dehumanisation and H-bombs and ended with a second chorus based around the refrain 'No Future', those two killing, chilling words. What every post-Hiroshima generation – what every post-Hiroshima artist worth his salt – had hinted at; the subtext of songs like Dylan's 'A Hard Rain's A-Gonna Fall', Pete Seeger's 'Mack The Bomb', Malvina Reynolds's 'What Have They Done To The Rain?', Front Page Review's 'Prophesies', Bowie's 'Five Years' and of serious films of the fifties and sixties like *Split Second, Hiroshima, Mon Amour, The Day The Earth Caught Fire, On The Beach, The Damned, Seven Days In May, Fail Safe, Dr Strangelove* . . . and the Pistols had suddenly, dynamically, blurted it all out, what the bright bland world of sequinned DJs, 'good fun' entertainers and demurring politicians had tried to ignore for decades, the radioactive elephant in the room that no one talked about, the first and last post-war taboo, the fact that there simply was No Future. In the insane atomic age of Mutually Assured Destruction and fatal four-minute warnings, we the human race had No Future. 'You are a fool if you don't realise this' – this is the unwritten, unspoken line that caused most fuss. For loyalists, and royalists, for the non-liberal middle class and much of the working class, it was the final insult – far worse than the mere sexual shennanigans of the Stones or the satanic poses of Led Zep. 'You are a fool if you don't realise this . . . '

The music press papers all gave GSTQ four-star reviews in a show of solidarity that's not been repeated since for a major release, while the national press refused to give it any review space. Although John Peel gave it a couple of swift late-night plays, an Indpendent Broadcasting Authority ban, coupled with a BBC ban, swiftly ensured it could no longer be legally played on any British radio or TV station. This ban was so totalitarian that an embarrassed IBA directive, quickly echoed by a similar BBC document, emphasised that this act of censorship was only to 'apply at this particular time' – i.e. the month of the Queen's Jubilee, June 1977 – as this was then when 'the record might cause particular offence'. (Despite these weasel words, the reality was the Pistols' GSTQ single was to be off the UK airwaves for 25 years.)[29]

Despite an absence of obscenity, Thames TV refused to show a

29 By contrast, The Strawbs' 1973 anti-trade union singalong 'Part of The Union' (A&M) was just as political in many ways, yet that remained on Radio One's daytime play list right up until the point when it reached No. 2.

10-second advert for GSTQ – the latter consisting of Rotten informing the audience that the Pistols were back, 'with a vengeance!'. A 30-second radio ad was also rejected by the four biggest commercial stations in Britain. The Sex Pistols couldn't play anywhere – well, not with any advance publicity – their latest single was not listed on many of the charts. GSTQ was not even stocked by W.H. Smith – they left a gap in the chart spaces – and it was also banned from all radio and TV shows in Britain, the home of parliamentary democracy and free speech, and the Associated Press agency had publicly pledged they would not run any stories featuring the Sex Pistols, the UK's most famous – not to say infamous – band. In this overreaction lay the clearest indication yet concerning the future destruction of Britain's consensus society. The new right-wing Tories had, under Thatcher, failed to maintain a serious lead in the polls; Labour was still being feted by the press as the 'natural party of government', despite its wafer-thin Commons majority. The People's Party had, after all, won four out of the last five general elections since 1960.[30]

Yet the architect of these election victories, Labour leader Harold Wilson, had already been pressurised out of No. 10 in early 1976 – and his claims of being hounded by MI5 were the subject of ridicule everywhere, even in publications that were then suspicious of the security forces (notably, *Private Eye* magazine). These pressure claims had since been proved to be true, though of course that didn't help Wilson or his successor, Jim Callaghan, at the time.[31]

Britain's North sea oil was about to start flowing and, even with the suspicious deals that gave much of the money to American oil companies, this was still going to yield billions of pounds for the government, guaranteeing that whoever was in office during the

30 Their sole defeat during this period, the 1970s poll was probably due to a Labour turn-coat who was secretly bribed £35,000 – over £350,000 today – to reveal Labour's election strategies to Ted Heath's campaign managers.
31 This was all only a year after MI5's unofficial project Operation Clockwork Orange had helped destroy the Northern Ireland power-sharing agreement, as later revealed in the Peter Wright book *Spycatcher*. Operation Clockwork Orange succeeded in preventing a Labour government bringing peace to Northern Ireland. It also ensured that the 'Ulster troubles' would continue for another 20 years and claim a further 2,000 lives.

first flurry would hold sway for a generation.

Anything in the seventies that might rally young people in any direction apart from the right was therefore bad. Although punk rock's existence embarrassed the Labour government, it embarrassed the real centres of power more and helped justify almost any means that would get rid of the People's Party. The 'menace' of punk rock had, after all, appeared on Labour's watch.

It was into this atmosphere that the Pistols GSTQ was finally released on 26 May '77. Over 50,000 copies were pressed in advance and the magazine adverts – mostly full page – stressed the need for fans to get the single fast as it was likely to disappear soon (possibly, it was implied, for legal reasons). This was a stroke of genius by McLaren and Co. 'Anarchy' had been pulled early from the shops even before EMI deleted it; subsequently, the value of these singles had tripled in six months. With the even more controversial GSTQ having already been kicked off A&M, what price would the Virgin 45 be worth if it too vanished quickly?

The 65 kids at the 100 Club had become 400 in a good weekend at the Roxy and now – via EMI, Grundy and A&M – they'd become perhaps 90,000. And the latter number would, if many bought multiple copies, now mushroom to 250,000 or more.

Within days it was obvious that something special was happening. In an editorial that was almost understanding – 'WHAT'S BURNING UP THE KIDS?' – the *Sunday Mirror* now admitted that GSTQ was going to be the fastest-selling single of all time. It was 'likely' to top the charts during Jubilee Week – an added embarrassment, potentially, for the BBC, which was supposed to play that week's number one every week at the end of *Top of the Pops*. GSTQ was, of course, cheated out of the BBC's official top spot. Despite pressing plant demand being three times that of Rod Stewart's 'I Don't Want To Talk About It', the latter remained at number one during Jubilee week. This was mainly because an extraordinary edict was issued by the industry that week – that record shops linked to record labels, i.e. the Pistols' label Virgin, would *not* be allowed to contribute chart returns. Since Virgin stores at that time turned over hundreds of thousands of records a month, and since they were the only record chain to put up Pistols' posters and flyers, this was a major blow. In contrast with Virgin's window displays, the Top 10 boards used by W.H. Smith, for instance, only showed a gap where GSTQ stood – even the song's mere title was offensive when linked with the Pistols (this 'gap' gave a new meaning to the phrase 'blank generation'). Seven days later, the Jubilee was over as GSTQ's sales began to flag – and the new chart return edict was quietly dropped. Virgin's boss Branson – despite a reputation for controversy and various family connections with the law – made no public comment about this chicanery at the time. He wanted to make money out of McLaren's boys, not further their social challenge. But the final drama of the event only came on the day itself.

The Pistols' Jubilee Boat, looking like an invasion vessel from some ramshackle future, ploughed down the dark waters of an eerily deserted Thames while fireworks strafed the night sky all around.

The evening had started off in an equally surreal fashion (on a boat named after the monarch and decked with the banner '*Queen Elizabeth* Welcomes The Sex Pistols!'). Various members of The Slits leapt onto the overcrowded boat as it pulled away from the quayside.[32] Five songs into the trip and a fight briefly flared – a French photographer had barged into Wobble and in return got a slap before being held over the side. Sid was drunk by then and John Lydon had seemingly lost all interest in the event and what it symbolised, but, according to Dave Goodman, 'Malcolm was still up for it, he kept saying "Look that's Parliament there, let's just storm it – there's only a couple of coppers there now, let's do it, let's just take it! Take Parliament! How amazing that'd be on Jubilee Day!" He made the boat cruise past it three or four times.' Wobble concurs, 'I'll give McLaren that much, he really was up for it on the boat that night. There was no way he was gonna go quietly. Not from that boat.'

---

32 Nora, mother of The Slits' singer Ari Up, didn't manage to squeeze on the boat. According to Wobble, she was so furious that she hurled a battered three-piece suite she'd found in a skip off a bridge onto the *Queen Elizabeth* as it passed. By a minor miracle, no one was hurt.

But the boat was no longer alone – 'I thought that was great,' Roadent claims, 'when we started to get the river police boats following us, I thought, "Wow, we're hardcore now, they really think we're a threat!" '

The river police ordered the Pistols' boat to pull over to a quay where dozens more officers were waiting. McLaren, Dave Goodman and Wobble were soon the only ones insisting the police order be ignored – McLaren and Wobble trying to storm the captain's bridge before Wobble started chucking beer cans at the police. The captain pulled the boat over, Julien Temple filming anxiously all the while. After a tense stand-off, the band and their fans streamed off the boat, many to be manhandled by the police.

The group, and Richard Branson, were unhurt, but McLaren, after calling the police 'fascists', was violently arrested and beaten, as were Westwood, Reid and Debbie Wilson. Sid and the other Pistols got off the boat and away unscathed, more by luck than judgement, for policemen were looking for them. The next day, following the police bust of a river party given by the Sex Pistols, the most notorious group in rock history, not a single UK newspaper gave the event, or even the arrests, any substantial coverage. Only the *Daily Mirror* mentioned it, in a small, two-paragraph 'non-story' – for the British tabloids, this was a new angle in peace-time; this was naked self-censorship and, again, it didn't bode well for the future.

Following the police lead, Teds, football yobs and even some young City gents joined in the ultra-right's punk-bashing frenzy of the following weeks. Lydon and engineer Bill Price were attacked with machetes by a gang of both black and white youths in Green Lanes, north London, and Jamie Reid had his leg broken in a separate attack. 'That was such a heartless time, everyone was being very tough and ruthless,' says Sophie Richmond now. 'I didn't even let Jamie get a cab back when he came out of hospital, and I made him limp home to save us money too.'

As the clampdown continued, with assaults upon their friends and neighbours, the Pistols felt that they had been deliberately targeted in a pre-arranged manner. No one said the word 'conspiracy' but that's what most of them then believed, even though the tabloids had whipped up the feelings of their less discerning readers ('Punish The Punks!'), it is a fact, later revealed by ex-MI5 spy David Shayler, that MI5 did indeed have a 1977 file named 'Subversion In The Music Industry'. In the file were pages about McLaren, the Sex Pistols and 'other leading groups'. 'The people at the top are so distant and, in many cases, so paranoid that I could actually see a few of them thinking that this was all very serious and menacing,' says Roadent now, 'though I don't think they'd have learned much from tapping our phones. And I feel sorry for anyone who had to listen in to any of Bernie Rhodes's phone calls . . .'

Lydon and Vicious ended two West End trips barricaded inside shops and restaurants as mobs tried to get at them. 'I don't wanna sound paranoid but there was something a bit strange about one of those attacks,' says Wobble now. 'When these guys started on John [Lydon] and John Gray in that gay bar, Louise's, they really weren't expecting me to go for 'em as strongly I did. So, after a minute or two, they were like, "OK, OK, calm down, calm down, let's leave it." The way they behaved, the way they spoke, it was like they might have been cops, you know plainclothes cops or off-duty cops or whatever. Then, outside, later on, there was suddenly a whole coachload of people that were looking for us and somehow knew where we were. It was all very weird, thinking about it . . .'

A week after the Rotten attack, Paul Cook had his scalp opened by crowbar-wielding Teddy boys at Hammersmith tube station, producing the *Mirror* headline 'PUNK ROCK ROTTEN RAZORED!'. Later the Teds' activities were acclaimed on The Dixie Rebels' dimly disturbing single 'The Punk Bashing Boogie'.

While the National Front's brand of free speech was always protected in the pre-1990s British Isles – over 3,000 police officers were once assigned to guard NF leader Martin Webster during a solo march – punk free speech was different; it was the type of free speech that could actually cost you a lot.

As well as hundreds of beatings inflicted on punks, in Dublin one young punk rock fan was stabbed to death during the summer of 1977. In London, a couple of months later, Clash associate Henry

Bowles had his skull fatally fractured by bouncers at a Subway Sect gig in London's Pentonville Road. Days after John Lydon was attacked, his brother Jimmy had his eye cut in half. 'All this pressure is killing me,' declared their mother, Mrs Lydon. Two years later she would be dead.

The Pistols, not unnaturally, began to keep their heads down. Cook and Jones spent hours playing at Rehearsal Rehearsals while Lydon began to stay indoors for longer and longer periods. Sid, predictably, retreated further with his girlfriend Nancy Spungen into the heroin his mother had used for years, the heroin that Johnny Thunders had first offered him a few months before, the heroin that had been the centre of Nancy's life for years.

The New York scene that Nancy Spungen had once been a small part of had changed considerably since Hilly Kristal's 1975 'festival'. The Ramones had blown out the Pistols over the Anarchy Tour – a wise move in retrospect – and then cut their second album *Leave Home*. Despite repeating their debut's bad-taste joke – 'Now I Wanna Sniff Some Glue' was updated, until the public outcry got too much, into 'Carbona Not Glue' – The Ramones' *Leave Home* did contain the non-stop excitement of 'Gimme Gimme Shock Treatment' and the more lyrically conventional boy–girl battles of 'I Remember You' and the post-Beatles' 'Swallow My Pride'. They were still freaks to America's mainstream press – or, as the *New York Times* put it, 'they speak up for outcasts and other disturbed individuals'.

Meanwhile NYC rivals Television – *sans* Richard Hell since 1975 – had scored a record deal of their own with Elektra, the 'traditional' home of edgy, left-field US rock from the days of The Stooges and MC5 onwards (and, like Iggy and MC5, Television were signed at the same time as wild-men The Dictators).

Four years after ex-school-boarders Tom 'Verlaine' Miller and Richard 'Hell' Myers had started The Neon Boys, the group's bastard son, Television, had finally got to release an album. The album and single were entitled *Marquee Moon*, a coldly brilliant debut that was more arty New Wave than punk, with the space and depth of its ten-minute title track (complete with a mid-tempo pace, ever-changing bass lines and duelling guitars). But Verlaine's reedy, occasionally soulful vocals held the listener's attention, as did the Smith–Ficca rhythm section and chilling numbers like 'Torn Curtain' and 'Venus' – the total effect quickly leading to the band being labelled 'the Ice Kings of Rock'. In the US, Verlaine's untutored voice and 'triple entendre' lyrics were guaranteed to keep the band out of the charts, but in the UK both the 'Marquee Moon' single and album skimmed the Top 30 (a better placing that the Pistols had scored up until that point – though the latter's notorious reputation was one reason the US acts, almost 'normal' in comparison, could then score airplay in Britain).

The seeds of Television's commercial failure – and cult success – had already been sown, however. After a successful UK tour with Television's polar opposites Blondie, drugs were being consumed *en masse* by most of the band and guitarist Richard Lloyd's resulting serious illness, endocarditis, meant his heart was, quite literally, starting to eat itself. He survived, but the second, solo-laden album *Adventure* – damned as second-rate Grateful Dead by most critics – was delayed as gigs were cancelled. By the end of 1978 they'd split.

One of Television's Manhattan competitors in early '77 had been the Patti Smith band – their reputation higher than ever after sell-out gigs in England and the critical acclaim there for 45s such as 'Gloria', 'My Generation' and a re-released 'Piss Factory'. But Smith's career was about to hit a major interruption – while playing live in Tampa, Florida, she had launched into the song 'Ain't It Strange'. This number reflected her, then current, attitude – 'Jesus, died for somebody's sins but not mine'. In 'Ain't It Strange', she would always dive into a big whirling-dervish-type spin, going round and round at high speed as she challenged God to do his worst – 'Gimme your best shot, I can take it!'. On a darkened Tampa stage her luck ran out – as she twirled round, she stumbled over a black monitor speaker and fell into the orchestra pit, smashing her neck into the planks and pipes that jutted out there. An audible bone crack heralded a flood of blood as a twitching Smith was strapped onto a stretcher and hurriedly wheeled away to hospital. The fall had caused a fracture in one of her neck vertebrae. While Patti slowly recovered, the forthcoming European tour was called off and her band ended up on welfare for a time. Smith would return, but her live act would never be as wild again. 'Gloria' and several other numbers were dropped as her onstage attitude shifted from 'craziness' to 'reconciliation'.

The darkest side of 'craziness' was starkly platformed on a single by another of New York's new 'punk art' bands, Talking Heads. After their wistful, almost poignant 'Love Goes To Building On Fire' debut on Sire records came 'Pyscho Killer', a throbbing, threatening classic that featured David Byrne's best Anthony Perkins impersonation.

Byrne had taken much from Jonathan Richman – including his Modern Lovers' keyboardist Jerry Harrison – but the resulting band were fresh-faced enough to be both arthouse and dance hall in 1977 (even though Byrne, blonde bassist Tina Weymouth and drummer Chris Frantz were all in their late twenties at the time). Their polished, almost delicate, debut album *Talking Heads* was produced by popmeister Tony Bongiovi. The latter's smooth work gave Bryne's urban angst, something to stand out from, and numbers like the eerily melodic 'Don't Worry About The Government' sounded like Jonathan Richman off on some paranoid holiday. This set was followed by the even smoother *More Songs About Buildings And Food* – though it did contain a stark, strong take on Al Green's 'Take Me To The River' – as the Heads swiftly became the 'thinking critic's darlings' (especially in Europe). It was American art school rock at its most thought-provoking.

But punk had moved beyond the US and mainland Britain even before 1977 – the future echoes had been washing round for some time – and a prime example of how far it had reached came with The Saints. This hairy Australian four-piece had started out in 1974 in a cheap rehearsal room in the cheapest part of unfashionable

Brisbane. Stooges type garage rock was the order of the day – the more basic, the better, though with the added modern bonus of guitar pedal distortion to open out the sound (at the same time as it muddied the 'top end'). By late '76 The Saints had 'regressed' enough to begin their punk recording career. It started with a private pressing of their thrashily desperate '(I'm) Stranded' single. Chris Bailey's throatily dry, leather-lung vocals and Ed Keupper's dourly entertaining buzzsaw guitar were the single's biggest plus points. Copies found their way to Sydney and then halfway round the world to London where a post-Pistols EMI were on the hunt for something, *anything*, that was vaguely punk – without, of course, being the Pistols. '(I'm) Stranded' was swiftly issued by EMI-Harvest and sold enough to encourage further records. The Saints' strongest number was their next 45, which rapidly became their only UK hit. 'This Perfect Day' was not the 1972 Lou Reed epic but a heavily accented original, a driving workout that was dourly exciting – Aussie Velvets in the late seventies with dumb-dumb Dee Dee style lyrics about 'not needing no one' to tell the singer 'what I don't already know'. It was given a *Top of the Pops* airing by the BBC, along with The Ramones' 'Swallow My Pride', in order to dilute the shock of the Pistols' *TOTP* 'debut' on the very same show – a debut that came via the Temple–McLaren pop promo of 'Pretty Vacant' (despite being 'only' there on video – and despite the Ramones–Saints punk sandwich – the Pistols still caused many complaints as well as a *Daily Mirror* headline, 'NOW IT'S TOP OF THE PUNKS!').

Much closer to home – at least, geographically – was Ireland. There, Bob Geldof had freaked out his strict Catholic teachers in his early teens by ordering copies of Karl Marx books – so it was obvious in 1976 that his new Dublin-based band would embrace the burgeoning punk scene, or New Wave as his nervous label Ensign usually described it. With a welter of Boomtown Rats armbands and flyers, the group descended on London in spring '77. By August their wild live appearances – with a manic, gleaming Geldof in striped shirts and keyboardist Johnny Fingers hamming it up in striped pyjamas – ensured that any record the Irishmen released would shift several thousand copies. The breakneck 'Looking After No. 1' did a lot more, selling over 75,000 and went into the Top 10. It also demonstrated – in Geldof's acerbic lyrics – the selfish side of punk: individualism, looking after No. 1, looking after yourself, Me! Me! Me! Or, I have no 'feelings' for anyone else, as John Lydon once put it.

The Rats scored several more chart places before Geldof's doomed-youth-in-concrete-jungle anthem 'Rat Trap', complete with honking sax, shifted 250,000 copies and went to number one.

In the north of Ireland there was another factor, the armed 'troubles': the unofficial civil war between the ruling Protestant majority and the large – and largely powerless – Catholic minority which had been claiming lives with increasing frequency since the summer of 1968. Communal and religious violence was the norm and there were two separate young tribes since virtually every school was divided into Catholic and Protestant. (Incredibly, the majority of schools are still single-faith, even today, in Northern Ireland.)

'I was then playing in a band called Highway Star,' says Jake Burns of Stiff Little Fingers now, 'but we really weren't very good musicians, we were very limited. We just never sounded enough like Lynyrd Skynyrd to get away with it.'

Liberation came from the unlikely direction of the British mainland and the new scruffy noises coming out of London. 'And then, God bless 'em, The Damned came along and Henry, our rhythm guitarist, got heavily into the whole punk thing, right from the off. I was buying Pub rock records by then, so were both veering away from the usual metal heroes. Henry bought the first couple of Damned singles and then the Sex Pistols' records and we were both like, "This is great, this is great, this is exactly what we should be doing!"'

But punk's divisive quality almost came into play at this point. 'The other guys in the band weren't so convinced, but I mean the big watershed was The Clash album – that was go out, cut your hair, stop mucking about time, y'know. Up to that point we'd still been singing about bowling down California highways. I mean, it meant nothing to me. Although The Damned and the Pistols were great, they were only exciting musically; lyrically, I couldn't really make out a lot of it. Quite how I made out Joe [Strummer] I'll never know, but I did – and to realise that they were actually singing about their own lives in West London was like a bolt out of the blue, y'know?'

Highway Star were now Stiff Little Fingers, the north's equivalent of Eire's Boomtown Rats, but SLF were still only playing other people's songs. 'An early SLF gig consisted of the first Damned album and as many Pistols' singles as we could get our hands on. We also did something by Iggy and The Stooges. That was Ali's influence. He got into the band because he was the only person we knew who had a Marshall amp . . . but there were no originals, none whatsoever . . . '

It took an outside influence to point out the obvious. Gordon Ogilvy was a music-loving *Daily Express* stringer reporting on the 'troubles'. Wading through blood-stained gutters and dodging bomb scares and bomb blasts were all part of Ogilvy's beat, but it was The Clash's arrival in Belfast that led him to connect with SLF. 'The Clash's arrival was previewed; they basically said this was going to be an important event and anybody with any interest in music should get themselves along there. That first Clash gig was actually cancelled, they couldn't get any insurance for the show and it [became] a typical Belfast reaction; we rioted outside the hall and that was actually my first ever radio interview, I remember being interviewed by somebody from Radio Ulster and I'm going, "It's a f—ing disgrace, that f—ing policeman, what's he hitting him for? He's done f— all." And we went round and shouted and screamed outside the Europa Hotel. Joe and Paul came out, but not Mick or Topper. They tried to pacify everybody and just got, basically, loads of abuse.'

Ogilvy was intrigued by the SLF letters and called the band wanting to see a gig – which wasn't that easy in the post-Grundy climate. 'We couldn't get booked into pubs or clubs and you also came up against the old sort of you're-not-proper-musicians [argument]. And I'm saying, "You f—ing booked us a month ago when we were Highway Star!" And the [venues] were like, "F— off, we're not interested now." So we had to hire halls and promote ourselves. One of the more popular places was a stable block outside a hotel called the Glen Makin, and we invited Gordon and his mate Colin along to see us. To be honest, I was only looking for free publicity, I hadn't got an eye on management at all, but Gordon in particular was very interested – and they mentioned straight away, "Have you got a manager?" I said no so they said, "Would you mind if we talk to you?" We met up the following week and went for a beer and they didn't talk about management at all.'

In fact the two older men were more interested in the longer term – which meant whether the band had any songwriting potential. 'They were more interested in talking about songwriting and what spurred us on. Gordon asked if I had written anything pertinent to where I'd grown up. Of course this was on the back of The Clash album and I'd written the song "State of Emergency", which was on the *Inflammable Material* album. I said, "Yes I have, I've written this." He then reached into his inside pocket and said, "What do you make of this?" And he handed me the finished lyric of "Suspect Device". I sort of read it and thought, "I can't believe it this is somebody thinking along exactly the same lines as me." I went home, wrote the music track and also in the same initial outpouring wrote "Wasted Life", probably in the same evening.'

At the time 'suspect devices' in Belfast referred to the small firebombs that the IRA were building into audio cassette cases (left in jacket pockets in clothes shops), they could cause fiery mayhem as they sprang into life after the stores had closed. It was a brave choice of song, and the cassette sleeve of the demo was equally 'cheeky'.

'I met them the following week,' says Burns, 'played both to them and they instantly put up £500 to make this thing. We booked a local jingle studio in Downtown Radio, which is a local radio station. We were in for two days . . . we didn't do the singing because I hadn't got any voice at that point, so we went back on the Tuesday night and did the voice when we thought it had returned enough. We were pressing the thing ourselves. We only had 500 of them and we were actually having to make the sleeves. So we were sitting cutting these bloody things out and gluing them together, it was like a small conveyor belt round a kitchen table. We had the radio on in the corner and we were listening to John Peel, sort of passing these things round, and there would come a point in the show where he would go, "I know I've played this a lot but here are Stiff Little Fingers," and we were like, "Don't play that f—ing thing again, I don't want to keep doing this!" We just couldn't keep up with demand and actually the first thing we did, when we made any money at all, was get sleeves printed commercially.'

After the numerous plays on John Peel's show, several labels were chasing the Belfast boys who'd dared to make their own indie record. They'd also dared to keep their religions secret; even now, few people are aware of who's Catholic and who's Protestant in SLF. This was partly because, as one young local put it in 1978: 'Punks don't talk about what their religion is here – to those involved here, punk *is* a religion.'

'I was still working at the time,' admits Burns. 'Island Records called and came and looked at us. Then they flew us across to London for as weekend to do demos. Everything was great, the guys that had flown over to see us were convinced, they were right up for it.'

SLF were even given soundman Ed Hollis, then riding high on the chart with his production of The Hot Rods' 'Do Anything You Wanna Do'.

'That convinced us that these guys were serious. They put us up in a swanky hotel and it was like, "Blimey, is this what's going to happen for the rest of my life?"'

Island quickly got to the point – 'I think they offered like a £35,000 advance, which was certainly more than enough to live on, you know? So that was great and we were told, "Quit your jobs, boys, and come to London now."'

A deal seemed inevitable, but, before it got that far, the demos happened to be heard by Island boss Chris Blackwell. 'And I think,' Burns relates, 'the basic objection was that they didn't know how they were going to market us in America. Which, to be fair, was kind of what most record companies were probably thinking about punk. So Island didn't want us. And we'd already left our jobs and it wasn't a laughing matter. We were actually on the verge of chucking the towel in. But Gordon was like, "Of course, you're not going to chuck the towel in, what on earth were you thinking of?"'

The next week, Ogilvy happened to be in the Rough Trade shop in Kensington Park Road, 'they were just one of the shops where we initially sold "Suspect Device" and they were like, "Oh right, you know we put out the odd record, we might be interested in helping you do a second single, we haven't got much money but we could possibly do that."'

An offer quickly arrived from 'gay new waver' Tom Robinson. 'The TRB group were willing to actually pay us to do the single, which was astonishingly generous. I also believe that Rough Trade said that they would put the record out, but they couldn't afford to record it and Gordon, who had moved to London at that point said, "Well that's OK, I think I can get some finished tapes." And he went round to Island Studios and said, "Oh, I'm from Stiff Little Fingers. I've come round for the 24-track masters." And they went, "All right, fine" and they basically just gave him the boxes and we just f—ed off with them. Allegedly!'

As a new UK indie, Rough Trade had the right semi-political vibe – the most visible example of the current DIY ethos – though that wasn't what Burns remembers. 'Rough Trade were incredibly nice people, really, really nice to work with, but I still felt that we should be on a major. Rough Trade still felt like an extension of the kitchen table conveyor belt to me. When we went on Tom Robinson's UK tour I was fully expecting we'd get major label interest. But they wouldn't touch us, and so I remember talking to Geoff Travis and Gordon. "Nobody else is interested, why don't you just do the album with us?" And at that point they'd only ever done one-off singles and it was all kind of a leap in the dark, nobody really knew what we were. But Rough Trade took that risk.'

SLF's most famous seventies single was also recorded when they were with Rough Trade. The intriguing 'Alternative Ulster' – its mere title an affront to some in Northern Ireland's establishment –

was a 45 which blended tight, thrash rhythms with a poignant, almost acoustic, riff. The feedback from it, despite its failure to chart, was enough for all concerned to put their faith in an LP, the move that really cemented the Fingers' growing reputation.

'I think we just all looked on the album as an extended singles session really, which was probably all to the good, spontanaeity is what makes a record, y'know?'

In Manchester and London there were now several punk venues to give a platform to the spontaneous and the calculating, to the dozens of groups – and fanzines – that existed in the two cities. But in Britain's third city, Birmingham, things were a little quieter at first, a little more typical of the UK as a whole. 'I'd been wearing suede-head clothes in the late sixties, and I'd loved the look that immediately preceded it, the American look complete with GI hair-cut,' said Kevin Rowland decades later, 'but then, in 1973 and '74 there had been more of a move towards the forties and Robert Mitchum hair and trying to be cool and sophisticated and all that. Every city, every town, had a few people that were into all that dressing up, and Birmingham was no exception.'

Rowland had been born in London then moved to the outer sub-urb of Harrow and then on to the Midlands, although he had kept returning to the capital's centre on an irregular basis. Although a guitar player, he was also vaguely aware that his voice was stronger that most – he'd auditioned as singer for several bands in the mid-seventies before being considered, and turned down, by the Sex Pistols back in 1975.

Rowland's brief flirtation with Glam had continued with the Lucy and The Lovers band but, by the middle of 1976, he'd got the punk message and he turned the Lovers into The Killjoys, who soon had Rowland on vocals only, backed by a guitarist and two girls. They were as fast and talented as any of the Midlands' bands around, but Birmingham back then had its live music circuit dominated by just two or three families – none of whom liked, or would even tolerate, punk. Metal was the preferred choice for those venues that weren't caught in the pub rock or Country and Western ruts.

It took John Tully and his Barbarella's club to really give the city's punks anywhere to play, and by the time that venue had been joined by others, The Killjoys were playing in London. Their replacements as local heroes were the multi-racial Automatics with Jerry Dammers and Terry Hall – later the Coventry Automatics. This was a band whose line-up, and slightly smarter clothes, more closely reflected the city's make-up – and its post-Jamaican style. The Automatics' punky reggae sound took a different direction when new manager Bernard Rhodes gave them an hour of ancient ska and bluebeat on a cassette he'd borrowed from Acme's Don Letts. This inadvertently led them to the Special AKA name – and to the faster post-dub rhythms that would later become known as Two-Tone.

Rowland, though, had just missed the punk boat and June 1978 saw the sharp-dressing Killjoys finally disband. It was the same month that The Special AKA gave their new name its first outing, when they supported The Clash at Aylesbury's Friar's venue. By the end of the year, they'd be free of both the double-edged punk tag *and* Rhodes's inspirational but draconian style of management (group wages £15 a week plus chips and with use of a payphone at Rehearsals Rehearsals. . .).

June 1978 also saw the release of an independent EP on Enigma Records – Enigma actually being the main members of The Stiff Kittens aka Warsaw (vocalist Ian Curtis, bassist Peter Hook, guitarist Bernard Albrecht and drummer Stephen Morris). The group's new recording name was Joy Division – as tastefully taken from the brothels within Nazi slave labour camps – a band that *NME*'s Paul Morley had described, back in May, as being 'dry, doomy . . . depending promisingly on the possibility of repetition'.

The band's visuals, increasingly grey and industrial, began, like their often brutal music, to reflect a completely different world from the almost joyful 1–2–3–4 of The Ramones and their many imitators.

A whole new world of musical and cultural possibilities had been opened up when the Pistols – with a little help from The Clash, The Buzzcocks and The Ramones – had kicked down the doors in 1976. But, by the middle of '77, the original prime movers were having problems of their own, problems that went beyond the media's unofficial backlash.

SAN FRANCISCO'S WINTERLAND – Cheated

The river of new acts breaking through swiftly became a flood in 1977; The Jam was one, a three-piece from Woking who preferred wearing sharp sixties-style suits to safety pins. They'd started out as a four-piece around 1974, with school friends Paul Weller, Bruce Foxton, Rick Buckler and Steve Brookes getting together to 'jam' – hence the name – during lunch breaks before then going on to perform small-scale local events.

But then, 'Paul had seen the Sex Pistols play live in the summer of '76,' says Bruce Foxton now, 'and that was it for us, from then on things started changing.' And The Jam, now dressed in mod threads, played their first significant gig as support to the Pistols in October 1976. Only 65 people turned up – Weller cheekily asked Matlock, 'I thought you guys were s'posed to be big, what's gone wrong?' By then Brookes had been replaced on bass by Foxton (songwriter Weller could then concentrate on lead guitar and vocals).

With Weller's father, ex-boxer John, now acting as the group's manager, The Jam concentrated on high-profile live work in and around London, playing places such as the Marquee, the 100 Club and Hammersmith's Red Cow pub, where they were auditioned –

The Clash at Islington's Screen on the Green (Ray Stevenson)

Journo Jane Suck cuddles up to the godfather of punk, Iggy Pop (Ray Stevenson)

Vivienne Westwood and Linda Ashby camp it up on stage as Anton Corbijn snaps away. This October '76 Pistols gig at Notre Dame Hall was filmed by Janet Street Porter for LWT (Ray Stevenson)

Opposite page From rags to rags (and pursued by the Raggare): the Pistols live in Sweden (Redferns)

Above The aftermath of another shattering night at the Roxy, January 1977 (Ray Stevenson)
Right Don Letts, DJ and future filmmaker, sits with Roxy Club manager Andy Czezowski outside the Neal Street venue. Czezowski, an ex-Acme Attractions accountant, had already managed The Damned by this point (Redferns)

OVERLEAF *Left* Battered and addicted but not quite unbowed: Sid Vicious on stage with the Sex Pistols in the US, 1978 (Redferns) *Right* His sneering humour survived the US tour, but he had only months to live . . . (Redferns)

The Bromley Contingent, October '76, from left to right: fifteen-year-old 'juvenile' Debbie Wilson; future singer Siouxsie; her bassist Steve Severin; S&M expert Linda Ashby; 'trendy' Sue Catwoman; friend Sharon Hayman; art student and punk Simon Barker; queen of clubs Phillip Salon; future author Berlin Bromley (Ray Stevenson)

Steve Severin and Siouxsie Sioux in 1978 as they started the mood that was post-punk (Redferns) and promptly dismissed – by EMI (the latter still unsure of where they stood with the Pistols – let alone anyone else).

In February 1977, however, The Jam were snapped up by Polydor's Chris Parry, a man determined to grab a punk, or punk-ish, band since letting McLaren's band get away. However, after being reduced to tears by the Pistols, Parry was playing it cool – he offered The Jam a paltry £6,000 advance (they accepted but the deal was so bad that a vastly improved four-year deal was renego-tiated later – discreetly, in order to save everyone's blushes).

Weller was against rock's new revolutionary mood and, although he'd dropped The Jam's Union Jack backdrops (they were then too easily associated with the National Front), he later, provocatively, claimed he intended to vote Conservative at the next election, 'Cos all this change-the-world bit is getting a bit too trendy.' He was only half-serious, but it was enough to further damn the band in the eyes of the punk prime movers. Were The Jam nostalgic mod Tories? Punk was surely a crusade or it was nothing?

The debut single by Weller's boys, 'In The City', was released on 4 June 1977 and just scraped into the UK Top 40 at No. 40. This was followed one week later by an album of the same name, pro-moted by a 42-date UK tour and several TV and radio showcases. The Jam also gained some, albeit limited, daytime airplay – their superficially retro image no doubt helping reassure Radio One's ageing DJs. It all pushed the first album to No. 20, just as their sec-ond 45 got to the very edge of the Top 10. This was the fine, yob-romancer 'All Around The World', an exciting, choppy record, laced with Who-style 'Pop Art' sound effects – and the shouted word 'Oi!' (an inadvertent trigger point, albeit one that was prob-ably influenced by the same echoed word on The Clash's 'Career Opportunities'). The incredibly relentless 'The Modern World', with a brutal 'outro' as punchy as anything recorded before or since, was followed by the more restrained, and more tuneful, 'News Of The World', a modern blues laced with guitar trills. Both made the listings, the latter getting into the all-important Top 30 (the 30 bestsellers were then always included, if only visually, in *TOTP*'s opening countdown).

Paul Weller as songwriter, and his group The Jam, had now most definitely arrived, just as things were reaching crisis point for the band that had, at least partly, inspired them just a few months before.

After the violence and hysteria over the Queen's Jubilee and 'God Save The Queen', the Sex Pistols had retreated. With UK gigs difficult and full group rehearsals virtually non-existent, the band, privately, seemed to be dying (a mood that Sid's increasing embrace of heroin only intensified). The creativity that had surrounded the group in Glen Matlock's day was long gone; only 'Holidays In The Sun' – a brutal wild rocker that borrowed its main riff from Weller's 'In The City' – and Rotten's obscene attack on abortion, 'Bodies', would be written in the year after Matlock's departure. 'The band really did cease to exist as a creative unit once Glen had gone,' Sophie Richmond said years later. 'That was it – no new songs, very few rehearsals . . .'

The irony in this downward drift was the fact that the group had just scored a massive hit (No. 2 or No. 1 in every chart that counted), as the movement they'd started was beginning to dominate the British music scene. McLaren, until now busy lining up record deals in France and the US, finally snapped into action when band members spoke of leaving, and a hasty Scandinavian tour was arranged. Thirteen gigs were played, mid the usual bans and cancellations, across Norway, Holland and Sweden – the Pistols' 'Pretty Vacant' single crashing into the Swedish Top 10 at the same time as it repeated the same feat in the UK. The Scandinavian gigs usually ended with the group being mobbed by girls or attacked by Raggare, Sweden's violent Ted-style bikers.

Roadent, a teenager with a minor criminal record who'd been 'inside' for a few months, was present on the Swedish tour. He'd drifted down to London from Coventry in the late summer of '76, where he'd met, lived with and virtually joined, The Clash – less a roadie, more an in-house philosopher-cum-security guard. But nine months of Mick Jones's then rampant ego, and manager Bernard Rhodes's penny-pinching, had driven Roadent to work with Glitterbest, where the money was better ('and you actually got it *every* week, which didn't happen at Rehearsal Rehearsals'). He still recalls the impact of the tour: 'If World War Three had started in July 1977, that would have been on page two of all the Stockholm papers 'cos the Pistols were always on page one. Not that the size of the venues reflected this, often they'd be playing in 300-seater places without even a stage – there'd just be a rope strung out where the group were.'

Someone else who was strung out was one Sid Vicious – the games he played with new pal Roadent were increasingly dangerous. 'The main enemy was boredom in the end,' Roadent admits now. 'I'm afraid that Sid got his self-harm thing from me, watching me put out cigarettes on my arm, using a knife on the same bit of arm – things he copied, basically. We also used to have a little competition – they had these tiny little chocolate racing cars in Sweden and we used to see how many we could eat before we threw up. Did the same with bits of Kentucky Fried Chicken – you don't need too much of that before you chuck up, believe me.'

Aside from Roadent's departure, The Clash's other wounds were also self-inflicted in 1977. Offered £100,000 by Maurice Oberstein's CBS, Rhodes – backed by Jones – leapt at the chance, even though Chris Parry's rival offer of £30,000 included far more generous royalties. The problems with the CBS contract were so numerous that, in Roadent's words, '[it] was later used as a classic example of the kind of contract that no group should ever sign – the group had to pay for their own tours, recordings, remixes, artwork, expenses . . .'

At the end of January 1977, The Clash's signing to CBS became public knowledge, bringing instant criticism from some quarters, especially *Sniffin' Glue*'s Mark P, a man who'd always applauded The Clash's anti-corporate stance. He condemned the group for 'selling out' and cited 27 January as 'the day that punk died'. In February, the group went into CBS's London studio to begin work on their eponymous debut album, although the recording was delayed slightly after the police had arrested Roadent and some of the band's girlfriends on suspicion of burglary. Just as the Pistols had, initially, used their live soundman in the studio, so The Clash gave their stage mixer Mickey Foote his first big break as producer. Although raw and, at times, thin, *The Clash* comes close to capturing the energy and power of the band in 1976–77. It was to be Terry Chimes's last serious studio work with the band – his apolitical stance was no longer tolerable, hence his nickname on the album cover, 'Tory Crimes'. He himself casually threw in the drumming performance of a lifetime: every track is pushed along by a snare-splitting cascade of beats. Such was the album's raw earthiness that a horrified American CBS refused to release, let alone promote, the album in the US. This refusal held even after it had cracked the UK charts on the back of the White Riot Tour.

The latter was the first full punk tour of the UK that was actually completed. It started uncertainly and ended in arrests, wrecked halls and headlines but compared to the Anarchy Tour it was a cake-walk. The Clash were supported by the Subway Sect, The Buzzcocks, The Jam and the wild girls known as The Slits – with guitar from Viv Albertine and vocals from the micro-skirted Ari Up (who was then barely 15). The adventure started at Guildford. Immediately in front of the stage that night were 100 or so 'rugger-bugger' students and football yobs, there to jeer with their large paper safety pins and bags of rotten fruit. They drifted away from the Sect's above-average set, ignored The Buzzcocks, wolf-whistled at The Slits and half-heartedly nodded through The Jam. But they all swarmed back from the bar for the headliners – the latter now wearing the piped and multi-pocketed 'urban guerrilla' styles as designed by the talented young Nottingham fashion student Alex Michon and her pal Christina Kolowska.

As Strummer walked on, he was met by a chorus of boos and beer splashes. The Guildford Civic Hall's half-dozen security staff suddenly seemed to be busy somewhere else and a violent confrontation seemed inevitable as Strummer stared down the jeers. After a 30-second pause that seemed to take forever, his manic stare managed to reduce the hecklers to near silence – into the gap he howled, 'Larn-dahn's Burning!' and the venue erupted in a mass of cheers and pogoing. Within a minute, many of the front row troublemakers were nodding along with the music they supposedly hated

– by the end of 'London's Burning' some were actually dancing to the group they'd come to attack.

Helped by an *NME* freebie EP tie-in, The Clash's rawly dynamic debut album, produced by sound mixer Micky Foote and CBS engineer Simon Humphreys, hit the Top 20. Not that, with their contract, this was to bring the band any extra money.

But it wasn't just the financial aspects of the contract that caused grief. While the group were free, artistically speaking, to record whatever they wanted, it was down to CBS how and when these recordings would be released. 'White Riot', the debut 45, was about the experience of being in the August '76 Notting Hill Carnival riot – caught between Rastas and police. As Strummer later put it: 'The police stopped and searched us for bottles and bricks and then we got stopped by Rasta looking for pound notes – but all we had was bricks and bottles.' It was about black culture having its own defence points while, 'white people go to school where they teach you how to be thick'.

To clarify the situation – several overly earnest student union groups had already tried to blacklist The Clash – Strummer spelt out the band's stance: 'People should know we're anti-racist, anti-violence . . . '

'White Riot' came out at the end of March 1977 and charted early in April as the first album began its climb into the charts. 'White Riot's mannered sound was closer to pop, or pub rock, than anything else the band were ever to issue, with a chorus like Slade on speed. Strummer's full-on vocals, the stompalong chorus and the alarm bell ending did make it stand out a little. (There was an even earlier, weaker, demo version cut at Polydor's in-house studio in November '76, where staff engineer Vic Smith had the nerve to ask Strummer the ultimate middle-aged question of the early seventies, 'Can you not sing the words more clearly?'). The reviews for the first 45 were fair; it managed to scrape into the Top 40 and there was little else to compare it with – The Damned and The Stranglers seemed to lack credibility while the other 'big punk band', the Pistols, had only put out the Chris Thomas version of 'Anarchy'. But in mid-May '77, without consulting The Clash, CBS issued another single from *The Clash* album. The new 45 was the untypical 'Remote Control'. Although its lyrics were acerbic enough in places and the ending kicked out musically over the 'Ree-pressh-shun!' backing vocals, the band had never seen it as a single. 'Remote Control's various changes, mid-tempo nature and fairly standard rock gee-tar solo all counted against it – it seemed limp compared with the band's live act. Or when played alongside the Pistols' forthcoming 'God Save The Queen' track. Or even compared with every other track on The Clash's debut set.

And besides all that, 'We just don't think it's a hit,' said Jones, with disarming honesty. And he was right – album cuts like 'Career Opportunities' or 'Janie Jones' would have made better singles but, perhaps, for CBS, there were worries about their even stronger lyrical content (concerned with, respectively, youth unemployment and office corruption).

The Clash album was still selling well, however, when the White Riot Tour ended in early May at Finsbury Park's art-deco Rainbow venue. Despite requests, the manager had refused to remove the seats – The Clash fans did it for him, ripping out dozens of seats. 'WHITE RIOT!' screamed the *Evening Standard*, in a report that was splashed over two and half pages. The most touching moment, though, had been when a fan had given Strummer a shirt – and the latter had handed over his jacket in exchange. Also present that night were Billy Idol and Tony James of Generation X – they were there with ex-Crushed Butler drummer Darryl Read, who'd just auditioned for Generation X.

Despite the continuing press furore – 'PUNK WRECK!' screamed the *Sun* – the Rainbow's manager said the venue would still continue to hold punk gigs in the future. As Bernie Rhodes is alleged to have said at the time, 'There's always someone willing to sell guns to the Indians.'

And, within months, there were many more 'Indians' to sell guns to – The Hot-Rods, the ubiquitous Nick Lowe and the darkly soulful Graham Parker and The Rumour were all finally breaking into the Top 30 in 1977.

The Clash's answer to CBS's wrong-headed heavy-handedness on their forced release of 'Remote Control' finally came with 'Complete Control' some four months later. Its similar title gave the game away, and it was also a side-swipe at Rhodes, who'd once told Strummer and Jones he 'needed complete control' of The Clash's direction. A quick listen to the acetates soon told CBS what it was about but, after a few minor murmurs, the unperturbed label agreed to the release and the group were finally allowed, in *NME*'s words, to 'bait their masters'.

From the start, 'Complete Control' sounds like a modern classic, with its strong yet scratchily brash guitar riff and four-to-the-floor beat (a beat that inadvertently anticipates both The Clash's move towards the dance floor and the NRG and House beats that were to boom so spectacularly in the mid- to late eighties).

Strummer's barking vocal piles in, telling us the 'true and dirty' tale of corporate treachery as it leads us towards the moment, just after the half-minute mark, when the whole track explodes into life. From that point on, it moves forward relentlessly, with Strummer's words being at once both naive and knowing, before finally turning on the contemporary mass market that had failed, thus far, to 'support' The Clash. The breakthrough artists of the past – Presley, The Beatles and the Stones – had been supported, why had 'Joe Public' failed the new groups now? Was it because he was 'controlled in the body' and mind?

The dub production touches – discreetly echoing the word 'rocker' just after two and a quarter minutes – showed a utilisation of that tradition that was as successful as the more obvious notion of covering the Junior Murvin's reggae gem 'Police And Thieves' for the debut album (though the latter was also chosen for its five-minute-plus length, in order to get the set over the half-hour mark). These touches were the last traces of Lee Perry's 'co-production'. He'd worked alone before original Clash producer Mickey Foote was called in to 'ground things' a little. The all-out dub versions of 'Control' that Perry mixed, 'amazingly good and amazingly deep' according to Roadent, were never issued.

But 'Complete Control' is, ultimately, a rock'n'roll record and on that level it succeeds beautifully. The beats and fills of new drummer Nick 'Topper' Headon weave in and out of Simonon's supple bass lines and Strummer's gruff tones, while Jones's chords and mini-solos shoot off all around them. The Bo Diddley-on-speed finale confirms the stature of the work.

It was released on 16 September 1977 and made the Top 30 after three weeks. Despite this success, it received virtually no daytime airplay – Radio One, Capital and the regionals were not going to have their obliging friends at CBS HQ so publicly mocked – and it dropped off the listings completely a mere seven days later. As with many other recordings of the time, Joe Public didn't get that much chance to hear the music he was unwittingly rejecting.

Elvis Costello was never quite a typical Joe Public guy, though he was still working 9 to 5 and honing his unpublished songs in the evening, when he heard The Clash's first offerings. 'I thought it [their debut LP] was terrible. I thought, if that's what music's gonna be like, I'll quit,' said Costello later, 'but I decided to listen to it, thinking if I can't get into this current stuff then maybe I should give up trying. I listened to it on headphones virtually non-stop for some 36 hours and then sat down and wrote "Watching the Detectives" all in one go.' 'Watching . . . ', a threatening near-reggae shuffle, became Costello's first Stiff Records hit six months later. Three solid rockers followed it into the charts. First out was the savage '(I Don't Want To Go To) Chelsea', with its insistent staccato rhythm section and raw guitar riff (and lyrics that jibed at 'swinging' Chelsea, the place where Knightsbridge meets reality, the place where 'they call her Natasha but she looks like Elsie . . .'). Then came the bluesy, pounding 'Pump It Up' and the anti-playlist anthem 'Radio Radio', which the BBC and Capital actually broadcast a few times before realising the joke was on them.

Costello's sweet'n'sour songs now, finally, had a market, an outlet. The former petrol-pump attendant and cosmetics computer programmer, real name Declan McManus, was now free to pursue the career he'd always wanted. The Pistols had changed the lives of Strummer and Jones – who, in turn, were changing the lives of others.

But, like The Ramones, The Clash in particular would always feel – *pace* 'Complete Control' – that their audience was never quite big enough, their impact not as massive as that made by the sixties' bands. But in that they were probably asking for the impossible; their stance was too strong, the market too controlled – and the music cottage industry was fast becoming a serious, conservative business by the late seventies. Notwithstanding that, there *was* an undoubted impact that went far beyond rock'n'roll. 'The Clash represented then, and *still* represent now, a rite of passage,' Kosmo Vinyl insists. 'It's not an empty experience, they – The Clash – thought about stuff and they looked fantastic – *and* they stood for something. Joe Strummer was a very non-judgemental person and that's rare in any human being. Many people, myself included, have lived our lives to a higher standard because of Joe. I've raised my kids differently. To those that saw it, to those that saw him, Strummer had a big effect, bigger than Jagger. Seriously. Much bigger than Jagger . . . '

By mid-October 1977, the Pistols' *Spunk* bootleg – essentially the Denmark and Gooseberry studio sessions – had caused horror at Virgin by beating the official Pistols album into the shops. *Spunk* caused a minor furore as well as being hailed as 'the real Pistols album' by the likes of *Sounds'* Chas de Whalley and *NME's* Tony Parsons. The identity of the bootlegger in question has always remained unknown, however. Goodman had only got £60 expenses for the Denmark Street recordings and might have been out for revenge but for the fact he'd stayed friendly with Glitterbest, who also had copies of the tapes. Plus there was the usual, understandable, producer's vanity. 'I'd never have allowed stuff of mine to go out like that,' Goodman said, a quarter of a century later. 'It just wasn't properly mastered, was it?'

Although Richard Branson's CV was far from perfect (he'd once been fined thousands of pounds for an import–export fiddle), his PRs always insisted that *Spunk* was not some kind of insider piracy. As bootlegs of the bootleg began to appear – soon they were turning up in the USA in numbers – the police were called in. They tracked the records down to vinyl pressing plant Lyntone, which was subsequently fined thousands of pounds, but they'd merely been duped – the search for the real bootlegger intensified. Although a crate of *Spunk* later turned up at Compendium Books – a hang-out for various Glitterbest staffers in the past – via an Israeli DJ, the search ultimately proved to be in vain.

The Pistols' official *Never Mind The Bollocks, Here's The Sex Pistols* album – a smooth if powerful Chris Thomas production – astonished many by jumping into the listings at Number 1 in November '77. It was the first time this had happened since The Beatles' 1963–67 heyday.

The Pistols' debut set had taken its title from a catchphrase Steve Jones had borrowed off the 'Hot Dog Twins', two hard-drinking East End boys who'd attended early Pistols gigs – when McLaren and Jamie Reid heard Jones tell a puzzled Soviet journalist, 'Oh, never mind the bollocks, mate,' they instantly exchanged glances. Here was the perfect outrageous – possibly illegal – title (and the band *were* indeed taken to court where, with the help of top lawyer John Mortimer, they were eventually exonerated).

Asked by McLaren to 'make the album look like a goddamn soap box', Reid responded with a shockingly bright yellow sleeve with a bright punk back and kidnap-writing titles, plus the Pistols' now official blackmail logo. All four 45s were crammed on the LP – a move which pleased older, album-oriented buyers but which appalled the young fans who had already spent their few pennies on the singles. By now the Pistols had charted with Matlock's classic 'Pretty Vacant', while Matlock himself was touring with the band he'd put together with Slik's Midge Ure: the power-pop-driven Rich Kids who attracted, for a time, many of the charts' younger consumers.

The Pistols' follow-up to 'Vacant' was 'Holidays In The Sun', which was banned on London's main station Capital because of Rotten's line comparing holiday centres with the Belsen death camp – a lyrical move which, combined with the 430 King's Rd love of swastikas, gave the wrong impression to many of those too young or too simplistic to appreciate irony. 'That was McLaren's biggest mistake, I think,' said record dealer Don Hughes years afterwards. 'I think he got 99 per cent of it right but the swastika thing was just wrong. And it got taken wrong by various football yobs and bone-heads – they weren't gonna understand talk about irony. To them it was a thumbs-up to racist thought.'

The *Evening News* had already annoyed McLaren with the head-line 'ROCK'S SWASTIKA REVOLUTION!', which linked punk to the far right National Front. McLaren instantly responded with a letter blasting the 'scummy' NF and the *News* for giving them free publicity – but, in a way, the tabloid was right to sound the alarm. Before the late seventies the far right's various motley groups had always, publicly at least, disowned the Nazi roots that had obvious-ly inspired some of them. But by the end of the decade, the latest racist organisation, the British Movement, was openly boasting of their Nazi connections while decrying the official so-called 'Hollywood version' of the Second World War.

McLaren, meanwhile, prepared an American tour in conjunc-tion with the band's new US label Warner Bros (they'd signed the Pistols for quarter of a million in the summer). Both Warners, who wanted a slow build, and McLaren, who liked the underground element, thought the band should ignore the two fledgling American punk centres of LA and NYC. Instead the Pistols opted for a Deep South tour that was to end on the other side of the country, in San Francisco. Strategically, it was a mess, criss-cross-ing badlands that had hardly heard of the Pistols, and – Rotten aside – the band left with much trepidation. For Sid, this was mainly because of the enforced absence from Nancy and the enforced absence from heroin – the tour minders, mostly 'Nam veterans, had been told to keep Vicious away from drugs at all cost. Rotten, on the other hand, was quietly convinced that his persona was about to conquer the USA. A new British Invasion . . .

Blood had flowed and flashbulbs popped when a female American fan had headbutted Sid. Petty violence was wrongly thought to be a friendly 'punk gesture' in the US, like spitting in some parts of the UK punk circuit. But while punks, art students and self-styled 'space cadets' made up much of the American audience, there were also those who really did come to maim or kill – over 300 handguns were confiscated on the door during the Pistols' US gigs.

After some early skirmishes – like whacking a violent heckler with his bass in San Antonio – Vicious's desperation finally got the better of him. For the last few gigs he appeared with the words 'Gimme A Fix' scratched on his chest, the letters spelt out in dried blood and Magic Marker ink.

'Look at that,' sneered his former friend Rotten, 'a living circus.' Despite all of Malcolm's alleged encouragement – 'that's the way a Pistol behaves, Sid' – Vicious felt more and more isolated. Cook and Jones buried themselves in beer and groupies, while the increasingly aloof Rotten-Lydon 'spent most of his time on the coach talking with the Warners' staff', according to Sophie Richmond. 'He really did. Not that I noticed that much – I was too busy looking out the window; it's quite beautiful driving across America when it's snowing and you're tucked up all warm on a coach . . .'

As the headlines proved, the Pistols were making more waves than The Ramones or Talking Heads ever had. 'When I saw *New York Times* guys there I couldn't believe it,' admits photographer Bob Gruen. 'I said, "What the hell are you guys doing here? It's just a rock band!"'

And the smacked-out shook-up Sid was definitely the star of the show now – only it wasn't much of a show any more . . .

The bad-tempered San Francisco gig of 14 January 1978 turned into the Pistols' last ever gig as a working band. Once again, Steve Jones had to cover for the band's damaged bass player. 'I was sick as a dog that night,' Jones says now, 'and things were definitely coming to a head. Rotten was doing his thing and all Sid wanted to do was get high and I was hanging out with Cookie – everyone had just gone off in all different directions. I remember when we were trying to write a song and it was when that "Belsen Was A Gas" thing was going on. And I remember thinking, "this is shit" – it was just too much, even for us, it was too much too soon . . . I just wanted to get away from it all . . .'

Rotten also tried to get them to work on his song 'Religion' – an outdated attack on religion in general, and Christianity in particular, that at first had had the subtle title 'Sod in Heaven'. Sid was enthusiastic: 'It's about God, it's a real attack!' he'd excitedly told radio presenters in San Francisco that week, when speaking of the band's 'new song'. But it was never to be performed live by the Pistols, Cook and Jones basically refusing to get involved in yet another tune that struck them as struggling to be outrageous for the sake of it.

After the final encore, a tired Rotten had sneered a last few words at the Winterland crowd, his kiss-off now almost legendary after being platformed at the end of the *Swindle* film. 'A-ha-ha! Ever get the feeling you've been cheated?'

The Pistols' American tour was now over and the Warners' minders duly left. Vicious immediately picked up a local groupie, wandered into Haight Ashbury and promptly overdosed. Road manager and fledgling sound mixer Boogie revived him long enough to bundle him onto a plane back to New York. Sid, skilfully using a blend of vodka and extra-strength valium, managed to overdose on that flight too.

As Cook, Jones and McLaren partied in Brazil with well-known Great Train Robber Ronnie Biggs, Rotten was vehemently telling reporters that he'd 'split the Sex Pistols'. Sid, meanwhile, found himself alone in the hospital of New York's La Guardia airport, snowed in by a fierce blizzard. He'd been in his favourite gang, the Sex Pistols, little more than ten months – and now he was alone again, more alone that ever in fact. All that awaited him in London was Nancy and her battered collection of dirty needles – and some movie sessions that would later be screened around the entire world.

In Rio, McLaren and Temple filmed Cook and Jones with Biggs, various hookers and a Martin Bormann lookalike (Hitler's deputy often appeared in Russ Meyer's movies – this was thus an in-joke at Meyer's expense, an in-joke that had a political sting in its tail, given Latin American governments' *penchant* for providing safe homes for Nazi war criminals). Cook and Jones wrote, and performed, the crude but pile-driving 'No One Is Innocent' with Biggs – the latter was still wanted by the UK police he'd escaped from ten years before. The song was initially called 'Cosh The Driver' in a tired attempt to excite even more outrage. (During the Great Train Robbery, the train's driver had actually been coshed and subsequently spent years as an invalid before dying young.)

Just to make sure the Rio trip would add some spice to the forthcoming, and still officially untitled, Pistols' movie, the unholy trio cut a version of 'Belsen Was a Gas'. Despite a tight sax solo and a pop video containing several girls dressed as Amazons, courtesy of The Slits, this recording remains a Pistols' low point both musically and lyrically.

Life is never that easy as an ex-anything in the music business, but for Sid Vicious, a musically mediocre clothes-horse, semi-performer and heroin dependant . . . it was just about impossible. At Sid'n'Nancy's Pindock Mews flat, the hopelessness continued – The Clash's Topper Headon became a full-time heroin addict while staying there and Sid's 'friend' John Shipcott died from a heroin dose in the lounge in August 1978. Meanwhile, Nancy threw herself back into prostitution to help make ends meet. On stage, Vicious could still summon a touch of the old threatening charisma . . . but he wasn't on stage any more. Instead, Sid sat by the phone, waiting for it to ring. But, beyond the odd reporter wanting his side of the Sex Pistols' break-up, no one ever called.

That is, until McLaren returned from Rio, with more filming plans for his proposed Sex Pistols movie. During all the interviews Sid had given that spring, he'd described McLaren as 'a lying, thieving wanker' . . . but junkies rarely continue to bite the hand that just might feed them. And, unlike anyone else in the business, McLaren was offering work for cold hard cash. His main worry was whether Sid would stay coherent long enough – or alive long enough – to finish the project. The film was now finally known as *The Great Rock'n'Roll Swindle* with the poetry and pornography of the *Who Killed Bambi?* script being sidelined – in part because its director, US 'soft-porn king' Russ Meyer, had annoyed both McLaren and Rotten before being fired. The million-dollar budget came partly from Glitterbest, partly from film financiers and partly from Warners. There was also a minimal, but key, contribution from Branson's Virgin. The director was McLaren, by default, with ex-film student Julien Temple acting as assistant and, on occasion, second unit director.

At the core of the *Swindle* storyline was McLaren – ably accompanied by his small art school pal Helen Wellington-Lloyd – the media manipulator of his age, casually explaining to the audience the lessons needed to get to the top of the rotten rock'n'roll tree, the best way, in other words, to exploit and 'insult your own useless generation'.

Meanwhile, with saving the film a priority, some last desperate attempts were also being made to save Sid from heroin and the early death that now seemed inevitable. 'I would talk to Sid for hours,' says Sophie, 'telling him what he should do and how he had to get off smack and why he should live. He'd always nod politely and listen and I really thought I was getting through to him. But, as we all know now, the minute I left the room, my words went with me . . .'

Several Glitterbest staffers now decided that mere words weren't enough. Instead they kidnapped a drowsy Nancy Spungen and whisked her off in a cab heading for Heathrow. They'd already booked her a single flight to New York and the hope was that she would only revive fully when over the Atlantic. In the few days or weeks without her, Sid could start a serious heroin cure. That, at least, was the hope.

But, as Sid lay sleeping uneasily, the last great plan that might conceivably have saved him began to unravel. With the cab still trundling slowly through central London, Nancy regained full consciousness and, after looking round, began screaming blue murder: 'Rape! Kidnap! RAPE! I'm being KIDNAPPED!'

The worried cabbie began to make noises about coercion and Nancy was dropped off near South Molton Street. The Glitterbest boys pursued her for a few hundred yards then gave up. Within the hour she was back beside the still slumbering Sid, the latter unaware that he'd slept through his last chance for a longer life. A month later the couple were in New York where, in Nancy's words, 'the smack will be much cheaper and much better'.

On the other side of the US, in sunny California where the Pistols had split, a new scene was stirring. Culturally, its roots were more tangled than punk in New York – the West Coast looked to England as much as it did the rival East Coast and, politically, it was more conservative (albeit under a veneer of political correctness). In fact, many West Coast punks took punk symbolism literally and drifted towards fascism – something that records like Black Flag's 'White Minority' did little to help, whatever their makers' intention (the Black Flag name was an anarchist magazine reference while 'White Minority' was actually an ironic quarter of their 1980 *Jealous Again* EP). Even the name of the biggest West Coast band of the late seventies was ambiguous in that sense – the Dead Kennedys' tag was much more of an offence to liberals and leftists than it was to the American right, who saw it as an amusing affront to the political dynasty they hated most. This wasn't the Kennedys' intention and it again showed the lesson of London: sheer outrage might be OK in a bedsit, rehearsal studio or tiny club but once unleashed in the outside world it was another game completely. Like a face-covering tattoo commissioned when drunk, it all looked different in the cold light of morning.

The DKs consisted of guitarist East Bay Ray aka Ray Valium, bassist Klaus Flouride and drummer Ted, while the front man for their July '78 live debut was Jello Biafra, who'd just returned from a trip to Britain. There he'd witnessed first hand the various convulsions of London punk, and he'd also seen and heard enough to know that his high-pitched voice was no longer a drawback for a performing artist – with punk, the rules were flexible or non-existent. Anything this serious, Biafra also decided, had to have a dark sense of humour. Appropriately enough, the Kennedys' live set featured such sensitive numbers as 'Too Drunk to F—' while their first single was the sarcastic, high-energy anthem 'California *Uber Alles*', a frantic, stuttering attack on CA's liberal Governor Jerry Brown (whom, the DKs imagined, would soon use death camps to enforce his love of 'suede denim' and macrobiotic food). As they realised the growing strength of the right, the DKs, especially Biafra, began to take more of a stand with singles such as 'Nazi Punks F— Off!' and 'Holiday in Cambodia'. Such sentiments made airplay – and record company relations – even more difficult. Their first few recordings were therefore issued on their own Alternative Tentacles label and their comparative success with this venture was to encourage dozens, and then thousands, of others to follow suit. By then the DKs themselves were signed to a Miles Copeland label and Biafra was taking some time out for stunts such as running for mayor of San Francisco in 1979 (part of his manifesto was the compulsory wearing of clown suits by businessmen – despite some hysterical press attacks he managed to come fourth out of ten).

California's other big punk band of the time, The Dickies, were seen as the West Coast's answer to The Ramones, with their lighter sense of fun and their frantic three-minute covers of rock and pop standards (their 1978 debut had been a breathless version of Black Sabbath's 'Paranoid' coupled with the sarcastic 'I'm OK, You're OK'). They'd formed in '77 with tunes that were as fast, as bizarre and as short as those played by 'da brudders' from Queens NYC. They rapidly signed to A&M Records, who were desperately looking for something to prove that they hadn't been burnt too badly by the Pistols. And The Dickies were happy doing 100 mph covers as typified by the relentless mindless rush of 'Nights in White Satin'. The UK single sleeve for 'Nights in White Satin', which of course was issued in white vinyl, featured the group dressed in white top-hat and tails splendour. It looked somewhat out of place, partly because it was a bastardised version of the US sleeve, wherein the group had decided to take the song title (semi) seriously. The original US cover featured the group in white KKK outfits, complete with a burning cross. A classic example of sick American punk humour – you'll laugh, you'll cry, you'll hurl . . .

The West Coast scene these two groups inadvertently spawned was though, ultimately, more positive than negative. The 1978–81 recordings made by them, and others, soon gelled into a collective message to America's youth, and it mattered little whether you lived in New York or New Brighton or New Orleans: their message was that of the pissed-off street kid, 'Just let me do my thing – or else.' Consequently, the Kennedys' debut album *Fresh Fruit For Rotting Vegetables* pretty much lived at the top end of the independent charts for the best part of a year, while causing the national chart a fair amount of grief too.

But, outside of the tiny CBGB's set, these were still very early days for US punk; to break beyond cult status – and the cities of New York, LA and 'Frisco – would take a lot longer in such a vast, business-minded country. No one was to become more aware of this than The Ramones.

Eighteen months after the 'brudders' debut LP, the Sex Pistols were still outselling The Ramones in their own country by almost five to one. This was despite the New Yorkers' own fairly healthy sales in the UK, with the chart single 'Sheena Is A Punk Rocker' –

something of a novelty hit despite its catchy verses and definite chorus – and lesser successes such as 'Swallow My Pride' and 'Don't Come Close'.

The implosion of the Pistols after their US tour, and Sid's increasingly publicised problems with drugs and violence, undoutedbly damaged punk in the USA, in the short term at least. If the Sex Pistols, kings of punk, were dead, why should the press give space to a corpse, and a threatening one at that? The Ramones, with their leather gang image, came off worse, with gigs and TV shows postponed or, in a few cases, cancelled.

After several comparative duds came the cheap but fun Ramones film vehicle *Rock'N'Roll High School*, a movie for which the boys were paid a mere $5,000 but which inadvertently led them to legendary producer Phil Spector. The 1979 album with Spector, *End Of The Century*, seemed a good idea. Although previous albums like *Rocket To Russia* and the softer *Road To Ruin* had received good reviews, neither had cracked the US Top 40 and a change of direction seemed necessary. But tumultuous studio sessions with Spector cost over $200,000 as the warped genius of pop production drove the boys to distraction by spending an entire day on the album's opening chord. Later, he'd listen to playbacks of the same track over and over, for five or six hours at a time, and at earthshattering volume (no wonder his engineer, Larry Levine, had a heart attack). Eventually an argument with The Ramones led to Spector pulling a gun on them. Later they were punished by being locked in the studio for hours on end.

The final album, a flawed masterpiece, attracted some good notices. Its cover of the Phil Spector–Ronnettes' 1964 smash 'Baby I Love You' became The Ramones' second, and last, UK Top 30 entry in February 1980 (even though the backing track was not, it later transpired, played by The Ramones but was knocked out by Spector's usual session men).

Despite high-energy one-offs that knocked pranks ('Somebody Put Something In My Drink') and the new president-elect Reagan ('Bonzo Goes To Bitburg'), The Ramones were not to trouble the singles chart again. Instead, they were kept afloat by a slow but steady stream of concert ticket and album sales – mainly to the students the band had initially despised.

GUNTER GROVE –
Under Heavy Manners

After the Pistols' implosion in early '78, Johnny Rotten began to put together a new group. After a brief Jamaican 'A&R holiday' sponsored by Richard Branson, who was keen to hang onto Virgin's most (in)famous singer, Branson himself went on the trip, along with Rotten friends Don Letts and the black Pistols' photographer Dennis Morris. The latter two would be deeply, if unofficially, involved in Rotten's new group. The official members of the new group were old pal Keith Levene, finally finding a home for his brilliant if deranged guitar arrangements, and bass ace Jah Wobble, who'd been practising with a four-string since his mate Ronnie Britton had acquired one for him in '77. They were joined, after a messy series of auditions, by ex-Furies drummer Jim Walker, a Canadian who'd studied jazz in Boston.

These were the men in Johnny Rotten's new band, Public Image Limited – except that McLaren in 1978 was legally claiming the name Rotten as well as the name Sex Pistols (the latter claim had some justification – McLaren had indeed come up with the Pistols' name, a monicker that Rotten himself had always disliked).

Being forced to use his original name gave John Lydon the aura of a man reborn, a man rediscovering his roots. By now he was pretty much regarded as a hip saint by the music press, and a lovable rogue by a slightly more cynical national press. It was a transformation that had begun as early as the late summer of '77, when he'd been granted a two-hour radio special with Capital's Tommy Vance. Lydon had used the opportunity to denounce mindless violence – and to play a wide variety of music (everything from Doctor Alimantado reggae 45s to olde worlde ballads by the then unknown Keith Chegwin). The next week was marked by a succession of day-time DJs remarking on 'what a nice guy' Lydon seemed to be. As 1977 turned into '78, Sid Vicious slipped further into heroin addiction – and it was a slide that took place in public. McLaren, meanwhile, was willingly allowing himself to be portrayed as the master swindler – a portrayal that was never wholly acurate – all of which made 'Honest John' Lydon seem a model of integrity, especially after the Pistols' split had distanced him from the industry's *bête noir*, McLaren.

Lydon rapidly used up this goodwill, but it did help get PiL off the ground – the name was shortened to initials by Public Image photographer, and ideas man, Dennis Morris, who'd first snapped Lydon during the SPOTS Pistols tour. By the time PiL started to put together the tracks that would become their first album, punk in Britain had started to stagnate a little. The *1–2–3–4!* three-chord thrash had become as clichéd as the teenybopper love song or the 'Progressive' 20-minute guitar solo (as had punk's safety pins and spiky hair uniform). Many UK punk groups were trying, during 1978–79, to be more hardcore, more consciously 'working class' than thou – which led some down the route taken by neo-fascists Screwdriver and the less politically active 4-Skins. The new name for this prole punk was Oi and, although it promoted some bands of talent such as The Exploited, the hardcore tended to the right and, in many cases, the racist far right (extremes that many felt the new sub-genre's chief champion, *Sounds'* irrepressible, and somewhat irresponsible, Garry Bushell, should have done more to challenge).

There were, however, still some innovative noises bubbling through – Siouxsie and The Banshees had grown from a clever gimmick into a fully fledged band with original ideas all their own. Songs had daringly different tempos and arrangements – the space and low bass of dub was often combined with art-rock guitars and Siouxsie's unique vocals (cold and impersonal, yet somehow passionate as well).

They had seemed certain to be signed to a major label in 1977, but the group's past Nazi imagery and stark new sound was still held against them and the few offers they did receive, such as Decca's £8,000 advance with eight per cent royalty, were felt to be beneath a group who were among the 100 Club originals.

There was even a 'Sign The Banshees' graffiti campaign, coordinated by Nils Stevenson. His brother Ray had offered to issue their records himself – 'I had a kind of label, and distribution,' Ray said 25 years later, 'and The Banshees had so many fans by then, even among music journalists. It was pretty obvious they would get plenty of good reviews and sell thousands of records. They'd have made more money in the long term and they'd have kept more control over their work. But, after the Pistols and The Clash went to EMI and A&M and CBS, Nils wanted to take them to a major, I guess. Plus I think he had a touch of sibling rivalry when it came to myself, as Dave Woods later told me – every time I made a suggestion Nils tended to end up doing the exact opposite!'

On Valentine's Day 1978, The Banshees triumphantly returned to the 100 Club for a gig which was briefly interrupted by former Welsh punk Steve Strange – then a member, alongside a reluctant Chrissie Hynde, of the short-lived Moors Murderers – who leapt onstage and shouted, 'Free Myra Hindley! Free Hindley Free!', a reference to Britain's most well-known, and most hated, child-killer. Mister Strange was given short shrift by Siouxsie – 'Castrate Myra Hindley – and f— the Moors Murderers!' she snarled, as she pushed the future Blitz king offstage.

The Banshees' set was notable for being the first time a new song was played: the bright, dancey 'Hong Kong Garden'. The latter was dedicated to a local Chinese take-away whose staff, according to Siouxsie, 'put up with a lot of racist abuse, and drunken stupidity, from the Saturday night beer boy crowd'. It was unlike any other number they ever did, but Dave Goodman's demo of it was enough to persuade Polydor A&R Alan White that he should try and sell

The Banshees to his bosses. Once word got out that Polydor might be interested, Radar Records suddenly started talking about making an offer and a small bidding war began. 'Our deal was good, but a lot of bands at that time did get really shit deals,' Nils said later. 'They did that just to get product out and I wasn't bothered – I just knew I had something really hot and I could hold out and it would be fine. Also, I think record companies were scared of Siouxsie and The Banshees, much more scared of them than, say, The Lurkers or Sham 69. The Banshees really put the shits up them for some reason. I guess Siouxsie was intimidating and I was a bit scary, we were kind of crazy at the time.'

By the summer of '78, the group had, finally, been signed to Polydor. 'Hong Kong Garden' charted in August, soaring into the Top 10 the next month as their intense debut album, *The Scream*, was mixed down. The latter was far more reflective of their artier, more sparse approach, though it did also contain their best single-that-never-was, 'Love in a Void'. The latter was a fast, romping switchback ride of a record – the favourite encore of every punk with McKay's strident guitar, Severin's pumping bass and Siouxsie's slammed out lyrics about the 'dumbness' of loving 'in a void'.

'It was supposed to be a democracy,' says Ray Stevenson, 'because every time I photographed them they'd say, "Don't just focus on Siouxsie, don't just emphasise her, we're a band, y'know, a democracy." But, of course, they weren't really. They were called Siouxsie *and* The Banshees, they could just as easily called themselves The Banshees, couldn't they? If it was really a democracy, that is.'

New guitarist John McKay – he'd joined in '77 – and drummer Kenny Morris certainly didn't consider it a democracy and, halfway through their first serious Polydor tour, the disenchanted duo disappeared into the night. As with Eno and Roxy Music before – or Morrissey and The Smiths afterwards – it is now impossible to tell whether they could have continued as a working unit. And, if so, whether they could have gone on making quality music of some originality.

'It was very much me, Siouxsie and Severin that made all the decisions,' Nils admitted later. 'That's why Mc Kay and Morris got pissed off and f—ed off. We'd literally put all the money from our advance into that tour, including their money as well. We'd all agreed, 'cos we'd earn a bigger percentage from the box office and all that, so we booked the whole tour, all the deposits and every-thing were down to us. If anyone sued us, we were f—ed. We had no insurance and they f—ed themselves really. I've never under-stood it. I still don't get it. We tried to placate them but . . . '

Siouxsie and Co. managed to get through the tour with a little help from their friends and continued to issue imaginative albums such as *Ju Ju* and *Kiss In The Dreamhouse*, with singles to match – the magical 'The Staircase (Mystery)', the swirling 'Playground Twist', the icy, John Heartfield-inspired *'Mittageisen* (Metal Postcard)', the bouncily, sarcastic 'Happy House' and the furious 'Spellbound' – but their thunder was, to some extent, stolen by the very movements that they themselves had accidentally started: the New Romantics and Goths. As one of the very first punk bands to develop a really new sound, The Banshees faced the problem of all trailblazers: you were the first and now you've been around a bit you're not so new . . . so what, and who, is next?

PiL's own 1978 hit-and-miss debut album *First Edition* contained the almost catchy chimes of the first eponymous PiL 45, a zesty rocker that was more eerie than punky – a Top 10 hit despite Lydon blowing out Mickie Most's *Revolver* TV show over stage fright. *First Edition* also had rambling yet exciting 'Anna-Lisa', plus two versions of the Pistols' last desperate song, the clumsy anti-clerical rant 'Religion' – one sung in total poetry style acapella by a singer who was beginning to take himself a bit too seriously. It was an interesting album, though its eclectic quality and strange humour attracted the ire of the Oi boys, but it was the last album the orig-inal line-up would issue.

In January '79, following the badly organised, and subsequently violent, live shows at Finsbury Park's Rainbow, Jim Walker walked out. 'We'd been promised an equal stake – 25 per cent each for me, Rotten, Wobble and Levene. That's what the press were told, that's what we were all told. But when it actually comes down to the deal, Rotten's lawyer tells us it's actually gonna be 52 per cent to Rotten and the rest of us will just have to divide what's left. The other two moaned but wouldn't do anything about this rip-off. I did something – once the album and those first few gigs were finished, I walked straight out. The atmosphere had changed anyway. Once the money arrived we were merely Lydon's lackeys, there was very little respect. His Gunter Grove place was very dark, very depressing – this messy little oasis of speed, heroin and hate just off the King's Road.'

Despite Lydon garnering nearly £100,000 in Public Image advances from Virgin, Warners USA and Japan's Toshiba EMI, Walker claimed then, as now, to have received no PiL performing royalties.

The 1979 PiL album *Metal Box* was made without Walker – only Wobble's bass-playing gives it the necessary continuity, as session drummer followed session drummer followed auditioning drummer (one of the latter was a 19-year-old Martin Atkins, later to become a Public Image stalwart). The first 60,000 *Metal Box* copies in the US and UK were issued on three 12-inch slabs of vinyl encased in a real metal box – a specially commissioned film can, an idea of Dennis Morris's that didn't save him from being 'expelled' from the PiL inner circle a few weeks later (at the request, Morris maintains, of the talented but insecure Levene). The album itself remains a brave, at times innovative, effort – the definitive Public Image release for most critics. The Wobble-inspired 'Socialist', a rumbling wordless piece, was only eclipsed by the flickering 'Poptones', with its original 'looped' riffs and Rotten's high, unreal singing. It was all a little disturbing but, then, so were the words, the story of a true-life kidnap case (the victim later helped police trace her attackers by remembering the tape they played in their car). The 'Radio Four' cut was also a little unsettling, with its lyricless synths and slow hypnotic beat.

Aside from *Metal Box*, the last PiL release to make waves was a single written for Lydon's dying mother, 'Death Disco's most memorable features are probably his high, almost pleading vocals that sing of seeing it – death, presumably – in 'your' eyes. Lydon later said his mother had laughed upon hearing it. Tragic, funny and threatening – perhaps the perfect summing up of early PiL (a near-legend, built on two interesting albums, many awful ones and a New York riot sparked by a huge video screen that hid PiL from view).

'Death Disco' is an exciting messy jam of a record; Jah Wobble's deep, deep bass keeps the rhythm going, although Keith Levene's guitar cork-screwing off into a take on Tchaikovsky's *Swan Lake* adds a little left-field gimmickry.

Helped by TV appearances on *Juke Box Jury* – where Lydon insulted the host before storming off – and *Top of the Pops*, a show the Pistols had never 'played' and which The Clash had always sworn to avoid – 'Death Disco' made it into the Top 20 (one of the most bizarre, and interesting, recordings to make it thus far).

Another group tarred – or anointed – with the 'bizarre' label were the Manchester-based Joy Division, formerly Warsaw, whose controversial name had been borrowed from Ka Tzetnik's harrowing book of the Nazi camps, *The House of Dolls*, the book from which Curtis quoted the spoken insert used in the JD song 'No Love Lost'. Manchester at that time was a depressing backdrop of a city; the factories had begun closing down and the future seemed as grey as the endless Edwardian terrace houses on the ground – or the equally colourless tower block 'terraces in the sky'. To infrequent visitor Dave Goodman, much of the area looked, in 1976 and '77, like a 'bloody great bombsite . . . Coronation Street via East Germany or something . . . '. Hard drugs – or the fascistic far right – began to look like an increasingly appealing option to a small but vociferous minority of the up-and-coming generation.

The newly christened Joy Division had made their live debut on 28 January 1978 at Manchester's Pips disco, the band now comprising bassist Peter Hook, drummer Steve Morris, singer Ian Curtis and guitarist Bernard Sumner. Although the group's members were both puzzled and angered by the mounting speculation over their name change, they themselves refused to be drawn into the argument. This decision, however – although justified in the group's eyes, given that they felt their lyrics to be anti-fascist – did little to appease their detractors, or, conversely, did little to distance them from the right-wing radical elements that began infiltrating their shows.

In May 1978, Joy Division began recording material for a proposed debut album, which was done in collaboration with RCA's Richard Searling and John Anderson. Anderson's decision to add synthesisers to the finished mix did not go down well with the group, however, and, as no one could agree on the remix, the material was shelved indefinitely and thus became a ready source for bootleggers. The material would 'officially' resurface years later as the *Warsaw* album. By this time, the group was also unhappy with their manager's failure to procure sufficient bookings, and he was replaced by Rob Gretton, whom Sumner had first began making overtures towards when the group had performed at Rafters in the Stiff Records Test/Chiswick Challenge.

Tony Wilson had also been present that night and it was as a result of Curtis's constant haranguing of Wilson over the latter's failure to invite Joy Division onto TV that the running order was rearranged, with Joy Division going on last and stealing the show. It would be five months before Joy Division finally made an appearance on Wilson's TV show *Granada Reports* on 20 September, when they performed the hauntingly brilliant 'Shadowplay', by which time the presenter had become fascinated by the group, swiftly signing them to his new Factory Records label. The original Factory contract with Joy Division was written by Wilson and signed in his own blood – he knew enough about Joy Division by then to realise what kind of commitment was needed. This signing ceremony took place before several bemused pensioners and a couple of darts players in a down-at-heel Salford pub.[33]

On 18 October 1978, Joy Division headed into Rochdale's Cargo Studios with producer Martin Hannett, where they recorded two songs, 'Digital' and 'Glass', for a Factory compilation EP which sold out within two months of being released. In 1979 Curtis was on the cover of *NME*, but the year would prove bittersweet, however, for he was also officially diagnosed as epileptic.

Epilepsy is a disorder of the central nervous system which results in periodic losses of consciousness and can often lead to brain damage. Although Curtis was placed on medication, his condition would become an ever-present concern for the group – Curtis would occasionally fall victim to fits brought on by in-house strobe lighting (although, conversely, his condition would inspire Curtis to write 'She's Lost Control').

On Valentine's Day, 14 February 1979, Joy Division received their first radio play on John Peel's Radio One show, having recorded the session the previous month. Peel was at his most influential during the years' 1976–79, although both he and his co-producer John Walters had rejected the chance of doing a Pistols live-in-the-studio session, they swiftly made up for their caution, and from spring '77 onwards they championed new music across the board, their show reaching levels of eclecticism that have never been matched.

The resultant post-Peel publicity led to Joy Division securing a prestigious support slot with The Cure at the Marquee on 4 March. The following month saw the group head into Stockport's Strawberry Studios with Hannett in order to record their debut album, *Unknown Pleasures*. Peter Saville, who had designed the poster for the group's first gig at Wilson's new music venue The Factory – and had since become a Factory director – was brought

---

33 Wilson had become the most important man on Manchester's music scene by then – a combination of 'promoter' John Curd and 'artist' Malcolm McLaren, his Factory label the records to buy, his Factory nightclub – later to morph into the legendary Hacienda – the place to be. And it was Wilson who, in 2005, inadvertently gave one definition of post-Punk sounds, 'Punk, and the Pistols, were great because they came along and said "F— off!" to all that blandness, but then, and I'm really quoting Bernard Sumner here, someone had to come along and say, "I'm f—ed", to basically express more complex emotions.'

in to design the album's cover, a printout taken from the *Cambridge Encyclopaedia of Astronomy* of 100 consecutive pulses produced by the CP1919 Pulsar, known to astrologers as the 'dying star logo'. The album was released the following month and received good reviews in the music press. Demand was so high that Factory was unable to keep up with orders and had to call in help from EMI.

In July the group returned to the studio with Hannett but, of all the tracks recorded, only 'Transmission' was released as a single, which, although it received equally positive reviews, failed to chart. That same month saw the group back on TV when Wilson invited them to perform on Granada's *What's On* (an arts programme with similar format to that of *So It Goes*), and in September the group appeared on TV again, this time performing 'She's Lost Control' and 'Transmission' on BBC 2's *Something Else*, a music and topical magazine programme made by, and aimed at, the nation's youth (although promoting JD's music – then alternately droney and thrashy – was probably not what the BBC's bosses had originally had in mind).

October and November was a busy period for Joy Division. The group embarked on a 24-date UK tour supporting The Buzzcocks – the latter now chart regulars after the success of soaring pop punk anthems like 'Ever Fallen In Love (With Someone You Shouldn't Have Fallen In Love With)' and 'What Do I Get?' – popular records of real distinction. These had been cut without Howard Devoto, who by now had started Magazine. Magazine's fine first single – the spirallingly stark but pacy 'Shot By Both Sides' – reached the edge of the UK Top 40 in March 1978, as the music press lavished praise and space on Devoto.[34] The single's title was seen – mistakenly – as being Devoto staking out a space between the new punks and the old Prog rock farts.

Joy Division recorded their second Peel session on 26 November. It was aired on 10 December and included the group's most famous

34 But Magazine were different anyway. Sales of albums like *Real Life*, *Secondhand Daylight*, *Play* and 1981's *Magic Murder And The Weather* were enough to get them 24 weeks on the listings. After 1981, though, Magazine were not to trouble the bestseller lists – or the music press front pages – again.

work 'Love Will Tear Us Apart', which would be voted the all-time No. 1 in an *NME* readers' poll years later. In January 1980, the group embarked on a European tour, taking in Holland, Germany and Belgium, where Curtis renewed his acquaintanceship with a Belgian girl called Annik Honore, whom he had first met back in November.

In March, the group and Hannett went into London's Britannia Row studios to record the group's second album, *Closer*, which would go on to reach No. 6 in the UK album chart, and earned enthusiastic reviews for both group and producer, as well as leading to discussions with Warner Brothers, and the prospect of their first American tour in May.

During the first week of April, the group played four shows over three consecutive days, which naturally took its toll on the group, especially Curtis who suffered an epileptic fit during one of the performances. On 7 April, Curtis, possibly in a bout of depression over his ailing marriage, took an overdose which was later perceived to have been a cry for help, rather than a genuine suicide attempt. The vocalist survived, but UK dates scheduled for the rest of April and early May had to be cancelled. Although the singer was feeling well enough to shoot the video for 'Love Will Tear Us Apart', he and the rest of the group refused to mime to a backing track, so the frustrated editing team were left to match up video footage of the group's live performance to the music. The song itself is haunting – a performance we cannot ignore in light of subsequent events. But the track also has musical strong points beyond those expressed in its singer's dark, bassy voice. The stop-start drums, shuffling rather than exploding, the accented guitar pushing through the piece's moody, bluesy chords, the sadly bright keyboards – all add to a single of breathtaking clarity and sadness. And it's there in the vocal: Curtis knew he was going to take his own life soon and, on hearing this, we know he knew.

On 2 May, Joy Division played what would be their last show at Birmingham University, a live recording of which later featured on the second side of the *Still* double album, and contains the only live recording of the song 'Ceremony'. Sixteen days later, and just two days before the group were due to depart for America, 23-year-old Curtis committed suicide by hanging himself at his Macclesfield home. The pressure of the forthcoming tour may have been a factor in this, as was his epilepsy and his fascination with both psychiatric disturbance *and* the Holocaust. (It's a little known fact that, even now, many Holocaust scholars commit or attempt suicide – depressed beyond measure by the subject they're studying.) His wife Deborah later said, on the subject of Ian Curtis's books, 'He seemed to spend all his time talking about, or reading about, human suffering.' This was modern urban blues at its darkest.

Another typically atypical cutting edge Manchester band was The Fall. Like Joy Division they were fans of sixties American art rock – The Stooges, the Velvets, The Doors. And, like JD, The Fall's genesis began in June 1976. On 4 June '76 the already dour 19-year-old Mark E. Smith – then working for an import–export firm – came across the Pistols during their first sojourn to Manchester. They had a strong impact on Smith, as on virtually everyone else present, and he spent much of the rest of that year trying to gather enough like-minded musicians to form a group. Eventually he found Una Baines, Karl Burns, Tony Friel and Martin Bramah.

Mark E. Smith toyed with the idea of calling this new band The Outsiders before settling upon The Fall, another name taken from the novels of Albert Camus. The Fall made their somewhat inauspicious live debut in May 1977, in a restaurant basement on Manchester's King Street where the ceiling was so low that the group's taller members were forced to adopt a near-crouching position. Their second live outing took place on 3 June at Manchester's Squat Club, at an event billed as a 'Stuff the Jubilee Festival'. By June 1978, by which time the group had developed their own unique sound – centred around repetitive riffs over which Smith delivered his lyrics in a style more usually used by a reggae toaster – they were being championed by John Peel, who was quick to invite the group into the studio to record what would be the first of several Peel sessions.

The Fall's philosophy was summed up in the lyric, 'Northern white crap that talks back'.

In August 1978 they released their debut EP *Bingo Masters Breakout*, a disc which had Baines's cheap Snoopy keyboard stabs, Burns's dour percussion, Friel's menacing bass and Bramah's spiky guitar supporting the in-yer-face Smith. Smith had based the whole set on a joyless night he'd spent with his parents in a local bingo hall. But his interpretation of the night's gloomy industrial 'fun' garnered enough positive reviews and sales to ensure that Smith's no-nonsense group of 'druggy, scruffy poets' would have a future. Although Smith had wandered around parties in 1973–74 with a swastika armband on – purely as a sick joke, he said – The Fall had played quite a few Rock against Racism benefits before their first recoding was issued. But, like The Clash before them, The Fall too were to become more than a little disillusioned with RAR's bureau-cracy and its determination to treat gigs purely as recruiting oppor-tunities. Smith's trip – and this applied to all the original line-up since they all contributed words initially – was at one and the same time more basic and more exotic. To put it simply, they were direc-tly telling the story of the growth of narcotics in the north – Smith swiftly graduating from pot to mushrooms to acid to speed (just as hundreds of thousands of others were starting the same journey in Leeds, Sheffield, Manchester, etc.). In fact The Fall's *Live at the Witch Trials* album was all about speed and the euphoric, and ulti-mately shattering, effect it could have. By then The Fall and Mark E. Smith were firmly established. The least brand-oriented man imaginable had successfully launched a musical brand.

One brand name most people would have run from was the tag 'Maoist'. But extreme politics were something the Gang of Four enjoyed promoting. They were post-Clash agitprop punk-funk rockers, men who'd been to art school – mostly – and who'd stud-ied Marxism too (the original 'Gang of Four' were the architects behind China's bloody cultural revolution of the sixties and briefly took over the country after Mao's death in September '76). Music's

Gang of Four were heavily influenced by Bertholt Brecht's 'Theatre of the Absurd' and consisted of vocalist Jon King, bassist Dave Allen, guitarist Andy Gill and drummer Hugo Burnham. While, post-'77, punk veterans like Steve and Mick Jones were happiest digging out classic rock riffs, vintage guitars and 'warm' valve amplifiers, the Four preferred abusing 'cold' transistor amps as they pursued robotic beats and angular performances that gave no special prominence to any particular instrument: 'This is democratic music.' Their debut EP, *Damaged Goods*, appeared in 1978 to rave write-ups over the total 'originality' of tracks such as 'Love Like Anthrax', with its disparate stereo rants.[35]

Within 18 months, Allen's tight punk-funk bass lines, and Gill's experimental guitar had confounded their new-found media friends by moving in a more conventional direction. By the time of the 1980s rocking *Solid Gold* set, Burnham admitted later, the band had become 'The Clash without the cowboy suits' – and, like Strummer's boys, they were a successful touring act in the one country they'd been persistently putting down, the USA.

One group that had a lot in common with the Gang of Four were The Mekons. Like the Four, The Mekons were northerners; like the Four, The Mekons were diametrically opposed to both the fading rock mainstream and the new thrash-punk clichés; and, like the Four, they had studied at Leeds University under T.J. Clark (the Fine Art head who'd once been a member of Britain's own branch of the Situationist International – an organisation that was rapidly eclipsed, and then replaced, by more informal pranksters such as King Mob).[36] The Mekons' reputation was built on their manifesto – no names, no individual identities, no photos, no jams – and two very different singles, both of them issued in 1978 on the tiny Edinburgh label Fast Product. The first was the unbelievably loose 'Never Been In A Riot' – a song many fans thought was full of

35 The critics seem to have forgotten that Generation X had used the same two-channel trick on their surprisingly powerful cover of John Lennon's 'Gimme Some Truth', part of a Peel session broadcast in 1977.
36 By contrast with the leftist university, urban Leeds was then the one big northern stronghold of the openly Nazi British Movement.

macho regret, the reverse of its 'nervous' intention according to the many M-people (Kevin Lycette, Tom Greenhalgh, Jon Langford, Andrew Corrigan, Mark White and Mary). The second was the sadly swaggering 'Where Were You?', a bitter song of unrequited love, shot through with plaintive, hurt sarcasm – wondering if the no-show girl would 'be my wife? Would you love me?' – which subsequently turns threatening. Musically, it built up and up, like a helter skelter in reverse. Love anger – or the need for 'non-economic' contact – was also at the heart of another Mekons' track from '78, the ridiculously short 'Letter's in the Post'. This is a number that lasts less than 35 seconds, though its Brillo-pad guitars and messy, direct vocals leap out at the unsuspecting listener – this is not music you can easily ignore. Peel sessions and Virgin albums rapidly followed – The Mekon manifesto, perhaps understandably, splintering all the while – but the world's and, some said, the band's attention had wandered elsewhere by the time Branson's label stepped in . . .

Wire was another 'non-punk' punk band that often played short tracks, i.e. under one minute. They had faint but real connections to both the intelligent end of Glam and to Prog rock – and to the Pistols. Wire had first come together in the late, hot summer of '76, a quintet of Fine Art students who though intrigued by, and perhaps secretly inspired by, the Pistols, Clash and Buzzcocks were determined to go their own way, to create songs that were arranged and 'conducted' *differently*. Original guitarist George Gill decided the group's 50- to 90-second compositions were a bit *too* strange, however, and after five months of gruelling rehearsals he left to join the more straightforward Bears. This move left vocalist-guitarist Colin Newman, guitarist Bruce Gilbert, bassist Graham Lewis and ex-Art Attack drummer Robert Gotobed to carry on practising songs that had little length 'and no solos'.

Newman had once been given lifts – from Watford to London – by Brian Eno, a friend of one of his art lecturers; Gotobed had been a percussionist for the punky pub rockers known as The Snakes; guitarist Gilbert was 31 in '77, so all of them were practically pre-historic in the climate of the time. But they looked young and Wire's urgent energetics did win over an initially indifferent Roxy crowd, supporting the besuited, three-chorded Jam – a contrast if ever there was one.

In June, Wire made their vinyl debut on EMI Harvest's *Live At The Roxy* collection – alongside The Buzzcocks, The Adverts, X-Ray Spex and Eater – a move that brought them into contact with Nick Mobbs, the EMI A&R who'd helped sign Pink Floyd and, a decade later, the Sex Pistols. Mobbs and his A&R junior, and would-be producer, Mike Thorne, both became enamoured of Wire's unusual song structures and promised them an album deal, virtually on the spot. Wire's *Pink Flag* LP was subsequently issued by Harvest in November '77. It featured a staggering 21 tracks – including '12XU' and 'Mannequin' – numbers that covered less than 35 minutes of vinyl, all encased in a daringly simple cover (a grainy colour pink of a lonely flagpole bearing a pink, er, flag). The sheer other-worldliness, and 'architectural quality', of the material led to some great reviews – 'is this the album of the year?' – and a January '78 Peel session, which then garnered further, positive press. This Radio One session featured a new take of '106 Beats That', a song about the band's search for the perfect 100-syllable lyric – pub rock it wasn't.

The left-field 45 'I Am The Fly' – the band were the flies 'in the ointment' – was followed, months later, by 'Outdoor Miner', a single recorded and mixed in a sixties' West Coast style, again demonstrating the group's artistic breadth. Their carefully put together 'anti-rockist' songs, once incredibly short, were now hitting the five- and six-minute mark. All of which encouraged Thorne to think he might just have the next Pink Floyd under his production belt – albeit in an incarnation that preferred grey, and black, to pink. On the second album, *Chairs Missing*, Thorne brought all his connections into play, encouraging the band to make their guitars sound like keyboards and vice versa as he plugged the group into the latest American FX pedals. And, all in all, Thorne *did* manage – for the first time in his studio career – to create a noise that was both glossy and glassy, the perfect epitaph for a gleaming, shallow new age. But it didn't crack the Top 30 and it was fast becoming obvious that the band never would. Their third collection, *154*, showed Wire at their most esoteric – and they compounded this by 'promoting' it in a very unconventional way; by playing songs from *other* albums in London's arty Jeannette Cochran Theatre. EMI began to lose interest and by June 1980 various members were cutting solo works. It was, in hindsight, the end of an era . . .

The sounds made by PiL, The Banshees, The Fall, Gang of Four, Joy Division and the 'Punk synth boys' – the edgy early Human League, Gary Numan's slightly more rockist Tubeway Army, Belgium's tuneful Telex, *et al.* – began to be given a new tag: Post-Punk. This was fine until people began to take it seriously as an exact musical genre – for, as Simon Reynolds, its finest chronicler, later said, it was far too wide for this, being more of an attitude than a quantifiable series of chords, keys or tempos.

CHELSEA HOTEL –
She's Somethin' Else

There was once a low-heel bohemian glamour attached to Bank Street, back in the days when John Lennon and Yoko Ono spent a few months living in a two-room apartment there. But that was at the start of the seventies; by the end of that decade it was more bum than bohemian, more heroin than heroic.

Smack was, of course, a huge part of the seventies' NYC music scene: The New York Dolls, Johnny Thunders's Heartbreakers, Richard Hell's various groups, The Ramones and even, to a slightly lesser extent, many of the Blondie band were saturated with it.

In the first half of February 1979, No. 63 Bank Street, NYC, was home to one Michelle Robinson, a young actress who knew all about smack, a young actress with no Oscars and even fewer movies to her name.

Between the odd bit of theatrical work, Ms Robinson divided her time between go-go dancing and escort work. And hard drugs. On the morning of 2 February 1979, in her small flat, in an even smaller bedroom – the most distinguishing feature of which was an unwashed swastika t-shirt in the corner – lay Michelle's new boyfriend, sleeping peacefully.

Not a pimp or a dealer this time, but a fully fledged bona fide rock star, a household name, a real live rock'n'roll somebody – a someone who might just lift young Michelle out of this low-life existence . . . only it had been about six months since he'd had a real career. But there was hope – in just over one month's time he would have a Top 3 UK single that would clock up sales of over 390,000 in Britain alone, plus hundreds of thousands more world-wide, bigger than any hit his old group had ever had. He would, in the intervening weeks, also have the front page of many US, and virtually all the British, newspapers.

The only problem that cold February morning was that he wasn't actually sleeping. He was dead . . .

By the age of 21, Sid Vicious was a washed-up, heroin-dependent, booze-soaked mess. He'd come to New York City at the suggestion of his long-term girlfriend Nancy Spungen, partly because the heroin was cheaper in NYC, partly because they'd harboured vague dreams about relaunching 'Sid Vicious: Punk Legend' in the city of dreams.

Only in New York City in 1978, British punk didn't count for much yet, largely because it was still waiting to be discovered by all but an elite few (a select throng who mainly, of course, preferred their own, local heroes).

But Sid Vicious was still a t-shirt-selling icon, a one-time member of the Sex Pistols – to many, *the* Sex Pistol – the most explosive rock band ever. He had been, in short, the face of British punk, a crazed obnoxious Action Man made flesh during the Pistols' US tour.

After that US tour and the Pistols' implosion – and after months of smacked-out idling – the first solo *Swindle* filming with Sid took place. It was in Paris during March 1978, with Nancy along for the ride, a spaced-out Liz Taylor to his menacing, mumbling Richard Burton. Sid was to become the 'new' front man for the non-existent Sex Pistols. In a style best described as piecemeal, Sid semi-rewrote the words of 'My Way', a song that might have been written just for him. He recorded it only after refusing to do Edith Piaf's ancient musical calling card 'Je Ne Regrette Rien' ('I Have No Regrets').

The following week, still in Paris, Sid shot a promo for the song wearing some kind of thrown-together evening dress – white tux, black jeans plus girl's garter. In the promo Sid delivered his best performance ever. It was a bit fake, several takes hacked together in the editing suite and the finish – pulling a gun and shooting his mother – was fake too. It was a shot of an actress playing Sid's mother Anne Beverley, filmed several weeks later in a London cinema.

But the promo had impact, from Sid's swaggering intro and his hyped-up moves right through to the bloody, guns-blazing finale. Serge Gainsbourg was among the spectators as it finally wrapped and it became the talk of Paris's café society, as did Sid's filmed stroll through the Jewish quarter (complete with the swastika t-shirt). The cameraman that day, a Vietnam War veteran, described the Sid assignment as 'being as difficult as dealing with the war in 'Nam'.

Just to prove the point, Vicious returned to the crew's hotel and physically attacked McLaren after one argument too many. Malcolm was now finally willing to sign the paper saying he no longer managed Sid Vicious. Back in London, Sid threw himself into his last *Swindle* scenes: one day was spent in bed with Nancy, another on a wild motorbike ride through suburbia, another was spent peddling tacky Pistols souvenirs on a mock Jubilee merchandise stall. It was a strange film and it affected everyone differently. While new bods like Eddie 'Tenpole' Tudor seemed to be enjoying themselves, others were suffering. 'I didn't have a good time doing the acting in the *Swindle*,' Steve Jones admitted recently. 'That's when I actually started to f— up, that's when I first got stuck into smack. So it was all a bit of a f—ing nightmare and it just f—ing hit me that, that whirlwind, for however long it was. That's when I dove in, doing smack. I was just doing the movie for something to do really. I never read a script. You just show up and they say, "You've got to say that" and that's what I did – I mean it shows. I don't think I ever read the script of *Who Killed Bambi?*'.

As filming on the *Swindle* drew to a close, Jones and Cook began to talk about starting another band. Meanwhile, a plan was brewing in the mind of Nancy. If she managed Sid, looked after him in a way that only she could, her boy would be a major star, not in horrible little England but in the big Big Apple, across the pond in the USA. In New York, New York . . . where she had connections, where the heroin was purer – and cheaper . . .

Sid was undecided. Of course, they would need money to travel anywhere, and everything McLaren had given him had quickly found its way into a heated spoon and just as quickly into their collective arms. They'd been to talk to John Lydon a few times, but their midnight visits began to annoy his Gunter Grove pals. On the last occasion, one of Lydon's pals pulled an axe and dealt out a few nasty bruises with the blunt end. Sid fell heavily against a boot-scraper, the pain of the bruise adding to the humiliation of the cuts. Now there was nothing and no one for him in London, and so Sid agreed to the New York trip.

Sid and Nancy pitched up at the Chelsea Hotel, a low-class hotel on the wrong side of The Bowery, where drug-addicted yestermen dreamed of brighter days. Getting paying gigs for Vicious was nothing like the breeze Nancy had imagined it would be. In fact, she was reduced to offering sexual favours and taking whatever money was given. It didn't amount to much, but then nor did the gigs. Dwindling audiences watched Sid – a punk 'superstar' some of them were barely aware of – go through the motions over a number of evenings at Max's Kansas City, now just an after-hours drinking club for the Lou Reed and Iggy Pop generation.

By early October '78, the sham was all but played out and even Max's wasn't returning Nancy's frantic phone calls. But back home in 'horrible' England, Sid's electrifying version of 'My Way' had been a hit single and the money was rolling in, to the tune of $25,000, which was duly wired out by McLaren after his usual commission had reduced it to $18,750.

Suddenly, the black cloud had a silver lining. But no one comes into that kind of money at the Chelsea Hotel without making all kinds of interesting new friends – and that meant personal friendly visits from the dealers who'd laughed in Sid's face just days before. The Sid and Nancy bank was the bottom cupboard drawer of their tiny hotel room, a room that was often open all hours.

On the night of 12 October, they decided on some kind of get-together – 'Sid and Nancy At Home, Room 100, Bring A Bottle'. A few turned up, mainly hangers-on looking for a free drink. There were a few fellow junkies too, of course, and the odd C-list New York rocker.

Just before 10 p.m. they were visited by a drugs dealer named Rockets Redglare, a B-movie actor later to be famous for cameos in films like *National Lampoon's Animal House*. Rockets sold them a mixture of drugs, but nothing that the buyers considered too heavy. Heroin at that time was in short supply in Manhattan – much to Nancy's annoyed amazement – and the little that did exist was stamped on (diluted) until it didn't really matter.

Sid quickly decided on a cocktail of what Rockets was offering. He mixed it up, injected and then swallowed a large vodka. He passed out cold while Nancy held court with their scrapbooks and stories of better days – the Dolls, the Pistols, headlines, TV reporters, the distant good old days of the year before last . . .

By midnight, all the guests had left the room and Nancy prepared to join her man in oblivion, but as she entered the bathroom, Rockets Redglare – who'd left ten minutes before – allegedly returned with the only heroin he could find. Noticing Sid flat out and grey on the bed, Redglare decided to help himself to a bit more of the couple's cash. Nancy saw the attempted theft and flew at him, nails flailing – and copped a Bowie knife in her lower abdomen. She slumped to the floor immediately. With no one standing in his way, Redglare took everything but pocket change and left behind what he believed to be two corpses.

Sid woke from his semi-coma just after 8 a.m. The bed was soaked with blood. He followed the trail to the bathroom sink and, underneath it, found his world – his lover, manager and his fellow heroin traveller, Nancy Spungen. He ran to the phone and called an ambulance, but given the nature of the Chelsea back then, most 911 calls were answered directly by the police. With his girlfriend pronounced dead just before 9 a.m., Simon John Beverley was arrested and charged with first degree murder. He was just 21 years old. If the charge stuck, he was looking at seven years to life in New

York's tough Riker's Island Prison, and he genuinely had no idea if he was guilty or not.

Over the next few days, Sid got more news coverage than any Sex Pistol had ever seen before. It turned out that the drug cocktail he had taken should have killed him – it would have killed a horse. This was no doubt Redglare's intention. But Sid's tolerance was so high from years of abuse that he'd somehow escaped death again.

But this time it was no fun. This time his partner in crime was missing, gone forever, while he was going through drug hell. Within 48 hours of the news breaking, McLaren and Anne Beverley were in New York. The former talked of police fit-ups and tried to raise bail (after secretly bribing someone to wash Sid's knife, just in case), while Ms Beverley sold her story to the *New York Post* . . . although she did also visit her son every day on Riker's Island, where a name like Sid Vicious will always attract trouble (especially if you were built like Simon Beverley – he was promptly beaten and gang-raped: 'You think you're vicious, do you . . . punk?').

However, $25,000 bail was agreed and by mid-November Sid was walking free into the Manhattan nightlife, still unsure, still talking of 'being a dirty dog . . . I still miss Nancy so much, I dream I'm with her in bed and I wake up all hot and she's not there. She was everything to me . . . '

There was talk of suicide pacts, but he still went through the motions and got a new girlfriend, more arm-candy than lover, in the shape of Michelle Robinson, and, because some junkies never learn, he went straight back to shooting smack.

There was talk of gigs, but a suicide attempt and constant talk of 'joining' his Nancy pretty much put an end to any attempted cash-ins (any large-scale gig would have been stopped anyway, as a bail violation). Westwood seemed determined to exploit the scenario (she printed 'ironic' t-shirts of Sid's face in a wreath with the legend 'She's Dead, I'm Alive, I'm Yours' printed underneath).

Sid, meanwhile, attended a Blondie gig with Johnny Thunders, Richard Hell and Jerry Nolan, signed in every day at the local NYPD station and seemed to be getting himself together for what promised to be the media's trial of the year, perhaps the trial of the century. And then, one night, in a stupid fit of jealousy, Sid smashed a bottle into the face of Patti Smith's brother Todd – for the heinous crime of glancing at ex-stripper Michelle while they were in Hurrah's nightclub. This single act of foolishness was good enough to destroy Sid's parole so Christmas, New Year's Day and the whole of January were spent back in the noisy hell of Riker's Island.

McLaren was shrewd enough to know that any chance of getting Sid bail money from Virgin would be dependent on a new product so, with a trial set to start on 1 February 1979, he hired the services of the highly rated F. Lee Bailey (who, years later, would be part of the team that proved O.J. Simpson 'innocent').

Then Talcy Malcy – the nickname McLaren's pale skin had earned him one decade and a dozen lifetimes before – cooked up the plan for a secret Sid solo album. McLaren would fly back to New York with ex-Pistols Jones and Cook on 3 February to book a recording studio and then wait for Sid to come out on bail. The album's producer was to be the original Pistols' soundman Dave Goodman, the old firm reunited. With the plan in place, Richard Branson eventually agreed to put up $25,000 in bail money.

Meanwhile, in the Bowery on 31 January, seated at the bar of CBGB's, Rockets Redglare casually admitted to several fellow drinkers that it was actually he who'd robbed and stabbed Nancy Spungen – and produced a handful of her blood-stained dollars to prove it. But it would be years before his stoned statement made it out of Hell's Kitchen, by which time the principals were all either bankrupt or dead.

Lee Bailey informed Virgin on the morning of 1 February 1979 that the hotel room was covered in dozens of different fingerprints. The police case was thus full of holes and it was really possible that Sid might be completely innocent. And, even if he wasn't, there was still a good chance he'd walk. The champagne corks popped and the Glitterbest staff talked of a massive hit album, which all this publicity would surely drive to Number 1.

However, two things were to go massively wrong in the first 24 hours of February 1979. The first was that ex-Sex Pistols' front man John 'Rotten' Lydon chose this day, of all days, to inform his ex-manager that he was intending to sue him for unpaid royalties and for the band's name. Since they apparently had a lot to gain, people openly wondered why Cook and Jones took so long to join in Lydon's legal action against McLaren.

Apart from the weekly wages they were still getting, Nils Stevenson gave a lightweight reason, which may well actually have been the true one: 'There's a point that's always missed about Malcolm, and that is that he's really fun,' he said, years after their last meeting. 'When we've had a couple of bob, we've been down to health farms together and we've been to Paris, and we were working in LA together for a couple of years. You're just constantly doing the maddest things with him and that's why you stick around with him, because he's a great laugh, really funny and up for anything. Paul and Steve appreciated that, at the time they loved it.'

But there was a second, far more serious problem for McLaren and that was also connected with Sid. It happened in New York and it made everything worse. For F. Lee Bailey had shot through all the witness statements, cross-examined two of New York's finest with all the power of a hungry pit bull and had made a seriously strong plea bargain, all in less than half a day. His case was unanswerable: there was some circumstantial evidence against Vicious but even that was undercut, both by his affection for Nancy, by the lack of witnesses and by the sheer number of different fingerprints in the room where the death occurred.

By late afternoon, a dazed Sid Vicious was once again free. In the company of his mother Anne, Michelle Robinson, photographer Eileen Polk and assorted members of the rock'n'roll wild boys' club – Heartbreaker Jerry Nolan, Eliot Kidd and Peter Kodak – Sid headed for 63 Bank Street and a celebratory meal. With lots of booze and, of course, lots of heroin. The latter was, in this instance, scored by an associate on behalf of Anne Beverley, who didn't want her son breaking his parole again. After an hour searching the smack-starved streets, the associate finally bought the Chinese rocks in the Bowery.

He was asked who they were for and when he replied, 'Sid – you know, Sid Vicious,' he was given a different bag to the original one he'd been offered. It would be more than ten years later that Peter Kodak finally saw a magazine picture of Rockets Redglare and recognised him as 'the guy who sold the heroin for Sid'.

Back in Bank Street, the party was in full swing, with talk of the solo album dominating and, for the first time in months, Sid appeared to be in a more positive mood. He could beat this murder rap and still be a rock'n'roll star.

Sex'n'drugs'n'rock'n'roll' – and murder. It made Hendrix and the others look like Boy Scouts . . . Sid took a hit of heroin around 10 p.m., a 'good hit,' his mother later said 'because he was almost glowing, like with an aura'. In fact the hit began to look too good, so, fearing an overdose, Old Ma Vicious put the rest of the smack into her purse. The heroin Sid died from that night was 98 per cent pure, incredibly strong for a city in the grip of a drug drought, where 22 per cent pure was considered strong – information that once again leaves the finger of suspicion pointing in the direction of Rockets Redglare.

No one is 100 per cent sure if the first hit kicked in again or if Sid stole more of the drug from his sleeping mother's purse, but by the next morning he was locked into the deepest sleep of all, stone dead at 21, as the unwitting Ms Robinson happily made coffee for her rock star boyfriend . . .

On 7 February 1979, as Sid Vicious was cremated in New York (his ashes were later scattered by his mother around Heathrow Airport), a legal hearing began at the Chancery Court re: 'J. Lydon and others v. Glitterbest/Matrixbest'. McLaren seemed to have a chance of postponing the inevitable but one week later Cook and Jones, seemingly furious at the alleged misuse of monies owed to

them, changed sides. Twenty-four hours later, Justice Browne Wilkinson delivered his verdict, taking control of the Sex Pistols away from Malcolm and placing it into the hands of court receivers Spicer & Pegler. McLaren immediately flew to Paris in search of a record contract for an album of standards, while Virgin prepared to issue Sid's cover of 'Something Else'. Under the Sex Pistols' banner, its pre-orders were enough to put it in the Top 10, prompting Branson to rush release *The Great Rock'n'Roll Swindle* soundtrack album.[37]

A week later, 'Somethin' Else' entered the UK chart on its way to no. 3. The same month saw McLaren back in London, sending letters of complaint to the receivers about the latest *Swindle* film edit: 'a pathetic scrapbook butchered about by people with no direction. Stop it now!'

The next day, he had carried out his threat and walked off the film. The *Swindle* still contained the inevitable side-swipes at Rotten, some of them amusing, as well as much swearing and humping from Jones. There was also a wealth of newsreel footage that became poignant when it featured those who'd recently retired or died. In McLaren's own words it was, 'a very English, very "Carry On" of a film, basically the life and times of the Sex Pistols'.

After much discussion, the final credits of the *Swindle* would curiously name Julien Temple as sole 'writer and director'.

The *Swindle* and the Pistols were still considered very wild in 1980. The BBC's *Film '80* review show ended its series run a week early so it wouldn't have to review a film that was seen as being 'potentially difficult'. But its strange, arguably inaccurate, credits made it the perfect start to the eighties – a decade of increased public squalor and private wealth, an era of increasing apolitical apathy, a decade of deceit and hype . . .

---

37 This isn't your normal soundtrack album. Some of the film's music isn't present in any form, while several of the tracks on the double album are not heard in the film. Still, it was a chance for fans to finally hear how strong Goodman's productions were – both in '76 and '78 – on Pistol covers such as 'Substitute', 'Stepping Stone' and 'No Lip'.

NYC: -
London Calling

As the Official Receiver began to close in, McLaren fled to Paris. Work on some soft-core porn films gave him cash but, ironically, very little satisfaction. He wrote a screenplay – it wasn't quite as explicit as the unfilmed *Who Killed Bambi?* plot but, while the project didn't even reach the point of screen tests, McLaren did get several songs out of it, at least one of which ('Sexy Eiffel Tower') would surface within the year with his shortlived BowWowWow project.

As Julien Temple was taking the *Swindle* around California – where press praise included the comment 'The *Citizen Kane* of Rock Movies!' – a film with a much lower profile, and a much smaller budget, struggled to get any kind of release.

In its depiction of a small American town where dark deeds are hidden out of sight, Dennis Hopper's *Out of the Blue*, shot in 1979, was a great influence on both David Lynch's *Blue Velvet* feature film and on his successful American TV series *Twin Peaks* (and later the movie *Twin Peaks: Fire Walk With Me*). But Hopper's film is more realistic than Lynch's and its impact all the greater – its young hero happened to be both female and a punk (or punkette in the slang of the time). It had to be shot in Canada after being refused US funding and, when completed, it was actually banned from the American cinema circuit for a time. ('There are no families like this in America,' said one distribution spokesman in a statement worthy of Brezhnev's Soviet Union.) Rare footage of 1979

North American punk gigs, the young Linda Manz's believable Ceebee and Hopper's spot-on portrayal of a corrupt slob are some of the film's many strong points. It is a disturbing, uneven tragedy, excitingly shot, which also introduced Neil Young's 'punk' ballad '(Hey Hey) My My' to the world. This song mentions Rotten by name – the latter, now Lydon once again, consequently played it for months despite describing it as being 'total shite'.

The cultures of Hollywood, post-sixties America and late seventies Britain made a volatile mix.

The summer of 1978 had seen the first serious Clash ventures into the world of multiculturalism. They returned to their punky reggae essays with '(White Man In) Hammersmith Palais', a track that blended rock and a reggae sensibility more effectively than 'Police and Thieves' or 'Complete Control'.

Lyrically – as with 'White Riot' and 1976's Notting Hill riots – it concerned another night when Strummer had found himself out of place, this time with Don Letts while visiting the Palais, a famous west London venue. A night of black music had falsely led Strummer to believe he might be among fellow dub revolutionaries – but the DJ played 'Four Tops all night' and the place was awash with robberies and threats (hence the song's 'Mister, please just leave me alone' refrain).

The second Clash album, also delivered in 1978, was the uneven *Give 'Em Enough Rope* – cruelly parodied as 'Give 'Em Enough Dope (and watch 'em turn into the Rolling Stones)' by *Sounds*' Oi supporter Garry Bushell. It was produced by American Blue Oyster Cult producer Sandy Pearlman, even though The Clash's boot-boy roadie Robin Crocker punched Pearlman to the ground when he first approached their post-gig dressing room.

London Calling was their next set, delivered in late 1979, with Margaret Thatcher's Tories in power and the Mod revival – sparked by the *Quadrophenia* film – being briefly even bigger than the new

Two-Tone scene. In order to stand out in this strange new world, it was felt that *London Calling* would have to go some – and it did. *Rolling Stone*'s Album of the Eighties tag was OTT for *London Calling* but not wide of the mark – the set, produced by ageing rocker Guy Stevens, *was* one of the finest of the age. The powerful title track, its howls and feedback guitar balanced by a smoother bass sound and Headon's click track drumming, had poignant lyrics that looked back at the 100 Club and forward to the coming crisis: the song's protagonist lives by the river (but the ice caps are melting as the Thames rises . . .).

Alongside it were gems such as the pounding covers of Bobby Fuller's outlaw anthem 'I Fought The Law' and Vince Taylor's atmospheric 'Brand New Cadillac'. The double album was rounded off with the poignant yet defiant Spanish Civil War song 'Spanish Bombs' and Paul Simonon's blue-eyed reggae take on Jamaica's *The Harder They Come* gangster film, a moody number entitled 'Guns of Brixton'. The follow-up was a triple set known as *Sandinista!*[38] *Sandinista!* blended genres from punk to rock to reggae to blues – a mixture that looked forward to the new world music. The finest track was probably Mick Jones's plaintive but powerful 'Should I Stay Or Should I Go?' with its contrasting, Spanish, verses.

In 1981 The Clash, now almost pariahs in a UK obsessed with Two-Tone, Oi and New Romantics, returned to New York. Their previous Big Apple shows such as the Palladium in 1980 had seen the celebs queuing in the aisles. Everyone was there, from ex-rock revolutionary Wayne Kramer and former model Bianca Jagger to Blondie singer Deborah Harry and film industry stars such as actor Robert de Niro and director Martin Scorsese.

For their May '81 shows in Manhattan, The Clash faced a variety of problems. Drummer Topper Headon had become a proper hedonist and had barely got through the band's recent European tour (mainly because of his fearsome hard drugs intake, which had

---

38 The Sandinistas were the guerrillas who had just overthrown the 44-year-long Somoza dictatorship in Nicaragua.

led to Horseferry Road Magistrates Court and a suspended 12-month prison sentence). Although *Sandinista!* had sold over half a million copies, Epic had refused to back a 60-date American tour once they realized the band's new managerial situation – the acerbic Bernard Rhodes was back. The band's internal relationships were consequently strained and, to cap it all, there was a series of Fire Department clampdowns going on in the Big Apple's various rock venues. But Bond's Casino, at the Times Square end of Broadway, was available and they were also up for The Clash's latest idea – to tie in with their recent 'Magnificent Seven' single, the band wanted to play Bond's seven nights in a row.

Tickets for the seven shows sold out within hours and, on Thursday 27 May, the first show went ahead. To the surprise of all the British hacks present, the band went down a storm. His leg pumping up and down as per usual, Strummer piled through the epic 'London Calling' and the touching 'Spanish Bombs' – its heart-breaking guitar delivered by a tremulous Mick Jones – with its choruses about the nation's tragic civil war. Vince Taylor's classic rocker 'Brand New Cadillac' and the Bo Diddley-esque shuffle that is 'Hateful' also got the live post-Westway treatment, as did the hip-hop 'This Is Radio Clash', with its astonishing beat crash arrangement. The crowd were ecstatic, but when the band finally came backstage it was to find NY firemen running everywhere. It took a lot of pleas and counterpleas from the Casino's bosses, but The Clash residency was eventually allowed to continue at a much reduced capacity. The Clash played a staggering 16 nights and several matinees to fulfil their obligations to some 28,000 fans, which didn't stop a minor fan riot, covered by all seven New York TV channels.

For the second part of the residency, the band had top NYC graffiti artist Futura 2000 doing backdrops and raps onstage, while in the audience were the likes of de Niro and Martin Scorsese. The latter was so impressed with the boys he offered them some small parts in the moive he was then shooting, the de Niro–Jerry Lewis vehicle *King of Comedy*. Poet Allen Ginsberg and representatives of El Salvador's FDR rebels – who The Clash allowed to set up stalls within the venue – were among those attending. These nights were fast becoming a celebration in themselves, with Times Square, the heart of Manhattan, being bought to a virtual standstill every night for two weeks ('We took this town,' Mick Jones was to tell an *NME* reporter years later. 'We took Broadway, de Niro and his kids were here and the city stopped. The Clash were in town . . . ')

The Bond's residency ended with a sweat-drenched band taking several deafening encores as photographers and TV crews jostled for space at the side. The Clash *had* conquered New York City, the first British band to really accomplish the feat since the heyday of The Who almost a decade before.

The Clash were to open for The Who the very next year – in front of nearly 70,000 in the legendary Shea Stadium – but it was a last high point. By then Mick Jones was on his way out. The lyrics became more politically meaningful after Jones left the group but The Clash were no longer The Clash. 'He said he should check with his manager before writing songs,' said the more militant Strummer, a few weeks after Jones's departure. 'So I said, "Go write songs with your manager then! Piss off!" Leave.'

It was a decision that later had both men close to tears . . .

SELFRIDGES – Escaping the 20th Century

Our music wasn't arty. We were doing f—ing art. Punk was art. It was all art. (Colin Newman, *Wire*, 1999)

They [the media] take one little word out of what you say, blow it up, disregard all the rest and make you out to be what you actually are not. (Malcolm X, civil rights activist, 1964)

Punk is musical rubbish, it'll soon be forgotten, its apologists will consequently look ridiculous.
(Derek Jewell, *Sunday Times*, 1976)

Philosophers have often tried to understand the world, the point, however, is to change it. (Karl Marx, *Das Kapital*, 1850)

It was just f—in' great music, wasn't it? F—in' great. 'Cos what the hell's happened since? Really? Honestly? Just that *Pop Idol* junk. F— all, in other words. And those Pistols records were amazing – and as for The Clash, they were blinding. They were like The Who, they were a real class act. (Ray Winstone, 2006)

So many deaths and suicides – the casualty rate was high, as if such bright spirits needed to burn themselves out. Was it all worthwhile? Was it worth the sacrifice of talent, and the shocking sums of money poured down our throats into our protesting stomachs? Was it worth the waste of time? Oh yes! We had fun! Everything was positive, not waste at all. Compared to today's world-weary pessimism, it was a time of innocence and hope. Anything could happen, and, for some of us it did.

(Dan Farson, *Soho in the Fifties*)

Beauty will be convulsive or will cease to be.

(André Breton, *The Surrealist Manifesto, 1924*)

In 1996, the Sex Pistols got together for their Filthy Lucre world tour, a reunion that was allegedly going to net them over $2 million. 'But it's also happening,' claimed Lydon, 'because we didn't get a chance to say goodbye before.'

For some, it was the ultimate sell-out. Siouxsie and The Banshees split, blaming the news from the Pistols' camp for their final destruction. Anne Beverley couldn't face seeing the band reunite without her son Sid Vicious and, after carefully cutting up all her remaining credit cards, she locked her front door and took a fatal overdose. Sadly, it was the death she both wanted and thought she deserved. An overdose over rock'n'roll, the music she mistakenly believed had given her years of addiction some kind of meaning.

After a barely adequate start, and with a few of the usual bans and angry press conferences, the Pistols successfully played Finsbury Park before a crowd of 40,000. It was their best reunion gig so far, although it was still damned with faint praise in the *NME*, who labelled their performance 'Desperately fine cabaret'. Nils Stevenson spoke passionately afterwards though. 'The Pistols were playing in tiny clubs in '76 and then they disappeared. We never saw this, what should happen to a band that get big, we never saw it at the time. And now we have, and now we can get on with the rest of our lives . . . '

The band found themselves in London facing a last-minute vacancy for Wednesday 17 July (a show in Belfast had been cancelled, perhaps not unexpectedly). At the eleventh hour, the Pistols were offered the Shepherd's Bush Empire, an elegant three-tier hall of crumbling grandeur that had once been used by the BBC.

As the evening drew near, and with other music biz gigs and

parties cancelled or postponed for various trivial reasons, the Empire tickets slowly but surely became hot property. Maybe, in this, the tour's smallest venue, the Pistols might just possibly give a flash of their past brilliance? It seemed an impossible hope.

Alan McGee, manager of Oasis, the biggest UK band since the Pistols, attended, fully expecting it to be 'part comedy, part irrelevancy'. McGee even took along Noel Gallagher of Oasis and Chris McCormack of 3 Colours Red so he'd have someone to talk to when the gig got boring. But with Cook, Jones and Matlock playing better than ever, and with Lydon provoked by hecklers into a blistering performance, the Pistols were, in McGee's own words, 'simply stunning. They blew everybody away. Both Noel and Chris said, separately, "They are better than us." Granted they [the Pistols] are no longer a social phenomenon, and that they had to wait almost 20 years to play their music, and be judged on that, shows you just how much of a social phenomenon they actually were . . . I came along cynical and it was one of the best gigs I've ever seen. If you don't get it now, you would never have got it then. Britpop? More like Shitpop. You're welcome to your mediocrity. This band are our alternative royal family. God Save The Sex Pistols.'

To prove his sincerity, McGee amazed the UK music industry by spending over £4,000 repeating his words in a full-page advert in *NME*.

Six years on, the most important band since The Beatles played their third London gig in 30 years, during Her Majesty the Queen's Golden Jubilee in 2002, at the Crystal Palace sports arena. EMI–Virgin re-released 'God Save The Queen' and it was played on Radio Two during the day. There was an accompanying promo video, mostly vintage footage of the band miming at the Marquee in 1977, as used in the *Swindle*, which even got an airing on *Top of the Pops*. Everyone, it seemed, wanted to play at cultural revolution now that it was safe to do so.

With his credibility at an all-time high, Lydon went on the desert island *I'm A Celebrity! Get Me Out of Here!* TV show in 2004, blowing said credibility, probably forever. Afterwards, like other modern 'celebs' who were once 'music-related', such as Victoria 'Posh Spice' Adams, Lydon found he could always score space in the tabloids, but no majors wanted to put out his solo material. His erratic musical career, patchy after 1979, barely alive after 1981, ground to a complete halt.

Two years on from 2004, and 30 from the 100 Club – 2006. The Buzzcocks, Steve Diggle, Glen Matlock, Cocksparrer, Gary Lammin, Stiff Little Fingers, Sham 69 and The Stranglers continue to tour successfully. America's punky grunge bands of the 1990s are now either long-gone legends – like Nirvana, the band started by the late Kurt Cobain – or million-sellers, who can still sell out stadiums across the world (Green Day, Rancid, Bad Religion, etc.). Punk's liberation of female rockers has empowered everyone from punk-lite superstars like Avril Lavigne, and the spikier Pink, to up-and-coming acts like The Mescalitas and the young British singer Tat De Maria, focal point of the Tat trio.

At Selfridges, the store he used to play pranks on, Malcolm McLaren returns to lecture to sell-out crowds about his greatest adventure: the method and madness of 430 King's Road, the group and the genre it launched on an unsuspecting world. Before the lecture he chats to a few friends about *Fast Food Nation*, the classic anti-corporate tome that he's just helped turn into a major movie (co-produced with Jeremy Thomas, the original producer of the *Swindle*). It is, in the broadest sense, a green film – a parallel, perhaps, to Dave Goodman's work promoting solar-powered PA systems at Glastonbury and producing tracks on Mat Sargent's excellent *Sex'n'Drugs'n'HIV* CDs as part of an AIDS and drug charity project.[39]

---

39 *Sex'n'Drugs'n'HIV* features many of punk's more talented musicians – from the late Wally Nightingale to The Damned's Captain Sensible to Chelsea's Nick Austin.

After the Selfridges lecture, McLaren speaks of how he arrived at the band's name, of the TV personalities his shop supplied with rubber and leatherwear, of how big a star Sid could really have been, of how random so much of it actually was. 'You never really write the manifestos until afterwards. It's just easier that way.'

All around, the 30th anniversary of punk gathers pace in the music, and sometimes the national, press. BBC TV's *Breakfast Show* tells us it's 30 years since the Pistols first played the 100 Club; *NME* informs us it's 30 years since The Ramones debut album was released; 30 years since The Clash, The Damned and The Buzzcocks first played; 30 years since the Punk Festival, since the EMI signing, since the Bill Grundy 'Swear-In'.

And still, somehow, the controversy continues. Milder now, of course, but the critics on some of the British nationals still cannot stomach what even much of the US music biz has come to accept – partly through America's Rock'n' Roll Hall of Fame and its belated invitation to The Ramones, The Clash and, finally, the Pistols. The latter, among the first to be faced with the new, higher table-rate for guests, were looking at a bill for thousands and refused to attend (Lydon, with his usual good grace, compares the Hall of Fame with a 'piss stain').

John Robb's book *Punk Rock: An Oral History* becomes a catalyst for attacks. It is given mixed reviews as Craig Brown, Nick Coleman, Tim Willis and other broadsheet heavyweights weigh in to comment about how punk is beneath comment. In Brown's view, Glam rock and (gulp) even Bubblegum have left behind records to 'which people can still listen' but the same 'cannot be said of punk'. It's not often that a serious writer will extol the virtues of, say, the 1910 Fruitgum Company's 'Simon Says' at the expense of 'London Calling' or 'American Idiot' or 'Pretty Vacant' – or even falsely claim, as Brown does, that the mid-seventies' charts were 'full of fast, energetic groups' before punk (aside from the Feelgoods and, on occasion, Lizzy, exactly who is he talking about?).

But then punk can still cause an irrational reaction among some of the calmest reporters. Even Willis, while conceding the professionalism of The Clash and the 'brilliance' of the Pistols' debut album, goes on to describe punk as 'a non-event' laced with 'stupidity' and 'ignorance'. He ends his piece by displaying more than a little ignorance himself, loudly celebrating Jah Wobble's retirement from music, way back in the eighties. Which is fine, except that Wobble didn't actually give up music back then and, in fact, continues to make innovative post-dub albums (his 2006 US tour helped recent CDs rack up sales in excess of 25,000 – more than respectable in the age of the illegal download and CD-R bootleg).

In fashion, the latest high black Balenciaga boots, a snip at £700, are pure designer punk, as is much of the post-seventies work of Galliano, John-Paul Gaultier, Franco Moschino, Alexander McQueen, Rifat Ozbek, etc. The strappy, zippy, over-pocketed trousers that every other clothes store has been selling for almost a decade are also unquestionably punk.

Meanwhile, television pundits vote the Pistols' appearance on *So It Goes* ITV's Best Music Debut Ever, as the main Pistols' websites rack up millions of hits and several net polls now say the band's influence equals that of The Beatles.

Away from the web, at the British Library, staff preparing a display marking 50 years of album charts, vote *Never Mind The Bollocks* the Best No. 1 Album of All Time. 'Punk was a phenomenon,' says the Library's Head of Exhibitions Alan Sternerberg. 'We thought we were going to change the world.' Good, bad, brilliant, awful, irrevelant, earth-shattering – there still is no consensus on punk, even now.

But a phenomenon? A social phenomenon? Rock'n'roll wasn't supposed to do this, wasn't supposed to be this. It had begun as a hybrid of blues, swing, country and folk, the first two genres arriving in the shape of 'jump blues' or 'race music', i.e. rhythm'n'blues. Just the latest dance craze.

I need you, yes I do, don't make me blue, I'm for you. Boy Meets Girl lyrics of love and desire. Playful at best, banal at worst. But

John Lennon and Paul McCartney – together with Mick Jagger, Bob Dylan, Pete Townshend and Ray Davies – pushed the lyrics, and thus the attitude, in a whole new direction. They were aided and abetted in this by the likes of Smokey Robinson, Marvin Gaye and the Holland–Dozier–Holland team. And by the early performances of artistes like Martha Reeves and her Vandellas, who always ended tracks such as 'Quicksand' and 'Heatwave' in a delirium of bluesy ad-libs. Call-and-response, but wilder than at any time since it had come in from the cotton fields half a century before. Back to the blues.

The British Invasion acts had responded with their own blues: more articulate, as befits musicians from the home of Shakespeare, Dickens and Greene, but also more electric, more immediate and with words to match. Certain areas of popular music were soon no longer just carrying the usual mix of fashion and moon'n'June – suddenly there was poetry, irony, protest, passion, anger and outright lust.

Between 1959 and 1962, it seemed the only way to crack the Top 10 was with a groomed, pretty boy singer pushing lightweight pop ballads for a major label. By the end of 1963, such an approach was far more likely to fail. By the mid-sixties, rock was roaring and raging with an intelligence and insight that popular music had never had before. It was, and it represented, an entire lifestyle: the way people danced, dressed, thought, walked and talked. But new drugs and new pressures, both political and financial, had essentially killed it off by the end of the decade.

By 1975 it seemed it had gone forever. Glam had become more and more trivial – brickies in make-up pouting at ever younger fans – while all music deemed worthy of serious criticism was produced by privileged twenty-somethings with carefully tended flowing locks, limousines and thousand-pound keyboards. The revolts of the past – rock'n'roll, skiffle, beat – had been smothered, smoothed over, dealt with. It was the role of the economic majority to ape their betters and to buy the concert tickets and gatefold sleeve albums they were offered. Rock'n'roll had been shorn of its grubby roots and protest connections. The future was corporate, controlled, air-conditioned, mannered, administered by the same privately educated people who ran the rest of the economy, dead, dull, boring until punk finally, brutally, brought the seventies to life.

Rock'n'roll, at its most extreme, is among history's most dramatic music. It suited the desperate backdrop of the period between 1945 and 1989. In the seventies, the right took the decision to risk nuclear war by upping the Cold War ante and bankrupting the Soviets with a faster arms race, with more – and more vicious – proxy wars in Nicaragua, El Salvador, Angola, Mozambique, Afghanistan.

And it was in the seventies that punk erupted: post-war culture's entire life flashing before its eyes – rock's life flashing before its own bloodshot eyes with amphetamine-fuelled haste. Beat–beatnik–Vietnik–rocker–pop–pop art–mod–hippy jumbled together in a manic rush of titanic energy.

For the right, the win-the-Cold-War gamble paid off, ultimately, though the results weren't quite what had been ordered. Perhaps the Cold War was always destined to end messily, with the East leaking uranium, arms, migrants and mafia cash just as the West's Afghani chickens (among many others) came home bloodily to roost. These transformations have undoubtedly robbed modern music of its strongest facilitators, even if many of its protagonists were barely aware of any but its most obvious symbol, the Berlin Wall.

Back then, in record shops, non-classical music was divided into Pop, Folk and Jazz which meant there were surprises in every other rack. Now CDs are divided into a thousand genres and sub-genres and surprises are rare. There will again be quality 'rock'n'roll'

songs but the whole ramshackle genre will never mean as much as it did before the late eighties.

It was only in the last years of this period that modern music began to seep into every bar, every restaurant, every boutique, every primary school, every police car, every TV and radio advert. It was only then that amateur rock saxophonists and guitar players such as Bill Clinton and Tony Blair would edge towards real political power.

Both of these men had understood the appeal of rock to their own, and subsequent, generations. What had started out as a mere beat, the next Big Thing after Swing, had become the greatest fusion of rhythm, melody, poetry, fashion, design, erotica and street politics. It was, at heart, an entire lifestyle, an authentic 'Third Way', a path between the West's greedy but individualistic consumerism and the East's grey but collective humanism (just as, within pop, punk was a new 'Third Way' between the pretentious po-faced slog of most Prog rock and the shallow teenybop mindlessness of the majority of Glam).

Both Clinton and Blair then hijacked this basic concept to win and to use (and, to a lesser extent, abuse) governmental power. They were, they claimed, a 'Third Way': social justice with a business brain, the Free Market with social democracy.

Many of the original participants have felt a great loss of meaning since punk. The crusade, the revolution, was over. As pioneering TV presenter Dan Farson wrote of his times, in his *Soho in the Fifties* book, the casualty rate was high – and it has subsequently been even higher with punk. Adam Ant in and out of mental wards; Joe Strummer, Nils Stevenson and Dave Goodman all killed by their own big hearts; Anne Beverley dead by her own hand; Johnny Thunders, various Pretenders, Heartbreakers, Dolls and at least one of The Ramones lost to heroin (even young Andy Blade of Eater was a smackhead for a time); The Nips' Shane MacGowan awash in alcoholism for decades; Sid Vicious and at least five others of the *Swindle* cast dead within months of its final shoot – four before the cameras had even stopped rolling. And these are just those who attained some fame (or notoriety). Out in the suburban sprawls and dog-barking sink estates, there are many more 'victims' whose reputation never stretched beyond the end of their own streets.

Like the concept of youth itself, punk granted a freedom that could never be entirely fulfilled or maintained. But perhaps that's why this most disposable of cults has continued to grow in both stature and allure. The original punk explosion unleashed, in many cases inadvertently, the cultural talent of an entire generation. And it still stirs a hint of jealousy in the young – and nostalgia among those entering middle age – because it is, in the end, a bewildering paradox. At its best, punk remains the ultimate expression of the very phenomenon it had come to destroy – rock'n'roll: the people's music that became the people's protest, the people's poetry, the people's lifestyle.

Maybe the best vision of this paradox, of this whole 'distant outsider working within' legacy comes with distance, from an outsider. Dennis Hopper, the actor turned director who was once James Dean's apprentice back in the 1950s, was only vaguely aware of Punk New York, let alone Punk London, when it was starting out. Yet the finale of his film *Out of the Blue* sums up so much about both of them . . .

It is the tale of a bitter middle-aged truck driver – Hopper, naturally – who crashes into a high school bus, leaving his young daughter Ceebee to be raised by his junkie wife. Fast-forward to her mid-teens, high school troubles, punk rock – the girl's CB call-sign is 'Pretty Vacant' – and dad's release from jail. And more trouble.

In the midnight hour, the emotionally battered Ceebee drags her junkie mother out to the front seat of the disused truck owned by her father (the father who's just tried to assault his daughter). It is the same truck whose CB radio the small-town girl uses to chat to passing drivers.

Ceebee's Elvis obsession and punk moves have given her failing life some flimsy armour throughout the film, but now they have not been able to prevent it from collapsing entirely. In the real world, reality can be postponed but it will not be denied. While her messed-up mother moans about the coldness of the truck – and her daughter's cigarette – Ceebee lights an explosive's fuse.

As the older woman becomes hysterical, Ceebee swiftly reassures her: 'It's just a fuse, Mom, it's not connected to anything, Mom, it's just a punk rock gesture, Mom.'

That's the end, says her mother – now more angry than scared – That Really Is The End. That's right, says Ceebee with resignation, that's right. And we the audience see through her hopeless teenage bravado, see that she doesn't mean it, see that it is indeed all just a pose, all just a gesture, all just talk. A sell-out like everything else. A fake. She doesn't really mean it. We know it. We just know it . . .

And then the truck explodes into a spectacular fireball. Afterwards, the truck continues to burn, the flames flickering throughout the end titles.

STOP PRESS:
15 August 2006

CHERRY LANE MUSIC SIGN FORMER PISTOLS
Cherry Lane Music Publishing has announced it has entered into a US North publishing deal with former Sex Pistols Steve Jones and Paul Cook, in conjunction with the estate of Sid Vicious. John Lydon is not party to the deal and it is unclear how that will affect the company's attempts to capitalise on the Sex Pistols' back catalogue. Confirming the signing, Cherry Lane VP Creative Services & Marketing, Richard Stumpf, said: 'Creatively, the music of the Sex Pistols has been under-worked by the music business . . . that's now about to change. There are a handful of bands that are viewed as pillars of change and progress in their respective genres: The Beatles, Led Zeppelin and Van Halen come to mind. The Pistols are one of those few who have impacted their genre in a profound way and Cherry Lane is going to aggressively pitch their music to make sure the world remembers this.'

Bibliography

Greil Marcus, *Lipstick Traces: The Secret History of the 20th Century* (Secker & Warburg, 1989).

Jon Savage, *England's Dreaming: Sex Pistols and Punk Rock* (Faber & Faber, 1991).

Greil Marcus, *In the Fascist Bathroom: Writing on Punk 1977–1982* (Harvard, 1993).

John Lydon Rotten, *No Irish No Blacks No Dogs* (1994).

Legs McNeil and Gillian McCain, *Please Kill Me . . . The Uncensored Oral History of Punk* (Little Brown, 1996).

Paul Burgess and Alan Parker, *Satellite* (Abstract Sounds, 1999).

David Nolan, *I Swear I Was There!* (Milo, 2001).

Marcus Gray, *The Clash: Return of the Last Gang in Town* (Helter Skelter, 2001).

Tony Wilson, *24-hour Party People* (4 Books, 2002).

Terry Rawlings, *Steve Diggle's Harmony in my Head* (Helter Skelter, 2003).

George Gimarc, *Punk Diary: The Ultimate Trainspotters' Guide to Underground Rock 1970–1982* (Backbeat Books, 2004).

Dick Porter, *Ramones: The Complete Twisted History* (Plexus, 2004).

Simon Reynolds, *Rip It Up and Start Again* (Faber & Faber, 2004).

Pat Gilbert, *Passion is a Fashion: The Real Story of the Clash* (Aurum, 2004).

Mark Paytress, *Vicious* (Sanctuary, 2004).

Andy Blade, *Secret Life of a Teenage Punk Rocker* (Cherry Red, 2005).

Alan Parker, *Sid Vicious: 21st Century Icon* (Orion, 2007).

Punk Films

Punk Rock Movie (Dir. Don Letts, UK, 1977, Sex Pistols, The Clash, Siouxsie and The Banshees, Generation X, X-Ray Spex, The Heartbreakers, Subway Sect).

Jubilee (Dir. Derek Jarman, UK, 1978, Jenny Runacre, Little Nell, Toyah Wilcox, Hermine Demoriane, Orlando, Jordan, Adam Ant).

Punk In London (Dir. Wolfgang Buld, West Germany, 1978, The Clash, The Adverts, Miles Copeland, Chelsea, X-Ray Spex, Subway Sect, The Lurkers, Roadent).

Rude Boy (Dir. Jack Hazan and David Mingay, UK, 1979, Ray Gange, The Clash, Johnny Green, Barry Baker, Terry McQuade, Caroline Coon).

Rock'n'roll High School (Dir. Allan Arkush, US, 1979, PJ Soles, Vincent Van Patten, Clint Howard, Mary Woronov, Dey Young, Dick Miller, Paul Bartel, Don Steele, Grady Sutton, The Ramones).

The Great Rock'n'Roll Swindle (Dir. Julien Temple, UK, 1979, Malcolm McLaren, Sex Pistols, John 'Rotten' Lydon, Sid Vicious, Paul Cook, Steve Jones, Ronnie Biggs, Mary Millington, Irene Handl).

Breaking Glass (Dir. Brian Gibson, 1980, Phil Daniels, Hazel O'Connor, Jon Finch, Jonathan Pryce, Peter-Hugo Daly).

Punk Can Take It (Dir. Julien Temple, UK, 1980, UK Subs).

Out of the Blue (Dir. Dennis Hopper, US–Canada, 1980, Linda Manz, Dennis Hopper, Sharon Farrell, Raymond Burr, Don Gordon, Eric Allen).

The Fabulous Stains aka All Washed Up (Dir. Lou Adler, US, 1980, Ray Winstone, Steve Jones, Paul Cook, Paul Simonon).

D.O.A. (Dir. Lech Kowalski, US, 1981, Sex Pistols, Dead Boys, Rich Kids, Generation X, Terry And The Idiots, X-Ray Spex, Nancy Spungen).

Smithereens (Dir. Susan Seidelman, US, 1982, Susan Berman, Brad Rinn, Richard Hell, Roger Jett, Nada Despotovitch, Kitty Summerall).

Sid and Nancy (Dir. Alex Cox, UK, 1985, Gary Oldman, Chloe Webb, David Hayman, Debby Bishop, Andrew Schofield, Xander Berkeley, Perry Benson, Courtney Love, Coati Mundi, Iggy Pop, Circle Jerks, Pray For Rain, Edward Tudor-Pole, Tony London, Kathy Burke).

The Punk aka The Punk and the Princess (Dir. Mike Sarne, 1993, UK, Charlie Creed-Mills, Vanessa Hadaway, David Shawyer, Jess Conrad, Jacqueline Skarvellis).

The Filth and the Fury (Dir. Julien Temple, UK, 1999, John Lydon, Sid Vicious, Steve Jones, Paul Cook, Glen Matlock, Sex Pistols).

Westway to the World (Dir. Don Letts, UK, 1999 / 2001, The Clash).

End of the Century (Dir. Michael Gramaglia and Jim Fields, US, 2004, the Ramones).

Chaos! Sex Pistols' Secret History: Dave Goodman Story 1 (Dir. Phil Strongman, UK, 2006, Malcolm McLaren, Dave Goodman, Don Letts, Glen Matlock, Tony Wilson, Ray Stevenson, Eater, Roadent, Terry Chimes, Gary Lammin, Tat, Sex Pistols Experience).

Index

and early appearances of Sex
Pistols, 19, 23, 24, 106, 108, 115,
134
and name of Sex Pistols, 106, 217
and clothes worn by Sex Pistols,
107, 136
and Nils Stevenson, 109, 110
and Dave Goodman, 112, 113,
146–7, 148
and Nick Kent, 116
and publicity for Sex Pistols, 120
speaks to Tony Wilson, 125
confrontation with Ian Dury,
125–6
and television debut of Sex Pistols,
126, 127, 128, 129
and 100 Club Punk 'Special', 135,
137
and EMI deal, 140–1
and EMI recording sessions, 144,
145, 146–7
and Anarchy Tour, 149, 150, 165
and aftermath of Grundy interview,
154–5, 156, 157, 162
and termination of EMI contract,
166
receives calls from A&M and
Virgin, 172
contacts Sid Vicious, 172
and departure of Matlock, 172–3,
174–5
negotiations with A&M, 174
and firing of Sex Pistols by A&M,
175
makes deal with Virgin, 175
and 'God Save The Queen', 176,
180
and Jubilee boat incident, 181, 182
MI5 file on, 183
arranges Scandinavian tour, 198
and title of Never Mind The
Bollocks, 206
and use of swastika, 207
responds to accusations of punk
link to National Front, 207
and American tour, 207
in Rio, 210

and *The Great Rock'n'Roll
Swindle*, 211, 244
makes legal claim to the name
Rotten, 217
portrayed as a swindler, 218
attacked by Sid Vicious, 236
wires money to Vicious, 237
goes to New York after arrest of
Vicious, 239
hires lawyer, 240
plans secret Vicious album, 240
legal action against, 241, 242–3
at Selfridges to lecture, 252, 253
involved in movie of *Fast Food
Nation*, 252
brief references, , 7, 26, 53, 89, 99,
114, 122, 143, 209
MacLaren, Pete, 65
McLise, Angus, 29, 30
McManus, Declan *see* Costello, Elvis
McNeil, Legs, 62, 63
McQueen, Alexander, 254
Madison Square Gardens, 48
Madrid, 71
Battle of, 72
Magazine, 226
Magic Tramps, The, 55, 59, 60
'Magnificent Seven', 247
Maher, John, 120
Mahler, 78
Makin, Jim, 84
Malanga, Gerard, 48
Malcolm X, 249
Malpractice, 54
Man, Vince, 66
Man About The House, 151
Manchester, 5, 13, 111, 193, 223,
224, 228
Sex Pistols in, 115–16, 120–1,
126–9, 164–5
Manhattan, 28, 30, 40, 46, 47, 61,
92, 131, 238, 239, 246, 248
'Mannequin', 232
Mansfield, Mike, 150, 152
Manz, Linda, 245
Maoism, 68, 69, 229
Mao Tse Tung, 70

Morrison, Sterling, 29, 38
Morrissey, Paul, 31
Morrissey, Ray, 119
Morrissey, Steven, 121
Mortimer, John, 206
Moschino, Franco, 254
Moseley, Oswald, 74
Moss, Jerry, 175
Most, Mickie, 221
Motorhead, 77
Mott The Hoople, 52, 56
Mozambique, 256
Muhammad Ali, 48
'Mummy, The', 63
Murcia, Billy, 41, 45
Murray, Charles Shaar, 2, 53, 129, 134–5
Murvin, Junior, 203
Mussolini, Benito, 72
Myddle Class, 30
Myers, Richard *see* Hell, Richard
'My Generation, 46, 135, 185
'My Way', 235–6, 237

Nag's Head pub, High Wycombe, 15–16
Nashville Rooms, 19, 22, 24, 111–12, 115, 138
National Film School, 24
National Front, 117, 183, 197, 207
'Nazi Punks F——— Off!', 213
Nazis, 72, 136, 207, 210
NBC, 172
Nelson, Paul, 44
Nelson, Sandy, 40
Neon Boys, The, 55, 184
'Never Been In A Riot', 231
Never Mind The Bollocks, Here's The Sex Pistols, 206, 254
Newcastle
City Hall, 163
University, 51
Newgate Prison, 74, 75
'New Hormones', 173
New Jersey, 46
New Left, 35
Newman, Colin, 231, 249

New Musical Express (NME), 52–3, 108, 110, 116, 129, 132, 134–5, 174–5, 194, 201, 203, 205, 225, 227, 248, 250, 251, 253
New Orleans, 92
New Romantics, 221, 246
'New Rose', 138
News At Ten, 154
New Society, 143
News Of The World, The, 161, 164
'News Of The World', 197
New Wave, 15, 134, 185, 187
New York, 2, 30, 31, 35, 39, 42, 46, 47, 54, 57, 58, 59, 62, 90, 92, 94, 131, 150, 184, 186, 209, 212, 234–5, 237–40, 241–2, 246–8 *see also* names of locations in New York
New York Dolls, 6, 14, 40–6, 48, 49, 55, 59, 61, 62, 63, 77, 82, 90, 91–3, 94, 100, 101, 155, 234, 257
New York Post, 239
New York Times, 184, 208
Nicaragua, 256
Nico, 31, 32, 33, 38
Nightingale, Warwick 'Wally', 84, 85, 93, 105
'Nights in White Satin', 214
999, 2, 25
'1969', 37
'96 Tears', 18
Nips, The, 257
Nirvana, 11, 252
Nixon, President, 35
NME *see New Musical Express*
'No Elvis, Beatles and No Rolling Stones in 1977', 166
'No Feeling', 119, 122, 173, 174
'No Fun', 37, 99, 105, 145, 173
'No Future' *see* 'God Save The Queen'
Nolan, David: *I Swear I Was There*, 121
Nolan, Jerry, 45, 150, 239, 241
'No Love Lost', 223
'No One Is Innocent', 210